D1221878

SUSTAINABLE
Landscape Management

SUSTAINABLE Landscape Management

Design, Construction, and Maintenance

Thomas W. Cook

Ann Marie VanDerZanden

John Wiley & Sons, Inc.

This book is printed on acid-free paper. ♾

Published by John Wiley & Sons, Inc., Hoboken, New Jersey
Published simultaneously in Canada

For general information about our other products and services, please contact our Customer Care Department within the United States at (800) 762-2974, outside the United States at (317) 572-3993 or fax (317) 572-4002.

Wiley also publishes its books in a variety of electronic formats. Some content that appears in print may not be available in electronic books. For more information about Wiley products, visit our web site at www.wiley.com.

Library of Congress Cataloging-in-Publication Data:

Cook, Thomas, 1950-

Sustainable landscape management : design, construction, and maintenance / Thomas W. Cook, Ann Marie VanDerZanden.

p. cm.

Includes bibliographical references and index.

ISBN 978-0-470-48093-9 (cloth); ISBN 978-0-470-88039-5 (ebk);

ISBN 978-0-470-88041-8 (ebk); ISBN 978-0-470-88042-5 (ebk) ; 978-0-470-90527-2 (ebk); 978-0-470-90528-9 (ebk)

1. Landscape protection. 2. Grounds maintenance. 3. Sustainable development. 4. Sustainable horticulture. I. VanDerZanden, Ann Marie, 1966- II. Title.

SB472.3.C66 2011

712--dc22

2010010794

Printed in the United States of America

10 9 8 7 6 5 4 3 2 1

To my wife Marilyn who edited this sentence and my son Bryan who helped me with my computer.

T. Cook

To my husband Joe, and children Nina and Peter.

A. M. VanDerZanden

Contents

Preface

During our combined 46 (31 + 15) years of teaching landscape design and management, we have developed and refined our curriculum to reflect current research, incorporate contemporary issues, and meet course objectives to prepare students for successful careers in the landscape and golf course industries. The current interest in, and push for, sustainable landscape practices combined with our teaching and industry experiences have guided us in writing this text. Much of what is included in the text comes from our professional experiences, both in and out of the classroom. The 10 chapters in this text are focused on a select group of topics that provide the foundation for sustainable landscapes. Although the focus is on commercial landscape management, the principles described are also relevant to residential properties.

The chapters are organized to provide a context for sustainability and the impact it has on landscape design, installation, and management practices. Throughout the text, we have referenced scientific research that substantiates points and replaces myth or urban legend with data and facts. Chapter 1 provides background and a review of relevant literature on the sustainability movement and sets the stage for subsequent chapters to discuss sustainable landscape practices with some specificity. Chapter 2 describes the different factors involved in designing beautiful, functional, low-maintenance, and cost-effective landscapes. The chapter also touches on the landscape design process and how different design approaches can enhance sustainability. Chapter 3 moves from the design process to the construction process and materials selection. As part of materials selection, there is a discussion about plants, hardscapes, and irrigation design and installation strategies to enhance a landscape's sustainability. In some cases, existing landscapes can benefit from retrofitting, and this is the focus of Chapter 4. The chapter outlines a series of questions that should be asked as part of a site analysis, and then provides guidance on prioritizing areas to retrofit and key issues that often need to be fixed in mature landscapes to enhance their sustainability. Chapter 5 describes landscapes in the context of an ecosystem and highlights establishment strategies for new plantings and management strategies for postplanting succession. Chapter 6 discusses a number of environmental concerns including nutrient and pesticide runoff, leaching, and the impact of pesticides on humans and other nontarget organisms. Other topics in the chapter include air pollution from power equipment emissions and environmental concerns with depletion of resources. The chapter concludes with an interesting perspective on sustainability and environmental rhetoric.

Sustainable soils are the topic of Chapter 7, including a discussion of healthy soils. The chapter then moves on to outline sustainable options when developing soils for landscapes, including using on-site soils and the impact of adding amendments. The chapter concludes by describing the role of mulches in sustainable soil management. Planting, fertilizing, irrigating, and pruning of trees, shrubs, and beds are covered in detail in Chapter 8. Chapter 9 provides a comprehensive discussion of the role lawns play in sustainable landscapes. The chapter outlines the importance of matching grass type to growing conditions and how grass breeding programs have impacted which grass species are readily available. The characteristics of cool- and warm-season grasses along with grass-dicot plant combinations for sustainable lawns are described. From here the chapter addresses sustainable maintenance strategies of mowing, irrigation, and fertility programs. The final chapter in the text discusses sustainable pest management, in particular the components and effectiveness of integrated pest management (IPM) systems.

When it comes to sustainability, there often is no single solution to solving a problem or enhancing the landscape's sustainability. With that in mind, we tried to tailor this text to describe and illustrate sustainable landscapes, as well as provide examples of landscapes that are lacking sustainability in certain areas. The ultimate goal is to offer you specific and proven strategies that can be used to improve sustainability.

Acknowledgments

We are grateful to our friends and colleagues who generously gave their time to this project. Their contributions came in the form of discussing concepts for the book, answering specific questions, sharing information, providing suggestions, reviewing draft chapters, and generously sharing their extensive collections of images. In particular, we would like to thank Josh Schultes and Taylor Crampton, Iowa State University; Bob Grover, Pacific Landscape Management, Inc.; Al Shay, Oregon State University Horticulture Department; Brian McDonald, Oregon State University Horticulture Department; Dr. Rob Golembiewski, Oregon State University Horticulture Department; Mark Mahady, Mark M. Mahady and Associates, Carmel Valley, CA; Dr. Micah Woods, Asian Turfgrass Center, Thailand; Dr. Peter Dernoeden, University of Maryland Agronomy Department; and Mario Lanthier, CropHealth Advising & Research, Kelowna, BC. We are indebted to Joe for his amazing editing skills. Special thanks to Marilyn for ideas and conversations about the book.

Most important, we thank our families. Their understanding of missed dinners, late nights and weekends in front of the computer, and our general preoccupation for a year and a half made this book possible. We hope you all know how invaluable you were to this project.

About the Authors

Thomas W. Cook is Associate Professor Emeritus in the Horticulture Department at Oregon State University. For 31 years at OSU, he taught turf and landscape management classes, including introduction to the turf and landscape industry, turfgrass management, landscape management, pruning, irrigation design, turfgrass nutrition, golf course management, and senior seminar, and was the coordinator for the department internship program. He also served as the state turfgrass extension specialist working with industry professionals and conducted practical field research in turf and landscape management. As part of his teaching and research program, he developed the turf and landscape field lab near the OSU campus, where students could actively participate in a wide variety of research and practical activities as part of their studies. Currently, over 300 former students are working in the landscape, golf course, and sports field management industries nationwide.

Mr. Cook has been a frequent speaker at state, regional, and national meetings and has published numerous papers for regional and national magazines and peer-reviewed journals covering the topics of pruning, tree care, pest management, putting green maintenance, sports field construction and maintenance, drainage, water quality, and low-input alternatives for lawns.

He received his B.S. degree in Agronomy and Soils in 1972 at Washington State University and an M.S. degree in Plant and Soil Science in 1975 from the University of Rhode Island. From 1975 to 1977, he worked as a research associate in turfgrass at Washington State University in Puyallup, Washington, conducting weed control research. He moved to Oregon State University in 1977, when the turf and landscape program was created, and spent his entire career building the program.

A lifelong gardener, he was inspired as a youth by his grandmother Lena Jury and next-door neighbor Kenny Hove and later by his mother-in-law Mary Rossi. He lives in Corvallis, Oregon, where he and his wife Marilyn continue to build their dream garden.

Dr. Ann Marie VanDerZanden is Professor of Horticulture and a member of the Iowa State University Horticulture Department. She has taught landscape horticulture courses, including herbaceous plant identification, landscape design, landscape construction, and landscape contracting and estimating, for 15 years. In addition to her teaching responsibilities, she is an extension specialist for the nursery and landscape industry and previously served as an extension specialist in consumer horticulture. Her research interests include sustainable landscape practices, undergraduate teaching, and using new technology to enhance the learning experiences of students and nursery and landscape professionals.

She is a seasoned writer and has published numerous manuscripts on teaching and extension outreach projects in peer-reviewed journals as well as general-interest articles in garden magazines. This is Dr. VanDerZanden's third textbook. Her earlier publications include *Landscape Design: Theory and Application*, co-authored with Steven N. Rodie; and *Mathematics for the Green Industry*, co-authored with Michael L. Agnew, Nancy H. Agnew, and Nick Christians. In addition to writing, she has a number of speaking engagements each year, reaching members of the nursery and landscape industry and home gardeners. Many of her presentations focus on sustainable landscape design, installation, and management.

Professor VanDerZanden completed her academic training in horticulture science and earned her B.S. and Ph.D. from Washington State University and her M.S. from Cornell University. Prior to joining the faculty at ISU, she was a faculty member at Oregon State University and Illinois State University. She has worked in the green industry in retail nursery sales and production, landscape design and management, landscape sales, and landscape estimating.

She lives in Ames, Iowa, with her husband and children. She enjoys traveling the world to explore and photograph new gardens, but finds the greatest joy spending time in her garden with her family.

SUSTAINABLE
Landscape Management

chapter 1

Introduction to Sustainability

INTRODUCTION

Sustainable landscape management is a philosophical approach to creating and maintaining landscapes that are ecologically more stable and require fewer inputs than conventional landscapes. They are still artificial landscapes inserted into highly disturbed site environments and maintained to meet the expectations of owners and occupants. Sustainability is a relative concept and more a goal to strive for rather than a well-defined end point. There will never be truly self-sustaining constructed landscapes, only landscapes that are more or less sustainable than our current efforts. To better understand sustainability, it is useful to review the historical origins of the movement. This will shed light on why there is so much interest in the topic.

HISTORICAL PERSPECTIVE

The sustainability movement started shortly after the industrial revolution, beginning in the 18th century. As cities became more industrialized and the ability to extract and use resources increased, it was not long before cities grew to an unprecedented scale and the population began to explode. This transformation changed everything and quickly brought out detractors. It was 1798 when Thomas Malthus, an English country parson, penned his *Essay on Population*. In this writing, he questioned whether the earth could support geometric population growth (Malthus 1798). He feared the poor (the laboring classes) would reproduce faster than the world could provide for them, resulting in a total collapse of society. Malthus's essay sparked reaction and has been debated almost continually since it was published. The heart of the debate is whether nations can keep finding and extracting enough resources to support a constantly increasing population without running out.

The philosophical discussion deals with political and economic theory. Many of the major figures in the sustainable development movement have been economists. While industrialists were busy exploiting resources, there was always a skeptical economist who would raise his or her hand and say, "Wait a minute. I think we may have a problem." In 1865, William Jevons wrote *The Coal Question* (Jevons 1865). In Jevons's time, coal was the only functional source of energy. He hypothesized that as population (and demand for coal) increased, Britain would exhaust its reserves and the economy would fail. He proposed that the British economy would slowly decline and be displaced by other countries with more natural resources. In terms of coal, he was essentially correct. It never occurred to him that other energy sources would ever be economically feasible (which was a big mistake). Two things can be learned from Jevons: first, hard-and-fast predictions will probably be wrong; and, second, technology will attempt to solve any problem caused by misuse of resources.

The idea that there is a technological fix for every problem is debated among those interested in sustainability. Even though humankind has been incredibly resourceful in finding new technological solutions for energy resources, there is a nascent feeling among proponents of sustainability that the world cannot indefinitely rely on innovation to find ways to exploit the earth's resources. In their view, it is time to find ways to avoid depleting those resources and (perhaps) even enhance them.

Prior to today's sustainability movement, countries supported ever-increasing populations by extracting resources to produce food and other staples without regard for the environmental consequences. What these efforts were doing to the earth or how they might affect its capacity to provide for future generations did not factor into the equation. For example, the basic strategy for obtaining oil has always been to find new places to drill and to drill deeper. Oil companies have scoured the earth using an incredible array of technologies in search of more oil. Drilling occurs in climates and locations that would have been impossible a hundred years ago. As such, each new source seems to increase the potential for environmental catastrophes (e.g., the *Exxon Valdez* in 1989 and Gulf of Mexico in 2010).

EMERGENCE OF THE SUSTAINABILITY MOVEMENT

There is no verifiable starting point for the current sustainability movement. It seems to have converged from several different broad ideas concerning our relationship with the natural world. Some of the key figures who have contributed to the discussion include Frederick Law Olmsted and Calvert Vaux, John Muir, Theodore Roosevelt and Gifford Pinchot, Aldo Leopold, Rachel Carson, and Ian McHarg. Their history provides a better understanding of how the sustainability movement has evolved to the present. This discussion will consider the landscape management perspective.

Olmsted and Vaux

In the mid-1800s, Frederick Law Olmsted and Calvert Vaux partnered to develop the Greensward Plan for an urban park, now known as Central Park, in New York City. Even though the park was built on largely derelict land and required massive efforts to reconfigure the topography, these two artists produced a relatively wild and natural landscape that provided a welcome natural experience for the public. This came at a time when New York City was becoming increasingly industrialized and home to a huge labor force living in squalid tenement buildings. Population density was high, and workers were unable to escape the summer cholera epidemics. There were virtually no recreational options available to the working class. Life was hard for all but the wealthy.

Olmsted, the more dominant and vocal of the two, stood out as a passionate advocate for natural spaces in the city that would provide passive recreational activities for city dwellers. He viewed landscapes in the same manner as a naturalist would view a forest or prairie (Figure 1-1). Olmsted and Vaux's designs created apparent natural landscapes that were, in fact, manufactured. Interestingly, though Olmsted obsessed over plant materials, he felt constrained by his lack of knowledge of plants and their appropriate niches in the landscape.

Olmsted's and Vaux's careers (and those of Olmsted's sons) spanned a period of major public park development throughout the United States. Their efforts enhanced the public's awareness of the value of beautiful and natural-looking landscapes. During his 50-year career, Olmsted was involved in designing some of the most outstanding

(a)

(b)

(c)

Figure 1-1 The designs of Frederick Law Olmsted and Calvert Vaux often mimicked nature. These natural landscapes are typical of scenes created in their work: (a) mountain meadow, (b) lake surrounded by forest, and (c) towering trees in a forest.

and enduring public parks in the world. He was well ahead of his competition and today is widely regarded as the father of landscape architecture in the United States.

Preservation versus Conservation

Coming from a completely different perspective and emerging as a major voice during the last half of Olmsted's career was John Muir. Muir was a self-taught naturalist who devoted much of his life to extolling the virtues of the natural world and who lamented the defiling of the wilderness by humans. Muir felt wilderness should be preserved for its own sake (Figure 1-2).

A visit to Yosemite in California in 1868 fueled Muir's love of wilderness and nature. He spent much of his time exploring this region and quickly began

Figure 1-2 John Muir's view was to preserve wilderness by making it off-limits to all commercial interests.

to understand the negative impact of cattle and sheep grazing on fragile ecosystems. During this time, the nation was rapidly expanding, and opportunists were quick to exploit all natural areas as they sought their fortunes. This new breed of entrepreneurs disregarded the intrinsic value of natural areas and how resource extraction threatened to destroy nature.

Muir's efforts eventually led to the preservation of several wilderness areas, notably Yosemite Valley in California. Muir founded the Sierra Club in 1892, long considered one of the most powerful voices for preservation of wilderness. A split developed between preservationists like Muir, who believed wilderness should be left alone and appreciated for its beauty and spiritual values, and conservationists such as Gifford Pinchot and President Theodore Roosevelt, who believed that forests and wilderness areas should be preserved but also be profitably used for grazing, timber harvest, and other commercial activities (Figure 1-3). This difference in opinion continues today and is reignited whenever plans are announced for logging in old-growth forests or when areas containing endangered species are targeted for development.

Figure 1-3 Theodore Roosevelt and Gifford Pinchot believed wilderness should be conserved but still used for commercial resource extraction, such as the logging shown in this photo.

Emergence of the Land Ethic

In the 1940s, Aldo Leopold expressed a more philosophical view of the relationship between nature and humans. Trained as a forester, Leopold spent much of his career working with wildlife in the arid Southwest and later in the Midwest of the United States. Although he held strong opinions about how the earth should be treated, he was not entirely opposed to using natural resources for hunting and fishing or even mining. His opinion was different from the opinions of other environmentalists and his message less extreme than that of the preservationists.

In 1949, shortly after his death, Leopold's *A Sand County Almanac* was published. This collection of essays starts with the naturalist's year in Sand County, Wisconsin, followed by his experiences in the western states, where he observed human successes and failures in understanding ecosystems in a diverse array of climates. The text concludes with an elaboration of his philosophy about wilderness, conservation, and, ultimately, what he called "the land ethic." The land ethic is best explained in his own words:

> All ethics so far evolved rest upon a single premise: that the individual is a member of a community of interdependent parts. His instincts prompt him to compete for his place in that community, but his ethics prompt him also to co-operate (perhaps in order that there may be a place to compete for). (Leopold 1949)

> The land ethic simply enlarges the boundaries of the community to include soils, waters, plants, and animals, or collectively: the land. (Leopold 1949)

He goes into more detail in later passages:

> A land ethic of course cannot prevent the alteration, management, and use of these "resources," but it does affirm their right to continued existence in a natural state. (Leopold 1949)

> In short, a land ethic changes the role of *Homo sapiens* from conqueror of the land-community to plain member and citizen of it. It implies respect for his fellow-members, and also respect for the community as such. (Leopold 1949)

Leopold believed that people need to view the natural world in terms of a biotic pyramid (what today is known as an ecosystem), defined by interconnected webs of relationships among soil, plants, and animals. How humans impact the land affects, often profoundly, the relationships among all participants, and they need to be mindful of everything they do managing the "land." Even though Leopold's emphasis was on wild lands, his message is just as powerful when considering constructed landscapes (Figure 1-4).

Post–World War II

Reflecting on the times, it is interesting to consider that when Leopold was working, there were only about 125 million people in the United States. The nation had just emerged from the Great Depression and the Dust Bowl and had yet to develop the fertilizer and chemical industries of modern times. The dawn of the chemical age began just after World War II and had profound impacts on every facet of our relationship with the earth and all of its inhabitants. It is hard to imagine the sense of optimism that defined the postwar period from 1945 through the 1950s. In his description of this era in *The Life and Times of the Thunderbolt Kid*, Bill Bryson summarizes the period perfectly:

> Happily we were indestructible. We didn't need seatbelts, air bags, smoke detectors, bottled water, or the Heimlich maneuver. We didn't require child-safety caps on our medicines. We didn't need helmets when we rode our bikes or pads for our knees and elbows when we went skating. We knew without a written reminder that bleach was not a refreshing drink and

(a)

(b)

Figure 1-4 Aldo Leopold's land ethic promoted the idea that humans should be part of nature rather than in control of it. (a) Natural area accessible to people and (b) wildlife area in the middle of an urban development.

> that gasoline when exposed to a match had a tendency to combust. We didn't have to worry about what we ate because nearly all foods were good for us: sugar gave us energy, red meat made us strong, ice cream gave us healthy bones, coffee kept us alert and purring productively. (Bryson 2006)

In the midst of the euphoric optimism of the 1950s, the world embraced nearly all technological marvels. One of the biggest marvels was synthetic pesticides, or, more specifically, fungicides, herbicides, and insecticides. Having been developed during World War II, many products had just recently been released for public use. Significant among these was dichlorodiphenyltrichloroethane (DDT), an insecticide that promised to eliminate nearly every insect pest that affected humans and crops. At the time, it was considered safe for people, which meant that it could be used indiscriminately—and it was. By 1960, it was becoming apparent that users did not understand all of the implications of DDT, as well as other pesticides that were rapidly coming into the market. For one person in particular, widespread use of insecticides posed a real threat to the natural world that was without precedent.

Rachel Carson

Rachel Carson was a naturalist, marine biologist, and author. Starting in 1941, she produced a trilogy of "sea" books: *Under the Sea Wind*, *The Sea around Us* (1951), and *The Edge of the Sea* (1955). *The Sea around Us*, the most successful of the three, explores nearly every facet of the sea. Carson's ability to blend science with the awe and wonder of the natural world made the life aquatic come alive. The book demonstrated her vast scientific knowledge and her love of nature and ecology. It was after her sea trilogy that she began work on her last, and by far most influential, book. In 1962, just two years before she died of cancer, Carson completed *Silent Spring*. *Silent Spring* was a different kind of book than the public had grown to expect from her. Rather than awe and wonder, it was filled with anger and frustration as she took to task "man's assaults upon the environment" (Carson 1962). Specifically, she singled out "contamination of air, earth, rivers, and sea with dangerous and even lethal materials" (Carson 1962).

Carson focused primarily on indiscriminate use of insecticides (DDT, endrin, dieldrin, and chlordane, among others). She was fully aware of the problems insects posed to humans and crops and made this clear early when she wrote:

> All this is not to say there is no insect problem and no need for control. I am saying, rather, that control must be geared to realities, not to mythical situations, and that the methods employed must be such that they do not destroy us along with the insects. (Carson 1962)

She expanded on this later:

> It is not my contention that chemical insecticides must never be used. I do contend that we have put poisonous and biologically potent chemicals indiscriminately into the hands of persons largely or wholly ignorant of their potentials for harm. (Carson 1962)

She then went on to detail numerous examples of environmental catastrophes and human tragedies resulting from poor judgment and plain misuse of insecticides in the quest for cheap and effective insect control. Although she does profile problems associated with other pesticides, insecticides are the primary focus.

This iconic book was controversial when it was published and remains so today. It split the world into two distinct camps: those who valued the benefits of pesticides and those who believed pesticides caused more problems than they solved. In the nearly 50 years since it was first published, copious resources have been spent looking for evidence to support either view. Many magazine articles and several books have followed *Silent Spring*, challenging Carson's viewpoint (Bailey 2002; Makson 2003; Marco, Hollingworth, and Durham 1987; Whitten 1966).

The impact of *Silent Spring* has been immense. It was influential in banning the use of DDT and numerous other chlorinated hydrocarbon insecticides, in creating the U.S. Environmental Protection Agency, and in providing a blueprint for modern environmentalism. Along the way, Carson has been lauded for producing one of the most influential books of the century, cursed as a radical environmentalist who was wrong about many of the questions she raised, and blamed for the death from insect-borne illnesses of millions of people worldwide who otherwise might have lived if DDT had been available. Given her background in science, her distinguished career as a marine biologist, and her success as a nature writer, Rachel Carson cannot be dismissed as a mindless crank spreading doom and gloom without regard for the consequences.

It is remarkable how accurate she was in her analysis of how humans can create problems because of their failure to fully study the ramifications of their decisions. Her descriptions of fish kills as a result of widespread application of insecticides to control gypsy moths (*Lymantria dispar*) in forests stand out as systematic failures of public policy. Her book demonstrates the importance of studying problems thoroughly before acting and exercising healthy skepticism about new technology before it is adequately tested.

Design with Nature

In 1969, Ian McHarg, an urban planner at the University of Pennsylvania, wrote *Design with Nature* (McHarg 1969), which addressed many of the same issues raised by Rachel Carson. His discussion was in the context of our approach to the built environment. At intervals in his thesis, McHarg outlined in great detail various catastrophes of failed planning, which included a study of the New Jersey shore where lack of intelligent planning resulted in indiscriminate building of vacation homes on fragile dune areas. A major storm in March 1962 resulted in serious destruction of homes and roads throughout the development. McHarg's study explained the inevitability of this failure and showed that careful analysis of a site could enable us to develop areas mindfully, avoid destroying ecosystems, provide desired

Figure 1-5 This freeway interchange demonstrates our ability to impose our will on the land. Ian McHarg believed it was possible to design the built environment in harmony with the natural environment and avoid the problems associated with thoughtless development.

recreational opportunities, and facilitate a sustainable tourist industry.

McHarg's analysis demonstrates the power of careful investigation and the value of producing win-win solutions to solve problems, ranging from determining the least intrusive location for highways to developing metropolitan areas without spoiling watershed ecosystems or eliminating local agriculture (Figure 1-5). His approach required study of multiple factors such as historic features, scenic values, social values, geology, ecological associations, stream quality, forests, marshes, beaches, and wildlife. By creating a series of overlapping transparent maps, he was able to delineate areas suited to development and areas to be held "off-limits" to development. His efforts demonstrated that, in virtually all situations, it is possible to identify the most effective and least destructive way to develop an area.

McHarg was remarkably philosophical about the issues facing humankind. His writing is infused with lofty visions of the role of humans in protecting the natural world. One of his themes involves the concept of entropy, which, in simple terms, is an increasing state of disorder. Negentropy is the opposite; it refers to an increasing state of order. In his view, entropy is synonymous with destruction, and negentropy is synonymous with creation. According to McHarg, our goal, as participants in the world around us, is to create diverse landscapes appropriately sited and constructed in a way that fosters biological diversity and builds from native plant palettes. In other words, we should strive for negentropy. The common process of removing all existing features of a site and imposing an artificial structure and landscape complete with imported soils and plants chosen without regard to the environment to which they are adapted simply increases entropy. In today's terminology, landscapes imposed on a site rather than fitted to it would not be considered sustainable.

Earth Day

Concerns about the world and our ability to sustain life on earth became increasingly focused on our treatment of the environment during the 1960s. In

1970, Senator Gaylord Nelson of Wisconsin called for an Earth Day celebration on April 22. Earth Day was a national alert that promoted the idea that all was not well with the earth and change was needed. Predictions of doom were abundant and focused on the effects of overpopulation and impending starvation. The predictions included the loss of 65 million Americans by 1989 due to starvation; a loss of more than 80 percent of the world's species within 25 years; a 50 percent reduction in the amount of light reaching the earth; a severe reduction in the earth's temperature, leading to an ice age; and exhaustion of world crude oil supplies by the year 2000 (Bailey 2000). Although none of these scenarios came true (think back to William Jevons's predictions), they did awaken the public from its complacency and served as a warning of what might happen to the earth if no one is paying attention to its needs.

Our Common Future

An awareness of sustainability continued to evolve through the efforts of concerned environmentalists, scientists, and governments. In 1983, the United Nations created the World Commission on Environment and Development. Led by the former prime minister of Norway, Gro Harlem Brundtland, the commission produced a report, titled *Our Common Future*, in 1987. Among other accomplishments of the report, the commission defined sustainable development as "meeting the needs of the present without compromising the ability of future generations to meet their own needs" (World Commission on Environment and Development 1987). This definition, simple and vague as it is, reinforces the reality that if resources are overused or misused, there will be fewer resources for future generations to draw on.

In a follow-up book, *Signs of Hope*, Brundtland writes in the foreword:

> Our Common Future is a hard-won consensus of policy principles forming the basis for sound and responsible management of the Earth's resources and the common future of all its creatures. (Starke 1990)

Sustainable development has since become the banner for creating a world where everyone can live now and into the future. The concept was further detailed in a report titled the *World Conservation Strategy: Living Resource Conservation for Sustainable Development*, published by the International Union for Conservation of Nature and Natural Resources, the World Wildlife Fund, and the United Nations Environment Programme.

According to the report:

> For development to be sustainable it must take account of social and ecological factors, as well as economic ones; of the living and non-living resource base; and of the long term as well as the short term advantages and disadvantages of alternative actions. (*World Conservation Strategy* 1980)

This echoes the methods espoused by Ian McHarg and demonstrates that principles of sustainability apply not only to buildings, roads, and natural resources but to all aspects of our world, including our approach to landscape management.

SUSTAINABLE LANDSCAPES

Now that more people are taking the idea of sustainability seriously, there is a need to define specific practices and approaches that will move us in the direction of more sustainable landscapes. Much of this book will address the difficulties in balancing our desire to produce truly sustainable landscapes with the realities of designing, building, and maintaining landscapes. It will also address the issue of what to do with existing landscapes to make them more sustainable (Figure 1-6).

Efforts are currently under way throughout the industry to develop sustainable landscape practices.

(a)

(b)

(c)

Figure 1-6 Which landscape is more sustainable: (a) this totally sheared and mulched bed; (b) this beautiful arrangement of herbaceous perennials; or (c) this urban park with water features, natural grass plantings, and a modest lawn area?

Several organizations have (or are currently developing) standards. Opportunities to move landscaping practices toward sustainability are outlined in Figure 1-7.

Leadership in Energy and Environmental Design

The Leadership in Energy and Environmental Design (LEED) Green Building Rating System was first developed in 1998 by the U.S. Green Building Council. The rating system sets certification standards for building construction and, to a limited degree, landscape development associated with the building. LEED certification is awarded on a point system and addresses six basic categories (LEED 2009):

Sustainable sites
Water efficiency
Energy and atmosphere
Materials and atmosphere
Indoor environmental quality
Innovation and design process

Landscapes are addressed primarily under the "water efficiency" category with rating points allowed for reducing water use by 20 to 50 percent, using no potable water (or no water at all), and using innovative wastewater management technology. Points are also available under the "sustainable sites" category for reducing site disturbance through protection or restoration of open space, storm water management, and reducing heat islands associated with hard surfaces and roofs.

LEED certification recognizes landscapes as a component of the overall development of a building site but assigns somewhat arbitrary point values for landscape design strategies, leading to a "paint by

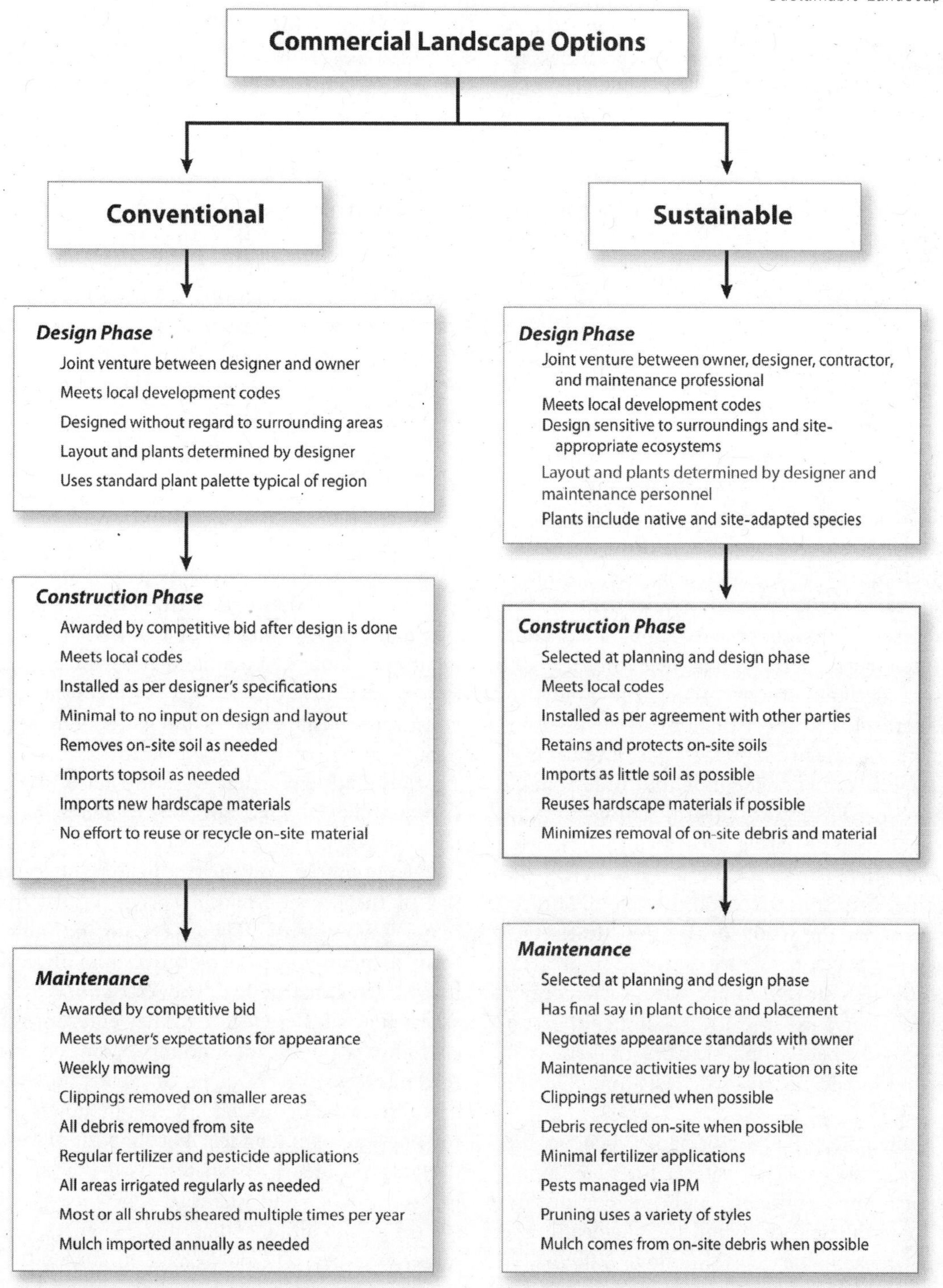

Figure 7 General comparison between conventional landscapes and sustainable landscapes.

numbers" approach to achieving the points necessary to earn specific certifications. It also involves only the designers in the certification process. Although it may be easy at the design stage to specify there will be no irrigation in the landscape, it may create numerous problems later for construction, establishment, and maintenance of the landscape. A more comprehensive and collaborative approach is needed to produce truly sustainable landscapes.

Sustainable Sites Initiative

In 2005, the American Society of Landscape Architects, the Lady Bird Johnson Wildflower Center, the University of Texas at Austin, and the United States Botanic Garden joined forces to develop sustainability guidelines for encouraging sustainable landscape development. The Sustainable Sites Initiative (SSI) interpreted the Brundtland report definition of sustainability as "design, construction, operations, and maintenance practices that meet the needs of the present without compromising the ability of future generations to meet their own needs" (Sustainable Sites Initiative 2009a). The intention of the initiative is to produce guidelines that "enable built landscapes to support natural ecological functions by protecting existing ecosystems and regenerating ecological capacity where it has been lost" (Sustainable Sites Initiative 2009b). As elaborated in Chapter 1 of the 2009 draft, the "Initiative's guidelines and benchmarks are designed to preserve or restore a site's sustainability within the context of ecosystem services—the idea that healthy ecosystems provide goods and services of benefit to humans and other organisms" (Sustainable Sites Initiative 2009b).

The guidelines and performance benchmarks identify five basic areas as criteria for determining whether sites are sustainable: soils, vegetation, hydrology, materials selection, and human health and well-being (Sustainable Sites Initiative 2009b). In attempting to elaborate on these areas, the SSI has opted for delineating desired outcomes rather than detailing prescriptive measures. Recognizing the lack of standardized practices that define sustainability, the SSI's hope is that the industry will innovate and develop its own strategies for sustainable practices.

Ultimately, the U.S. Green Building Council anticipates incorporating SSI benchmarks into the LEED Green Building Rating System. In its present form, the SSI focuses strongly on the design, construction, establishment, operations and maintenance, and monitoring and innovation phases of new developments. The need for ongoing evaluation is recognized due to the dynamic nature of landscapes. The SSI makes it clear that the initiative is a work in progress and will likely evolve over time.

Sustainable Maintenance

There are many facets of sustainable landscape management. In recent years, sustainable criteria for design and construction have become well defined, but what makes for sustainable maintenance practices is less clear. Currently, there is no blueprint for what constitutes sustainable maintenance. Further, maintenance is currently ongoing on the 99 percent of all existing landscapes that were neither designed with sustainability in mind nor constructed using sustainable methods.

Maintenance contractors historically have been out of the decision-making process until the landscape is completed. They have no input in design from a maintenance perspective and often are not involved in construction. They have no say regarding where new sites are located. They enter into the process after a significant amount of time, money, and resources have been spent to create the landscape and often when considerably less money is available for ongoing maintenance. They inherit all of the underlying problems associated with the site, including soil quality and quantity deficiencies, irrigation system design and installation deficiencies, and plant material issues. They also have to contend with the owner's expectations, which may differ from the design intent.

Figure 1-8 Current designs often include large water features and large lawn areas all kept green and neat and tidy. The corporate world embraces this look. Will their standards change any time soon?

Because aesthetic appearance is the criterion by which most judge a landscape, there is a premium on neat and tidy looking landscapes that distinguish themselves in this manner (Figure 1-8). The image projected by the building and grounds of a corporate headquarters is important to corporate stakeholders because, as the saying goes, "Image is everything." Over time, as owners come and go, maintenance contractors have to adapt to changing attitudes and trends. In short, maintenance contractors are forced to find ways to efficiently maintain sites that may have many built-in deficiencies from a sustainable perspective. Clearly, the challenges of maintaining existing landscapes are immense if the goal is to achieve sustainability.

Greenwashing

As the age of sustainability dawns, it brings with it those who claim to use sustainable practices or products when, in fact, they do not. The common term for this is "greenwashing," which is defined as "the act of misleading consumers regarding the environmental practices of a company or the environmental benefits of a product or service" (TerraChoice Environmental Marketing 2009). According to TerraChoice Environmental Marketing, the vast majority of products offered in a range of markets are guilty of greenwashing by committing one or more of the "seven sins" of greenwashing. The most common sins include:

Hidden trade-offs. Pointing out one positive attribute while ignoring other negative attributes

Vague claims. Claims that are so broad or ill-defined that they mislead consumers

No proof to support claims. Offering no proof that claims are substantiated by research

These sins can be used to promote services as "natural," "green," or "organic" when they are no different from conventional landscape maintenance practices. A healthy dose of realism is needed as the industry pursues the goal of sustainable landscape management. It may be that on many sites contractors are already practicing sustainable maintenance while others who claim to be sustainable are only greenwashing.

SUMMARY

To succeed, sustainability has to be more than just a fad. In this chapter, the historical glimpse of how sustainable ideas have developed over time demonstrates that interest in sustainability has been a relevant topic for a long time. In all segments of society, there are opportunities to develop sustainable approaches, which include constructed landscapes. At this point, there are few rules and many ideas. The search for sustainable landscape management strategies is just beginning and will continue for some time. Techniques will evolve over time as a result of both successes and failures. This book aspires to offer practical ideas and techniques, based on current knowledge, to begin the process of creating sustainable landscapes.

STUDY QUESTIONS

1. Define sustainability as it relates to landscapes. Are any constructed landscapes truly sustainable? Explain.
2. Thomas Malthus and William Jevons were both pessimistic about the future. How have their predictions played out so far?
3. How did Frederick Law Olmsted and Calvert Vaux view the role of landscapes (parks) in the context of the urban environment? What did they strive for in designing their parks?
4. John Muir and Gifford Pinchot were both intimately involved with the wilderness areas in the western United States. How did their views differ from each other? What was Muir's lasting legacy?
5. Aldo Leopold developed the land ethic. Exactly what is the land ethic and what does it have to do with sustainability? How did Leopold's ideas differ from Muir's?
6. What changes occurred after World War II that led to the current nonsustainable approach to landscape maintenance? Is conventional maintenance really unsustainable? Explain.
7. What did Rachel Carson do that has affected today's sustainability movement?
8. Explain Carson's attitude toward chemical pest control. In her view, what was wrong with pest control strategies in the DDT era?
9. What did Ian McHarg prove through his approach to landscape planning? Explain what McHarg meant by entropy and negentropy.
10. How did *Our Common Future* explain the concept of sustainability? How can that be interpreted in constructed landscapes?
11. What is LEED and what does it have to do with sustainability?
12. What is the Sustainable Sites Initiative trying to accomplish? What are the five areas it has designated to determine the sustainability of landscapes?
13. What challenges does the landscape maintenance industry face in attempting to develop more sustainable landscapes?
14. What is greenwashing? How does it threaten the sustainable landscape movement?

SUGGESTED READING

Background

Edwards, A. R. 2005. *The sustainability revolution: Portrait of a paradigm shift.* Gabriola Island, BC: New Society Publishers.

Leopold, A. 1949. *A Sand County almanac: And sketches here and there.* Oxford: Oxford Univ. Press.

McDonough, W., and M. Braungart. 2002. *Cradle to cradle: Remaking the way we make things.* New York: North Point Press.

McHarg, I. L. 1969. *Design with nature.* Garden City, NY: Doubleday/Natural History Press.

The Environmentalist Perspective

Bormann, F. H., D. Balmori, and G. T. Geballe. 2001. *Redesigning the American lawn: A search for environmental harmony.* 2nd ed. New Haven, CT: Yale Univ. Press.

Carson, R. 1962. *Silent spring.* New York: Houghton Mifflin.

The Skeptic Perspective

Bailey, R. 2000. Earthday, then and now. *Reason Online* (May), http://www.reason.com/news/show/27702.html (accessed June 8, 2009).

Lomborg, B. 2001. The skeptical environmentalist: Measuring the real state of the world. Cambridge: Cambridge Univ. Press.

Sacks, D. 2008. Green guru gone wrong. *Fast Company* (November 1), http://www.fastcompany.com/magazine/130/the-mortal-messiah.html (accessed June 8, 2009).

chapter 2

Sustainable Landscape Design

INTRODUCTION

A sustainable landscape requires as much attention to design specifics as a traditional design. The goal of quality sustainable design is to create aesthetic, functional, maintainable, and cost-effective landscapes that are well suited for a specific location or region. To accomplish this goal, the design process requires a clear articulation of the designer's intent for the site, detailed site assessment, and documentation of the site's features, as well as incorporation of design concepts that capitalize on existing site features. The overarching purpose of this approach to design is to maximize short- and long-term sustainability of the site.

This chapter will describe eight key factors in sustainable landscape design:

- The process of sustainable landscape design
- Selecting plants to increase sustainability
- Creating aesthetically pleasing landscapes
- Creating functional landscapes
- Creating landscapes that meet basic human physical and cognitive needs
- Designing to minimize maintenance
- Designing to enhance a landscape's short- and long-term cost effectiveness
- Integrating specialized design approaches to maximize short- and long-term sustainability

THE PROCESS OF SUSTAINABLE LANDSCAPE DESIGN

The landscape design process has multiple steps. Although the steps vary depending on the design, most projects have certain requirements: documenting information about the physical and environmental features of the site, determining how the site will be used, generating design ideas relative to this analysis, creating a preliminary design, gathering feedback from the client about the design, and creating a final design. Although design, installation, and maintenance are all integral to a successful landscape, it is essential to consider these three otherwise separate parts as a single entity throughout the design process. For example, a landscape that looks good on paper but does not account for an extreme slope on the site will be difficult to install and may have long-term maintenance problems due to soil erosion or irrigation or drainage problems. Figure 2-1 illustrates a typical design process. The figure also highlights steps within the process where input from installation and maintenance personnel could

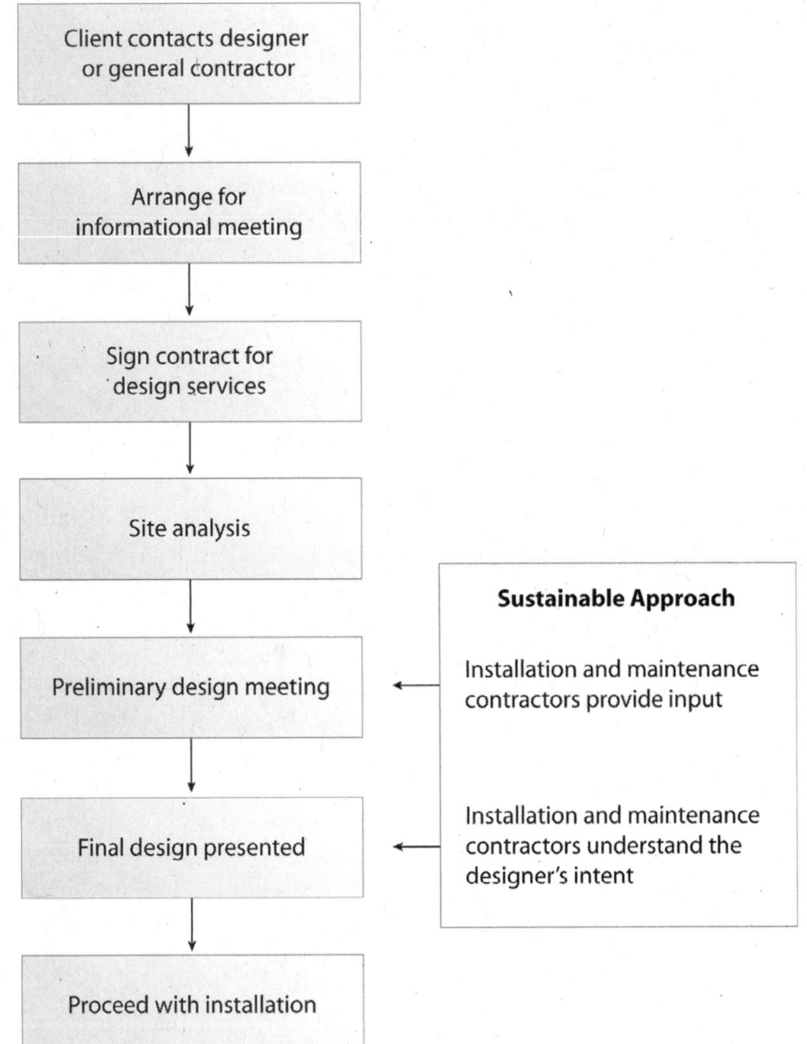

Figure 2-1 An illustration of the multiple steps involved in the landscape design process, including opportunities where the final design could be made more sustainable.

be useful in making the landscape more sustainable in the long term.

Documenting Physical and Environmental Features of the Site

Sustainable design solutions are derived from the designer's knowledge of site conditions and his or her ability to incorporate the pre-existing natural systems into the design. For a design to be successful, it is critical to fully understand the physical and environmental features of a site. Completing a thorough site assessment is the best way to document this information.

Soil type and conditions, wind characteristics, topography and drainage, and seasonal variations in sun and shade patterns require documenting, because each of these can have a significant impact on the

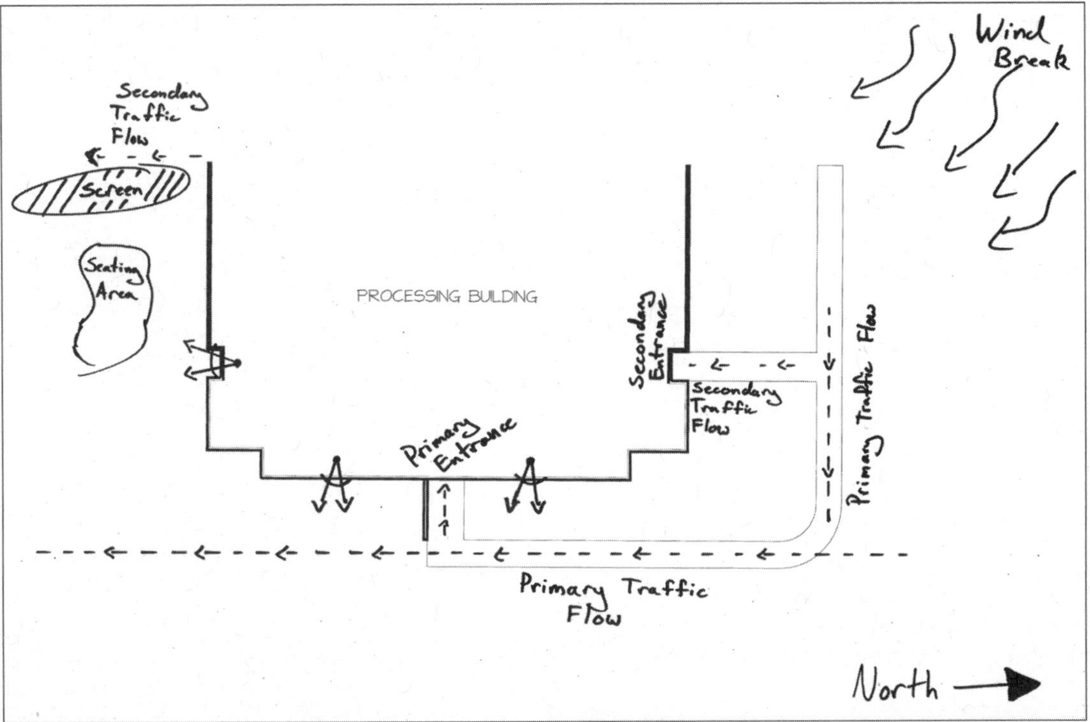

Figure 2-2 A completed site analysis of a new research facility, documenting important information (circulation patterns, views, etc.) relative to developing the landscape.

long-term survivability, which correlates to sustainability, of a newly installed landscape. When documenting the site location, issues on adjacent property should be noted. These include storm water runoff from the property, foot or vehicular traffic patterns, and the need for screening (Figure 2-2). It may not be feasible to address these issues initially, but they should be documented for future consideration. A final group of factors to document include site restrictions (easements and rights-of-way), on-site circulation patterns (vehicular and pedestrian), parking needs, and utility locations.

During the site assessment, the designer and client might also discuss design concepts that will capitalize on existing site features. For example, the site may have an area with poor drainage. The drainage issue might be identified as a problem to be solved through the construction of an underground drainage system. Or it might be viewed as an opportunity to create a wetland area in that space and select plants that thrive in a poorly drained growing environment. These initial discussions can help guide a designer as he or she moves into the next phase of the process.

Starting the Landscape Design Process

Landscape design is a fluid and iterative process (Figure 2-3). The brainstorming phase of the process is very dynamic. During this phase, designers generate multiple design options as they combine different design ideas with site information and initial input

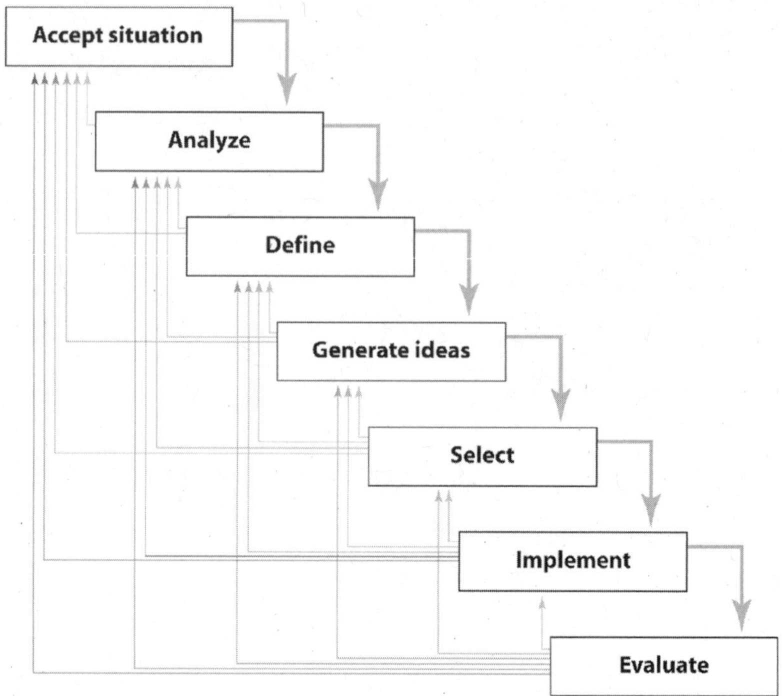

Figure 2-3 Graphical illustration of the landscape design process, showing the multiple phases and how previous phases are revisited throughout the process.

from the client. One design option often leads to another and yet another, until at the end of this phase a designer has multiple options that could be developed further. Some of these options are developed into preliminary designs to share with the client for his or her feedback. Feedback from the client then shapes the next phase as the designer makes changes and works toward a final design. Throughout the process, the needs of the client, the site characteristics and constraints, and the designer's intent should be integrated to create a beautiful and functional sustainable landscape design.

Design Intent

The designer's vision (design intent) for a site is the underlying premise for the design. Often the design intent addresses aesthetic and functional goals of the landscape. An additional feature of design intent relative to sustainable design is that it incorporates ecosystem services. In brief, ecosystem services are benefits we (humans) receive as a result of an ecosystem functioning properly. For example, higher temperatures created by an urban heat island can be reduced by the shade created from street trees. Ecosystem services are described in detail in Chapter 5.

In theory, a designer has a goal in mind when he or she creates a design and selects plants. For example, one area of the landscape may be conceived of as an enclosed space surrounded by layers of plants with low-growing ground covers and stepping up to taller plants. If this intent is not articulated to the maintenance professionals, the effect will be destroyed by limbing up trees and hedging medium-sized plants. Another example is mass plantings used to screen an objectionable view. If this intent isn't communicated and the maintenance crew shears the plants so they don't grow together, then a functional screen will not be created.

Designers must be able to explain the overall intent and how various elements of the design work together. This is particularly important on larger-scale projects, which may be installed in phases or have different personnel involved over the span of the project. If maintenance professionals understand the function of various parts of the design, the subsequent maintenance on the project should be more appropriate. The short- and long-term fate of the design shouldn't be left up to the discretion of the maintenance crew. In addition to improper pruning practices, typical unwarranted modifications to the design by maintenance professionals include plant substitutions, changing lawn and bed areas to make mowing more efficient, and removal of plants with important functional and aesthetic roles. Inadvertently, maintenance often redesigns the landscape to the point where it is unrecognizable from the designer's intent. Communication between the designer and installation and maintenance professionals is essential if the design is to reach its full potential.

The ultimate goal of a sustainable landscape design is to create an outdoor space that includes appropriate plant species, is aesthetically pleasing, has high functionality, requires low maintenance, and is cost effective. The development of the design should take into account each of these factors in order to achieve the best result.

SELECTING PLANTS TO INCREASE SUSTAINABILITY

Creating a sustainable landscape planting involves a complex array of considerations and decisions. Among them is matching the right plant to the site's growing environment. Although this is an obvious step, there are many considerations. A number of decisions are made when selecting plants: whether introduction of new plant material is necessary, the type of plant material to use, the origin and provenance of the plant material, and establishment methods (Dunnett and Clayden 2000).

A thorough site assessment is the essential first step in plant selection. The site assessment provides an awareness of vegetation patterns on the site as well as on the surrounding areas. Based on this information, a three-stage protocol for plant selection can be created. The protocol includes the following:

Identify and plan for what already exists. A fundamental objective is to enrich the existing ecological capital provided by existing vegetation.

Restore existing habitats that have been degraded through the construction process.

Create new habitats where possible and restore or create new connections between habitats. These links may be within an individual site or between the site and the surrounding area (Dunnett and Clayden 2000).

The objective is to create a plant community that needs minimal inputs of water, fertilizer, and pesticides and that requires less maintenance as it matures (Figure 2-4).

Figure 2-4 This rooftop landscape on top of a 25-story building was designed to re-create the natural landscape found in the Mountain West of the United States.

Growing Environment

In addition to soil type, other environmental conditions such as seasonal precipitation, sun and shade patterns, and microclimates have a significant impact on the growth and development of plants. Seasonal precipitation refers to the total amount of precipitation as well as the annual distribution of the precipitation. Although some areas receive adequate annual rainfall amounts to support plant growth, they receive a limited amount during the growing season. In these cases, supplemental moisture can be added through irrigation.

Sun and shade patterns change in a landscape throughout the day, the growing season, and over the lifetime of the landscape. For example, when a new landscape is installed, the overstory plants are often too small to shade the understory plants. The result is that understory plants get scorched from the summer heat and sun intensity because they are not protected (Figure 2-5). It takes a long-term approach to sequentially plant appropriate species over time so the plant community evolves as it would in nature.

Figure 2-6 The high light and heat intensity created in urban planting sites can make it difficult for plants to grow. Adapted street trees such as Armstrong maple (*Acer* × *freemanii* 'Armstrong') and 'Stella d'Oro' daylily (*Hemerocallis* 'Stella d'Oro') are good choices for this environment.

Figure 2-5 Shade-loving perennials such as hostas (*Hosta* spp.) will be scorched by the summer sun, because there is no overstory planting to provide shade.

Microclimates are a combination of many environmental factors (wind, shade and sun exposure, temperature, and humidity) in a relatively small area within a landscape. They are very site specific. Regardless of size, every landscape site will have a variety of microclimates that can affect planting conditions and survivability of plant materials. Built environments often have a number of microclimates due to the size and orientation of a building and the reflective (light and heat) properties of hardscapes (Figure 2-6). In some cases, these microclimates can be integrated to create unique planting areas; in other instances, they can contribute to an "urban heat island" effect and be detrimental to plant growth and development.

CREATING AESTHETICALLY PLEASING LANDSCAPES

An aesthetically pleasing landscape is often the primary goal of a client whether he or she is a homeowner or the owner-manager of a commercial

ACCOUNTING FOR MICROCLIMATES

During the initial site analysis phase, the location and extent of existing or potential microclimates should be documented. Once the conceptual site design is created, the designer should revisit the site and complete a comprehensive site walk-through to determine if the microclimates have been accounted for adequately. This more integrated approach to design will alleviate many of the short- and long-term problems that develop in a landscape when the design is created off-site without the necessary site evaluation and consideration.

DISCUSSION POINTS

The landscape in Figure 2-7 was created after extensive site evaluation. The designer selected plants appropriate to the site after analyzing the existing ecosystem, including the mature trees on-site. Discuss how site analysis can impact plant selection.

Figure 2-7 This native landscape was created by preserving existing plant materials and incorporating new species based on the site analysis.

property. Commercial landscape designs must account for business access, public safety, and the fact that much of the landscape is intended to be "drive-by scenic" as opposed to being used for specific activities.

In commercial settings, the visual impact of landscapes is very important and is often the first impression clients or customers have of the company. Beautiful landscapes can be an important part of the company's image. The interest in sustainability and "going green" over the past decade has led many companies to reconsider the impression made by their landscape. Some companies have limited their use of high-input plants such as annual flower beds and increased the areas that are maintained with fewer inputs such as irrigation. The result is an impression of environmental awareness, which their customers appreciate. For a detailed description of aesthetic landscape design theory and principles, see the suggested reading at the end of this chapter.

CREATING FUNCTIONAL LANDSCAPES

In concert with aesthetic design considerations, a designer must consider basic issues that affect the functionality of a landscape. A functional commercial landscape accounts for how the space will be used by employees, customers or clients, or, in the case of parks and plazas, the public. Functionality in most landscapes can be assigned to two categories: appropriately sized spaces relative to use and maintenance and suitable access points and circulation routes.

The individual spaces that make up a landscape need to be appropriately sized to accommodate how the client intends to use the area. Examples might include gathering spaces used during work breaks or for company functions. These spaces will need to be large enough to hold a specific number of people and should include durable materials that withstand substantial foot traffic. In the case of planting areas such as lawns and planting beds, the size and shape must be considered with regard to the equipment (mowers, edgers, and wheelbarrows) used to maintain the space as well as the irrigation system that will be installed. Suitable access points and circulation routes need to be designed for both foot and vehicular traffic. People or vehicles in the space should be able to move around comfortably within the area and move easily between adjoining areas.

Designing Lawn Areas

Lawns are best used where they serve a clear purpose in the landscape design. Examples of these might include delineating the entrance to a building or along an entrance drive, providing the foreground for a vista of distant landscape features, or serving as a site for passive and active recreation. Unfortunately, what often happens during the design process is that after the hardscape areas are configured and the planting beds are shaped, the area left over on the plan is deemed to be lawn.

In general, if the area in question isn't going to be walked on or sat on, is filled with potential mowing obstacles, or is placed on an extreme slope, it shouldn't be planted with turfgrass. In these examples, a sustainable choice would be to use ground covers or low-growing shrubs instead.

The first step in creating sustainable lawns is to design the area for maximum irrigation and mowing efficiencies. It is essential to design the irrigation system in parallel with the lawn area. It is much easier to adjust the size and shape of a lawn area on paper before the installation is under way. When they aren't designed in combination, the result is a poorly fitted irrigation system with stretched head spacing, reduced uniformity of coverage, excessive precipitation rates, and distorted spray patterns (Color Plate 2-1).

Hardscapes are any nonplant part of the landscape and include walkways; driveways; outdoor seating areas such as patios, fences, and walls; and site amenities (arbors, balustrades, seating, lighting, etc.).

Designers should consult with landscape maintenance contractors regarding the equipment that will likely be used to maintain the lawn. These professionals can provide guidance on the type and size of mower that will be used, including the dimensions of the mowing deck and information on the turning radius the mower will need. The designer can then adjust the lawn and planting beds accordingly. By addressing maintenance considerations before the project is built, there should be fewer maintenance problems over the lifetime of the landscape.

In addition to considering the irrigation system and mowing equipment, the design should also anticipate the impact tree and shrub placement will have on the lawn area. As these ornamental plants mature, they can significantly reduce the amount of sunlight that reaches the lawn. At some point, the lawn area or planting bed area may need to be reconfigured to account for these changes. Finally, when possible, lawns should be placed inside surrounding shrub beds so that overthrow from irrigation or fertilizer lands in beds and not on sidewalks and roads, which could lead to nonpoint source pollution of nearby waterways (Figure 2-8).

Figure 2-8 Surrounding turf areas with planting beds is an effective way to prevent water and fertilizer overthrow from reaching hardscapes.

Nonpoint source (NPS) pollution is pollution affecting a body of water from diffuse sources, such as polluted runoff from agricultural areas draining into a river or wind-borne debris blowing out to sea. Nonpoint source pollution is different from point source pollution, where discharges occur to a body of water at a single location, such as discharges from a chemical factory or urban runoff from a roadway storm drain (Wikipedia 2010).

Designing Planting Beds

Planting beds containing trees, shrubs, perennials, ground covers, and annuals are an essential part of most landscapes because they provide a necessary contrast to turf and hardscape areas in the design. Planting beds also provide yearlong interest with seasonally changing texture and color. Even the most simple planting bed composition is a valuable addition to the landscape (Figure 2-9). Similar to designing lawn areas, irrigation and maintenance need to be considered when designing planting beds.

Just as with lawn areas, the size and shape of the planting bed must be considered with regard to the irrigation system. Odd-shaped planting beds suffer the same irrigation inefficiencies as lawn areas due to stretched or compressed head spacing. Other factors that need to be considered are the location, expected growth rate, and mature size of plants in the bed. These factors will significantly influence what type of irrigation system should be installed and where heads should be placed. (See Chapters 3 and 8 for more details on irrigation design and installation.)

Figure 2-9 Simple low-water-use and low-maintenance planting islands enhance this downtown streetscape.

Part of the design concept should include grouping plants based on water and fertilizer requirements. This thoughtful arrangement can minimize the likelihood of overwatering or overfertilizing plants that require fewer inputs. Likewise, grouping plants with similar maintenance needs, such as pruning and deadheading, can reduce maintenance time (mainly by reducing walk time between beds). Providing easy access points into the bed and making sure the necessary maintenance equipment can also be used in the space will speed maintenance time.

Intensively managed floral displays are often important components of commercial landscapes, particularly near entrance drives and building entrances. These planting areas may be part of a larger planting bed or a separate area. What makes them unique compared to other parts of the landscape is that they are often changed out three or four times a year to provide fresh seasonal color (Color Plate 2-2). These small areas can provide a significant visual impact to the landscape. Although as individual spaces they may require significant inputs, their overall size relative to the rest of the landscape that is maintained sustainably is generally quite small. Concentrating inputs to high-visibility, high-impact areas can be a sustainable approach to design.

Designing for Access and Circulation

To facilitate access and circulation, landscapes include a variety of entrances (public and service), driveways, parking areas, and walkways that are appropriately sized and made of materials able to withstand vehicular or foot traffic. The spaces should be designed by licensed professionals to account for maximum traffic load, safety, storm water management, and other large-scale site considerations. Careful selection of hardscape materials can make these features functional and attractive additions to the landscape. (See Chapter 3 for examples of sustainable hardscape materials.)

Vehicular Access and Circulation

Commercial properties need to have service entrances, driveways, loading zones, and parking areas that are appropriately sized to accommodate trucks and other vehicles. Designs that do not account for this type of vehicular traffic often result in areas that are continually damaged and difficult to repair (Figure 2-10).

Designers should specify permeable interlocking concrete pavers, pervious concrete pavement, porous asphalt, or turf block when they are designing sustainable driveways and parking areas (Figure 2-11). These products can handle the vehicular weight, and they allow water to move through the material profile and into the ground, rather than horizontally across the surface and into the storm water system. Design professionals who specialize in these products should be consulted at the outset of the design process, and, in some cases, the design of these areas should be handled entirely by them.

Figure 2-11 This development used permeable interlocking concrete pavers for the street and eliminated storm water runoff from that area. Courtesy of Unilock, Inc.

Figure 2-10 This narrow driveway between two buildings does not provide adequate room for trucks. A single layer of wall block was installed to protect the plants and irrigation system, but it and the curb continue to be damaged by truck wheels.

Pedestrian Access and Circulation

Strategically placed walkways move people from the parking lot to the building entrance, while other walkways move employees through the outdoor space so they can benefit from the landscape while at work. The goal is to create a network of routes that effectively move people throughout the landscape.

Figure 2-12 A wide primary walkway is critical to effectively moving students across a college campus. This walk provides a direct route to the other side of the quad.

Most landscapes are designed with walkways classified as either primary or secondary. The walkway's function will determine which hardscape material is most appropriate. Primary walkways should be a reasonably direct route between two points (Figure 2-12). These walkways should be a minimum of 5 feet (1.5 meters) wide, although they are often wider to better accommodate pedestrian traffic and to be in scale with the overall landscape and building(s). Local building codes may dictate the minimum size for these walkways and should be determined prior to initiating the design process. Primary walkways should be made of a solid surface that is easy to walk on, that is able to handle wear and tear, and that is maintainable and accessible in all weather conditions. Sustainable hardscape choices for such walkways are similar to those for driveways and parking lots and include permeable interlocking concrete pavers, pervious concrete pavement, and porous asphalt. Secondary walkways tend to meander through a landscape and are not necessarily major thoroughfares. Because they have less traffic, they can be narrower [2–3 feet (1 meter)] and made of gravel or a thick layer of mulch. Gravel and mulch are sustainable options because both materials allow water to filter through and soak into the ground.

Hardscapes located in northern climates have the additional consideration of snow removal. Sidewalks need to be large enough to accommodate the type of snow removal equipment used on the site. They also need to be made of materials that are able to hold up well against typical ice-melting products used in the area.

Some designs will call for gates associated with walkways. These gates may be used to limit public access to a space, or they may simply be aesthetic. Regardless of their function in the landscape, they must be sufficiently wide to accommodate lawn mowers, wheelbarrows, and other maintenance equipment that need to be transported into the enclosed area.

CREATING LANDSCAPES THAT MEET BASIC HUMAN PHYSICAL AND COGNITIVE NEEDS

The Sustainable Sites Initiative (2009a) acknowledges the importance of addressing the physical and cognitive needs of humans in landscape site design. As part of the guidelines and performance benchmarks relative to sustainable site development, the initiative includes a list of nine site design criteria related specifically to human health and well-being. Although these criteria are quite different from the common sustainable design concepts most people are familiar with (reducing pesticide use, managing storm water on-site, etc.), they are equally important. Designers who thoughtfully address these criteria and incorporate them into their designs will develop a truly sustainable landscape. The criteria outlined by the Sustainable Sites Initiative (2009a) are:

Promote equitable site development.

Promote equitable site use.

Protect and maintain unique cultural and historical places.

Promote sustainability awareness and education.

Provide for optimum site accessibility, safety, and wayfinding.

Provide opportunities for outdoor physical activity.

Provide views of vegetation and quiet outdoor spaces for mental restoration.

Provide outdoor spaces for social interaction.

Reduce light pollution.

The first three criteria—promote equitable site development, promote equitable site use, and protect and maintain unique cultural and historical places—focus on the economic and social benefits of site development. They support the idea that sustainable site development can promote the long-term stability of local families and businesses and enhance a community's sense of place and history. Addressing these during the design phase can help a company become a "good citizen" of the community.

The fourth criterion—promote sustainability awareness and education—can provide an important public relations benefit for companies if projecting an image of environmental awareness is part of a company's core values. The goal of this criterion is to promote understanding of sustainability in ways that affect user behavior on-site and beyond (Sustainable Sites Initiative 2009a). Examples of how a company can achieve this include developing educational or interpretive elements that help site users (employees) and visitors (clients or customers) understand how on-site sustainability features can be applied to off-site situations such as to homes or schools (Sustainable Sites Initiative 2009a). Landscape designers can work collaboratively with the company's marketing and public relations department and professionals in the field of interpretive education to develop appropriate materials based on the landscape design (Figure 2-13).

The remaining five criteria are directly linked to physical and cognitive human needs and are discussed in more detail next.

Figure 2-13 The signage at this commercial site shows that this part of the landscape has been designed as a natural wetland area.

Provide for Optimum Site Accessibility, Safety, and Wayfinding

Humans don't like to be confused by their immediate environment. We prefer landscapes that are easy to enter, navigate through, and then exit. Safe, accessible, and legible sites encourage both use and enjoyment (Figure 2-14). The easier it is to use the site, the more likely it is that users will take advantage of opportunities for physical activity, mental

Figure 2-14 The pathways, bridge, and open areas make it easy to navigate through this landscape.

restoration, and social interaction (Sustainable Sites Initiative 2009a). In order for designers to adequately address this need, it is helpful to interview the people, often employees, who use the landscape the most. With this input in mind, the designer can create entrances into the landscape that are easy to find and welcoming. The designer can also design walkways and gathering spaces that are accessible, easy to walk on, and guide users throughout the landscape.

Provide Opportunities for Outdoor Physical Activity

Healthy employees tend to be more productive and have fewer health care costs; both are beneficial to a company's bottom line (DeJong et al. 2003). Physical activity can be added to employee workdays with a well-designed landscape. Regardless of the landscape's size, designers should locate desirable and accessible spaces to enable and encourage physical activity (Sustainable Sites Initiative 2009a). The design may include meandering pathways, public sidewalks, or even sustainable single-track bike trails if the site is large enough. Some companies have workplace wellness programs that focus on ways to improve employee physical and mental health (Wellness Council of America 2010). Consulting with company executives, a workplace wellness officer, and employees can provide designers with the necessary information to develop a landscape that encourages physical activity.

Provide Views of Vegetation and Quiet Outdoor Spaces for Mental Restoration

People like to look at nature and plants because it has a calming and restorative effect (Kaplan, Kaplan, and Ryan 1998). Designers can help people experience nature by providing visual and physical connections to the landscape. In addition to making sure the landscape is clearly visible from all windows, designers can also integrate small quiet outdoor spaces into the landscape. These quiet spaces should include seating, a way to minimize noise, and shelter from sun and wind.

Provide Outdoor Spaces for Social Interaction

An extensive body of research describes the links between social connectedness and human health and well-being. As part of a sustainable design, designers should include outdoor gathering spaces of various sizes and orientations to accommodate groups, for the purpose of building community and improving social ties (Sustainable Sites Initiative 2009a). The spaces should be able to accommodate groups of various sizes, provide different types of seating, include protection from harsh weather, and allow for visual and physical access to plants (Figure 2-15). Well-designed landscapes are a great way to foster social interaction.

Reduce Light Pollution

Light pollution is the illumination of the night sky by electric lights, which can be a significant problem in

Figure 2-15 The large tree adjacent to this sitting area provides shade from mid-afternoon sunlight, creating a comfortable space for employees.

urban areas. Light pollution can negatively impact the normal functioning of many species (including humans). Designers can reduce light pollution by minimizing light trespass off the site, reducing nighttime sky glow, increasing nighttime visibility, and minimizing the negative effects on nocturnal environments. Many of the newer outdoor lighting products are engineered to minimize light pollution. By choosing these types of products and locating them strategically throughout the landscape, the space will still be well illuminated but not give off excess light.

DESIGNING TO MINIMIZE MAINTENANCE

The next factor in sustainable landscape design is to consider alternatives that minimize maintenance. A low-maintenance landscape is one that requires minimal inputs of labor and of products such as water, fertilizers, and chemicals for pest control. Although the maintenance needs of a sustainable landscape are lower than those of a traditional landscape, the site will still need some level of ongoing care.

Designing to Minimize Maintenance Labor

Appropriately sizing areas, minimizing labor-intensive areas, and selecting the proper plants all impact the amount of work needed to maintain a landscape. For example, sizing lawn areas to be mowed by larger, more efficient mowers reduces the amount of time spent mowing a site. Using lawns in appropriate locations is another effective way to reduce landscape maintenance labor (Figure 2-16). Lawns planted on a steep slope that is difficult and dangerous to mow should be replaced with a ground cover or low-growing suckering-type shrub. These types of plants will stabilize the slope and prevent soil erosion but will not require the same level of maintenance as a lawn (Color Plate 2-3).

Eliminating areas that need to be trimmed using a string trimmer or edger can reduce labor inputs, as can using edging to create a functional barrier between lawns and planting beds. When designing a sustainable landscape, it is essential to choose a product that is long-lasting and does not need regular maintenance or replacement.

Placing the right plant in the right place during the design phase is critical to reducing the long-term maintenance needs of a landscape. A plant that is well suited for a particular growing environment with regard to soil conditions, light exposure, natural precipitation, and overall size will require minimal maintenance. Designers need to have a comprehensive understanding of these factors before beginning the design because plants that are poorly matched to a site will likely struggle to survive. One such example is planting rhododendrons (*Rhododendron* spp.) in alkaline soils (Color Plate 2-4). The designer should have specified another shrub species such as common snowberry (*Symphoricarpos albus*), Vanhoutte spirea (*Spiraea* × *vanhouttei*), or dwarf bush honeysuckle (*Diervilla lonicera*), all of which are adapted to alkaline soil conditions.

In other instances, poor plant selection by the designer will mean a plant needs constant and extreme pruning to keep it in a confined growing space. This is a common design problem with foundation planting where large junipers (*Juniperus* spp.) are placed in narrow beds. Selecting slow-growing plants and reducing or eliminating techniques that are maintenance intensive such as espalier and topiary will greatly reduce the amount of time spent pruning. Such steps also reduce the amount of landscape debris.

Another way to minimize labor is to mass plantings together. Massing plants can prevent light from reaching weed seeds, thereby preventing germination and reducing the need for weed control. Although appropriate massing can reduce weed germination, if plants are grouped too closely together, disease problems can develop because of poor air circulation around the plants. Designers need to balance these two issues.

(a)

(c)

(b)

Figure 2-16 (a) Designing lawn spaces to account for maintenance is essential. This narrow lawn strip between the street and the sidewalk just doesn't make sense from a maintenance point of view. (b) The tree stakes, lights, and limestone outcropping edge make this lawn a nightmare to maintain. (c) The flowing curves of this design combined with uninterrupted lawn make mowing this lawn easy and efficient.

Designing to Minimize Maintenance Products

Most landscape maintenance products (water, fertilizers, and pest control products) can be reduced through proper plant selection. A plant well suited to the growing environment will be healthier and require fewer inputs. Even sustainable landscapes, however, require some level of maintenance and, in some cases, may even require minimal inputs of water, fertilizer, or pest control.

Water

The need for supplemental water in a landscape can be reduced by incorporating plants native to the area or by including plants adapted to a similar growing environment. If supplemental watering is required, plants should be grouped according to their water needs. In doing this, plants with a higher water requirement get the moisture they need without overwatering their drought-tolerant or low-water-use landscape neighbors. Lawn areas that are properly designed to accommodate efficient irrigation systems, as discussed earlier in this chapter, are critical to reducing the amount of supplemental water used in a landscape.

Fertilizer

A common misconception is that plants require regular fertilizer applications for proper growth and development. Although plants do need nutrients in order to grow, they don't necessarily need fertilization. Many soils contain adequate nutrient levels to sustain plant growth.

Designers can reduce the need for fertilizer applications through careful plant selection. Many ornamental species are considered "tough" and are able to grow well in poor soils. Table 2-1 provides a list of shrubs and perennials that grow well in poor, compacted soils. Many of these species are also drought tolerant so they are doubly sustainable choices.

Pest Control

Inputs associated with pest control can be greatly reduced through proper plant selection, and disease- and insect-resistant plants should be selected whenever possible. Many plant tags now include information about a species' disease and insect resistance, and the majority of plant reference books and Internet sites also include this information. Several species available in the nursery industry today have been specifically selected because of these characteristics. Designers who incorporate these species in their designs can greatly reduce the need for pest control products over the life span of the landscape.

TABLE 2-1 Shrubs and Perennials Suitable for Growing on Compacted Sites

Scientific Name	Common Name
Shrubs	
Aronia melanocarpa	Black chokeberry
Berberis koreana	Korean barberry
Diervilla lonicera	Dwarf bush honeysuckle
Rhus aromatica	Fragrant sumac
Rhus glabra	Smooth sumac
Rhus trilobata	Skunkbush sumac
Sorbaria sorbifolia	Ural false spirea
Symphoricarpos albus	Common snowberry
Perennials	
Achillea millefolium	Yarrow
Alyssum saxatile	Basket-of-gold
Arabis albida	Wall rockcress
Cerastium tomentosum	Snow-in-summer
Dianthus deltoides	Maiden pink
Eryngium campestre	Field eryngo
Geranium maculatum	Spotted geranium
Geranium sanguineum	Blood red cranesbill
Helianthemum nummularium	Rock rose; sun rose
Nepeta spp.	Catmint
Perovskia atriplicifolia	Russian sage
Rudbeckia fulgida	Gloriosa daisy
Sedum spp.	Stonecrop
Veronica spp.	Speedwell

Source: Adapted from http://www.extension.umn.edu/distribution/naturalresources/DD7502.html and http://www.extension.umn.edu/distribution/horticulture/components/08464-boulevard-perennials.pdf.

DESIGNING TO ENHANCE A LANDSCAPE'S SHORT- AND LONG-TERM COST EFFECTIVENESS

The seventh factor in sustainable landscape design is to consider the cost effectiveness of a landscape. The cost effectiveness of a sustainable landscape has both short- and long-term implications. Landscape installation costs are up-front costs payable all at once. Maintenance costs, on the other hand, are ongoing and over time can be 10 to 50 times the cost of installation (Palmer 2009). In some cases, factors such as increased water restrictions, prolonged drought, and a tight labor market are forcing property managers to rethink their landscape installation and maintenance practices.

Short-Term Cost Effectiveness

Short-term cost effectiveness centers on choosing lower-cost installation procedures as well as lower-cost hardscape and plant materials. This doesn't suggest that inferior procedures or lower-quality products should be used, but rather the cost of a procedure or product should be compared to other viable alternatives. One way to create attractive and cost-effective designs is to integrate the existing elements on a site such as topography, plant material, and hardscapes whenever possible. This will help the designer capitalize on valuable site features as well as reduce costs because fewer new construction materials will be needed for the project.

Working with the Existing Topography

The topography of a site is an important design consideration and includes existing slopes and grading and drainage plans to modify these slopes to make the site usable. The technical expertise required to successfully alter a site requires collaboration with licensed professionals such as landscape architects and engineers. Careful manipulation of the site can enhance the landscape's sustainability by improving its functionality, reducing maintenance, and maximizing its aesthetic value.

The functionality of a landscape can be enhanced by altering slopes to improve drainage or to direct water to a specific site location. Another example is using grading to level an area for a building or to make walkway slopes safe and usable. Functionality and maintenance can be improved when lawn areas are graded to reduce the slope so maintenance is both easier and safer. Finally, from an aesthetic standpoint, grading can increase the visual interest of a site and create a physical barrier to an undesirable view.

Another design approach to a site's topography is to minimize grading and install other functional landscape features. For example, rather than doing extensive grading to a site to make it mostly level, a series of short retaining walls could be installed to create level terraces (Figure 2-17). Another example is to design a dry river bed that will move water away from a structure or hold water temporarily during heavy rainfall events (Figure 2-18).

Figure 2-17 Short retaining walls were used to create level terraces for plantings in this design. The series of terraces gives the site an enclosed feeling and reduces noise from a nearby road.

Figure 2-18 The dry river bed installed adjacent to this street serves as a collection point during heavy rainfall events and prevents storm water runoff from reaching the storm sewer.

Working with Existing Plant Materials

Often landscape sites have existing plant materials that can be incorporated into the landscape design. If these plants will be used as part of the new design, they need to be identified early in the site development process so they can be protected. One factor to consider when evaluating existing plant material is age. In general, younger, smaller trees can withstand more root injury than large mature trees. In some situations, it may be best to sacrifice older trees that will be more impacted by the construction and have a limited number of years left in their life span, in order to save more viable, younger trees. Capitalizing on this existing site vegetation can significantly reduce the initial cost of the landscape.

Working with Existing Hardscapes

Existing hardscapes, the nonplant part of a landscape, can be incorporated into new designs. Although retrofitting existing landscapes is more common on residential properties, there are still opportunities to employ these concepts to commercial or public landscapes. Existing brick, concrete pavers, and natural stone can all be reused to create new patios, walkways, or driveways (Figure 2-19). Reusing these existing materials is important from sustainable and economic perspectives, because transporting and dumping demolition debris impacts landfill space and can become a significant project expense. In some landscape renovations, existing hardscapes may be left in place and just added to rather than demolished (Figure 2-20).

New construction sites may have materials such as boulders or other types of stone that can be used for hardscapes. Boulders can be used to create natural-looking retaining walls or to provide accents in planting beds. Using these native materials can also enhance the "genus loci" (sense of place) of the landscape and help it fit into the surrounding physical context.

Figure 2-19 Limestone salvaged from a retaining wall demolition project was recycled to create this walkway.

Figure 2-20 The entrance to this building was widened to improve access by adding concrete pavers to the edges of the existing walkway.

Long-Term Cost Effectiveness

The most significant cost benefit of a sustainable landscape is the substantial savings in maintenance costs over the life of the landscape. These long-term maintenance cost savings can be seen in a comparison of two similarly sized [1,900 square foot (175 square meter)] landscapes in California (Sustainable Sites Initiative 2009b). One landscape was installed as a "traditional" landscape with turf areas, planting beds of nonnative species, and a user-controlled sprinkler irrigation system. The second, or "native," landscape included only climate-appropriate California native plants, low-volume drip irrigation with a weather-sensitive controller, and a system for capturing storm water runoff for groundwater recharge. Annually, the native landscape uses 80 percent less water, requires half as much maintenance, and generates half of the green waste of the traditional landscape (Sustainable Sites Initiative 2009b). The result is a sizable cost savings. A number of strategies to reduce landscape maintenance inputs were described earlier in this chapter.

INTEGRATING SPECIALIZED DESIGN APPROACHES TO MAXIMIZE SHORT- AND LONG-TERM SUSTAINABILITY

The final factor in sustainable design addresses the overall goal outlined in the Sustainable Sites Initiative (2009a), which is to protect and restore site processes and systems during the site design phase. The initiative "... envisions that sustainable landscape practices will enable natural and built systems to work together to protect and enhance the ability of landscapes to provide services such as climate regulation, clean air and water, and improved quality of life." To achieve this goal, the initiative has created a matrix that evaluates a number of design approaches related to the ecological components of a site.

A number of strategies can be implemented to achieve this goal, and some of these were described earlier in this chapter. Other sustainable approaches to site design outlined by the Sustainable Sites Initiative (2009a) include the following:

Minimize or eliminate potable water consumption for irrigation.

Preserve and restore native wildlife habitat.

Promote a sense of place with native vegetation and appropriate site-adapted species.

Manage water on-site.

Cleanse water on-site.

Minimize or Eliminate Potable Water Consumption for Irrigation

A number of strategies can be used to minimize or eliminate potable (drinkable) water used for irrigation. These strategies include using low-water-use plant species, high-efficiency irrigation equipment, and climate-based irrigation system controllers. Potable water can be preserved by using gray water, captured rainwater, or condensate water for irrigating.

While the goal is to reduce the use of potable water, this should not be interpreted as eliminating an irrigation system altogether. Eliminating irrigation systems reduces options during establishment and maintenance of the landscape. It may also lead to landscape managers pulling hoses around a site to water plants or having to retrofit sites with irrigation systems. The key is to design landscapes that can thrive with a minimum level of irrigation and to implement management strategies that include constant monitoring of water use in the landscape. Plant selection and grouping becomes critical so that plants with similar water requirements are grouped together. Irrigation systems should be sophisticated and allow for a maximum number of zones, employ precise flow control, incorporate newer head designs such as stream rotors instead of pop-up sprays, and use advanced controller technology that allows for multiple cycles and evapotranspiration (ET) management. Along with these solutions, discussions about water use and irrigation strategies need to be ongoing between designers, owners, and maintenance personnel.

Preserve and Restore Native Wildlife Habitat

A growing human population has led to urban development replacing native wildlife habitat in many parts of the world. As a result, populations of several native insect, bird, and mammal species have been displaced and often seek refuge in the suburban landscape. Providing the basics of food, water, and cover will attract many forms of wildlife to a landscape. For instance, plants that set fruit or seeds can provide food for birds and mammals. Foliage and flowers of other species are food sources for butterflies and beneficial insects. Often it is necessary to leave spent flowers on the plants so seeds can develop, although this reduces the overall aesthetic in some people's mind. Water sources for wildlife can be as simple as a birdbath or an elaborate pond or water feature. These large-scale water sources can be dramatic focal points in the landscape and meet the needs of local wildlife.

The type of cover provided in the landscape will impact the type of wildlife it attracts. Thickets of shrubs and large perennials will work for small mammals, while snags and dead trees provide cover and nesting habitat for birds. Another benefit of attracting specific wildlife is that birds and beneficial insects help reduce harmful or nuisance insect populations. Consult a local resource such as the Department of Natural Resources or Cooperative Extension for more information about wildlife in specific areas.

DISCUSSION POINTS

As part of the sustainability movement on many university campuses, grounds management personnel are being asked to reduce or eliminate the use of potable water for irrigation on campus. What strategies could they implement to achieve this goal? How should they prioritize the areas that are irrigated?

Promote a Sense of Place with Native Vegetation and Appropriate Site-Adapted Species

Native plants are widely promoted as being a key part of sustainable landscapes, and certainly using plants native to a particular region can increase the likelihood that those plants will do well in the landscape. Yet, aside from hardiness zone, few commercial landscapes provide the same environmental conditions found in native landscapes. The built environment where plants will be installed will likely have a modified soil type, altered drainage patterns, different sun and shade patterns, and even microclimates that result in temperature differences. Sometimes native plants are not well suited to this modified environment. Nonnative plants adapted to a particular growing area may be a better alternative.

Figure 2-21 A row of 'Autumn Blaze' maples (*Acer* × *freemanii* 'Jeffsred') lines this street. These trees are well adapted to the site and create a spectacular display in the fall.

Courtesy Jeff Iles, Iowa State University.

In the case of street trees, nonnative species and tree cultivars are frequently more adaptable to urban conditions than native species. Research has also shown that many of these nonnative trees often require fewer public resources to maintain than native trees (Ramstad and Orlando 2009). One reason red maple (*Acer rubrum*) and Freeman maple (*Acer* × *freemanii*) and their cultivars ('Armstrong', 'Autumn Flame', 'Bowhall', 'October Glory', 'Red Sunset', and 'Autumn Blaze', to name a few) make good street trees is because this species evolved in swampy environments with limited air in the soil for the roots to absorb (Figure 2-21). Because of this adaptation, they make good trees for urban environments, because the soils on these sites are often compacted with limited soil oxygen.

Cultivar is derived from the words *cultivated* and *variety*, often designating a product of plant selection or breeding (Acquaah 1999). Woody plant cultivars are asexually propagated, typically through budding or grafting, in order to perpetuate one or several attributes of a plant. A cultivar is genetically identical to all other plants of the same-named variety.

Using a combination of native and nonnative species can also reduce the impact of large-scale plant death due to insects and diseases. There are historical and current examples of plant populations, in particular trees, being wiped out due to introduced disease and insect pests. In the early to mid-1900s, native elm trees (*Ulmus* spp.) in Europe and North America were essentially decimated as a result of Dutch elm disease (*Ophiostoma ulmi*). Municipalities and commercial sites that had overplanted this stately species were left with little to no tree cover after this devastation. Currently, two recently introduced pests, the emerald ash borer (*Agrilus planipennis*) and the Asian long-horned beetle (*Anoplophora glabripennis*), have been destroying native and nonnative species. The plant hosts for the emerald ash borer, as its name implies, are ash trees, in particular, green and white ash, *Fraxinus pennsylvanica* and *Fraxinus americana*, respectively (Color Plate 2-5). The Asian long-horned beetle's preferred host species include *Populus* (poplar), *Salix* (willow), *Ulmus* (elm), and *Acer* (maple). By itself, a diverse mix of species in a plant community could not have prevented these widespread outbreaks. However, species diversity is essential to maintaining a sustainable landscape.

Creating Conceptual Plant Communities

A big-picture approach to using plants is to develop plant communities that replicate a native plant community. This conceptual plant community can include a combination of native and site-appropriate species adapted to the site. In nature, plant communities develop because plants grow in association with other plants with similar environmental requirements such as soil, moisture, and climate. Another feature of natural plant communities is the combination of different-sized plants growing together. The shorter plants in the community are adapted to grow in the shade of the taller grasses, shrubs, and trees. This natural integration of different species enhances the overall landscape aesthetic, provides wildlife habitat, improves long-term ecosystem balance, and lowers overall maintenance costs,

Figure 2-22 This commercial site in the Midwest was designed to re-create a native prairie indigenous to the region.

Figure 2-23 The downspouts on this commercial site empty directly onto a hard surface and contribute to the site's storm water runoff.

thus enhancing a landscape's overall sustainability. In recent years, more commercial sites are being developed to preserve existing plant communities or are being designed to re-create plant communities that were on the site prior to construction (Figure 2-22).

Manage Water On-Site

The ultimate goal of managing surface water is to have all natural precipitation or irrigation that falls onto a landscape remain and eventually soak into the soil. Irrigation systems should be designed and calibrated to apply the appropriate amount of water over a set time so runoff does not occur. The amount of precipitation during rainfall events, on the other hand, is difficult to predict so multiple design strategies may need to be considered.

The function of downspouts, to collect and direct water from the roof, contributes substantially to where and how quickly water from a large rain event enters the landscape or storm sewer (Figure 2-23). Downspouts should be oriented away from paved surfaces and directed to areas in the landscape, including plantings that can withstand large flushes of water during heavy storms. In addition to careful placement of downspouts, two other design strategies to manage on-site surface water movement are specialized grading of the site and reducing nonpermeable surfaces.

Grading

As described earlier, grading a site has many functional and aesthetic benefits. Often grading is done to move water away from a structure or hardscape in order to prevent damage. Ultimately, if water moves across the site, at some point it must be contained or there is risk of polluting off-site waterways. Grading the site to include swales (small dips in the ground) and berms (raised earthen mounds) can help prevent surface water from leaving the site (Figure 2-24). The swales will collect the water temporarily and allow the water to percolate through the soil, whereas the berms will create a physical barrier to the movement of the water to a different location on the site. In some cases, material can be added to the swale area to increase the initial infiltration rate of water into the soil.

Reducing Nonpermeable Surfaces

Whenever possible, a designer should select porous materials such as mulch, gravel, pervious concrete, permeable interlocking concrete pavers, or similar

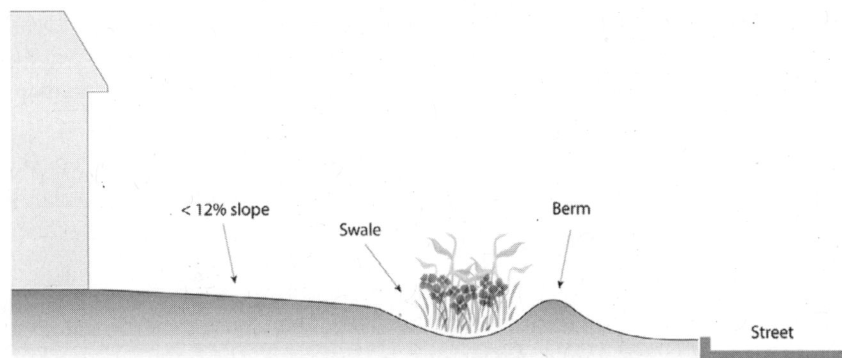

Figure 2-24 This cross section illustrates how water can be captured in a swale to limit storm water runoff, and how a berm can be used to create a physical barrier to storm water movement.

hardscape materials for the landscape. These materials allow rainwater and irrigation water to soak into the ground, which filters pollutants and reduces runoff from the landscape. Obviously, in some instances, these products may not be acceptable based on the type of pedestrian or vehicular traffic on the site, but creative thinking about the overall design should result in the integration of these materials where appropriate.

Cleanse Water On-Site

On-site water cleansing aims to filter pollutants and sediment from surface water runoff on the site. A number of technologies and strategies can be used to accomplish this, including directing runoff from all surfaces to soil- and vegetation-based water treatment methods such as vegetated swales, filter strips, and bioretention areas.

Rain gardens are a relatively new addition to the list of water-cleansing strategies (Figure 2-25). In brief, a rain garden is a specially designed and slightly depressed site where rainwater can be collected and allowed to slowly percolate through the soil profile. The rainwater is filtered through the soil and plant roots, removing impurities and soil particles. This results in cleaner water entering the groundwater. Many local and state agencies are encouraging homeowners and commercial property developers to build rain gardens in an effort to achieve cleaner groundwater. References on building, planting, and maintaining rain gardens are given in the suggested reading at the end of this chapter.

Figure 2-25 The small-scale rain garden shown here is an excellent way to collect water from hard surfaces, allowing it to filter through to the groundwater system.

SUMMARY

A sustainable landscape design is more than the conscious arrangement of outdoor space for human enjoyment and satisfaction; it will also result in a landscape with minimal inputs of water, fertilizers, pesticides, labor, and building materials. Designing a sustainable landscape means working toward a thoughtful balance between resources used, during both construction and maintenance, and results gained. Research indicates that sustainable design should meet basic human needs while consuming little energy, wasting no resources, and being culturally informed and biologically compatible (Wann 1996). Because of the complexity of achieving these goals, large-scale sustainable designs benefit from the input of numerous professionals, including land use planners, civil engineers, landscape architects, horticulturists, and construction and maintenance personnel.

STUDY QUESTIONS

1. Outline the typical landscape design process. Where can sustainable influences be incorporated?
2. Define "design intent."
3. What can a designer do to ensure plants selected for a design are sustainable?
4. Define "microclimate."
5. Define "hardscape."
6. Define "nonpoint source pollution."
7. Describe five ways designers can create landscapes that meet basic human physical and cognitive needs.
8. List five things landscape designers can do to reduce landscape maintenance.
9. Describe "long-term cost effectiveness" with regard to landscape design. What can designers do to enhance a landscape's long-term cost effectiveness?
10. Define "conceptual plant community."
11. Describe two ways designers can manage on-site water.
12. List 10 sustainable materials that a designer can incorporate into a design.
13. Describe the relationship among landscape design, landscape installation, and landscape maintenance. How should this influence design decisions?

SUGGESTED READING

Hartsig, T., and S. Rodie. 2009. Bioretention garden: A manual for contractors in the Omaha region to design and install bioretention gardens. City of Omaha, NE.

Northeastern Illinois Planning Commission. 2003. *Conservation design resource manual.* Chicago: Northeastern Illinois Planning Commission.

Smith, G. W. 2009. Sustainability and horticulture. Special Directory Section, American Nursery and Landscape Association, Washington, DC.

Starbuck, C. J. 2002. Preventing construction damage to trees. Publication G6885. University of Missouri Extension, Columbia.

VanDerZanden, A. M., and S. Rodie. 2007. *Landscape design: Theory and application.* Clifton Park, NY: Thompson Delmar.

chapter 3

Sustainable Landscape Construction: Process, Irrigation Systems, and Hardscape Materials

INTRODUCTION

Landscape design and landscape construction cannot truly be separated because issues that affect one segment affect the other segment. Because the design and construction processes involve multiple phases and often multiple personnel, good communication between parties is imperative in order to achieve design goals and the long-term success of the landscape. Ideally, the designer, the landscape contractor, and the landscape maintenance professional will communicate during the design development and installation phases to ensure project goals are achieved. In some cases, changes to the original design may be warranted to make the landscape more sustainable. Establishing a shared vision and a set of clearly stated goals that the entire team understands is critical to a successful landscape.

Sustainable landscape construction includes modifying conventional construction processes so existing vegetation and soil are considered a site resource and managed appropriately. It also includes properly designed and installed irrigation systems and integration of sustainable hardscape materials.

This chapter will discuss the following topics:

The conventional landscape construction process

A sustainable landscape construction process alternative

Sustainable irrigation design and installation strategies

Sustainable hardscape materials

THE CONVENTIONAL LANDSCAPE CONSTRUCTION PROCESS

The landscape construction process consists of multiple phases and varies depending on the size of the project, the location of the project, and the landscape contractor's preferences. Figure 3-1 illustrates the most common phases of a landscape construction project. As the focus of this text is sustainable landscape management, only the grading phase of the construction process will be discussed here. See the suggested reading at the end of this chapter for detailed information on the entire construction process.

Rough Grading

During the rough grading phase, the site is manipulated into the desired landform, which facilitates site drainage. In many cases, erosion control features are temporarily installed to limit on-site

Step 1

Preconstruction activities and site preparation

Step 2

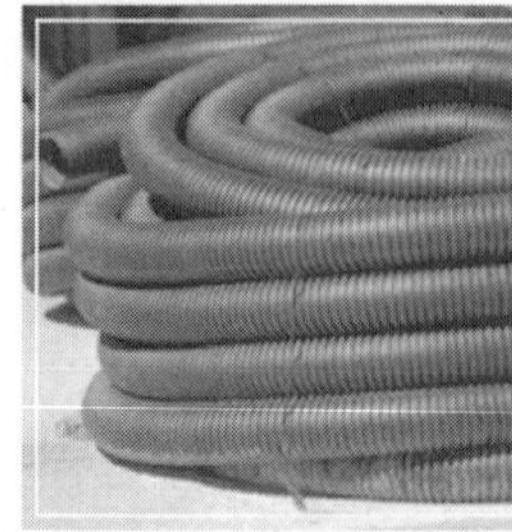

Rough grading, drainage, site utilities, irrigation, and distribution lines installed

Step 3

Retaining walls, stairs, and any paving completed

Step 4

Site structures finished

Step 5

Finish grading, fencing, and freestanding walls

Step 6

Site amenities, plant material, and turf

Figure 3-1 Diagram showing the most common phases of a typical commercial landscape construction project.

erosion and prevent erosion from impacting areas outside of the construction site (Figure 3-2). Once erosion control measures are in place, existing site vegetation, including turf, ground covers, shrubs, or other nonprotected vegetation, are removed. In this conventional approach, these materials are usually disposed of off-site. The next step is to scrape the existing topsoil and stockpile it either on-site or nearby for use later when the site is brought back to final grade. What remains is the subgrade soil, which may have poor structure, poor permeability, nonoptimal pH, or low nutrient content (Color Plate 3-1). Using heavy equipment, the subgrade is cut and filled to create the overall shape and contours of the site. This often entails grading to create

Figure 3-2 An erosion control fence can be an effective way to minimize on-site and off-site erosion during construction.

a relatively flat area for the building (Figure 3-3). The grade that is created at the end of this phase is called the "rough grade." The rough grade is usually 5 inches (410 centimeters) below the final or finished grade to account for the addition of topsoil for planting areas or the installation of paving materials (Figure 3-4). Additional erosion control measures may need to be installed at the completion of rough grading to provide further protection against on-site and off-site erosion.

In some cases, gravel is spread over the subsoil after the rough grading is completed to make it easier for construction vehicles to maneuver around the site. Although this prevents vehicles from getting stuck in muddy conditions, it also makes for very difficult planting conditions once the construction is complete.

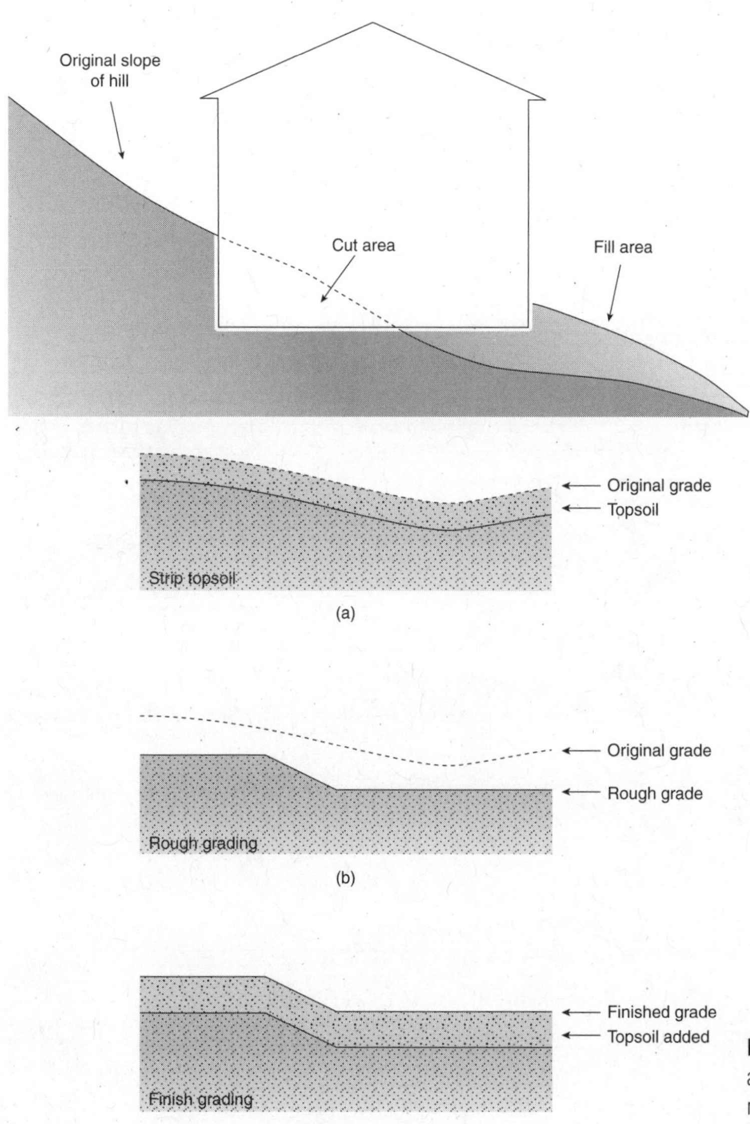

Figure 3-3 During the grading process, some areas of the existing topography are cut (removed), while others are filled with additional soil to change the overall site contours to accommodate the building and landscape.

Figure 3-4 Site grading is a sequential process as illustrated in steps (a), (b) and (c). Once the rough grade is established, the last step is to bring the site to final grade by adding topsoil.

SLOPE TERMINOLOGY AND CALCULATIONS

The outcome of site grading is a change in the site's topography, in particular, the slopes found on the site. Slopes are measured as a mathematical ratio between a vertical distance and a specified horizontal distance (Figure 3-5). Slopes are generally referenced as a ratio or percentage. In either case, slope represents a change in elevation over a specified distance. Table 3-1 provides basic slope guidelines for a variety of landscape settings. These guidelines must be considered during the grading phase of the construction project to ensure the site has maximum functionality and meets accessibility requirements.

Ratio

- H/V (horizontal distance/vertical distance)
- 20:1

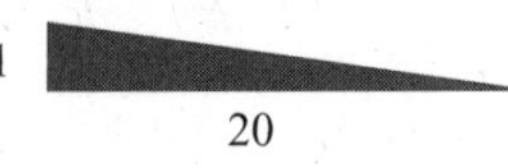

Percent slope: 20:1 = 1/20 = 0.05 = 5%

Figure 3-5 Diagram illustrating how to calculate the slope based on changes in vertical and horizontal distances.

TABLE 3-1 Slope Guidelines Relative to How the Landscape Space Will Be Used

AREA	MAXIMUM (%)	DESIRABLE (%)	MINIMUM (%)
Street	17	1–8	0.5
Parking	6	1–4	0.5
Service area	4	1–3	0.5
Walks			
Building approach	4	2–3	1
Major walkway	5	2–4	0.5
Ramp	8.33	6–8	0.5
Paved pedestrian areas (seating, plazas)	2	1.5	1
Lawn (mowed)	25	4–10	2
Lawn (mowed, adjacent to building)	25	4–10	2 (absolute minimum)
Unmowed bank	50	33	—
Swales	5–6	1–4	0.5
Playing field	4	3	2

Accessibility issues for the disabled:

- Maximum slope of 8 percent.
- 1.5 m long level landing provided for every 0.75 m of vertical climb (30 horizontal feet of ramp at 8 percent slope).
- Maximum cross-slope of 2 percent.
- Railing needed on both sides if slope is greater than 5 percent.
- Handicapped parking space access 2 percent or less in both directions.

Finish Grading

Once the site utilities (sewer, gas, electric, etc.), irrigation distribution lines, retaining walls, stairs, driveways, walkways, and outdoor seating areas have been installed, the finish grade is started. The finish grade is achieved by spreading topsoil, from the stockpile that was created during the rough grading phase, over the areas where turf and planting beds will be installed. The topsoil is carefully raked to the finish grade.

The Impact of Grading on Existing Soil

The techniques used to modify drainage patterns and create structurally sound foundations for buildings and hardscapes often result in planting areas that are not well suited for plant growth. As a result of completing general site work, the soil layers on a site are layered differently than if the soil were in its native state. As described previously, the topsoil is scraped off the building site; heavy equipment moves across the area during construction, causing soil compaction; and generally before the new landscape is installed, a layer of topsoil is brought in and spread across the area. Generally, this layer of new topsoil is not tilled into the compacted layer below, creating an interface between the two disparate soil types (Figure 3-6). The term "sandwich soil" is used to describe many urban soils where new construction has been completed because of the layering effect that is created.

Soil Compaction

Soil becomes compacted when aggregates and individual soil particles are pressed together with force. Compacted soils have higher bulk density, fewer large pores, decreased infiltration and percolation rates, and increased resistance to root penetration (Day and Bassuk 1994). This combination can be deadly to plants. Some plants are more tolerant of such growing conditions, but all plants will ultimately suffer from extended time in this type of growing environment.

Figure 3-6 Topsoil (the dark soil in this image) has a much different composition from subgrade soil and should be tilled into the existing site soil to prevent a soil interface problem.

In addition to being a poor growing environment, compacted soils also have the problem of precipitation (rain or irrigation) accumulating on the soil surface. This causes a crust to form on the surface as the soil dries out (Color Plate 3-2). Susceptibility to compaction is highly correlated to the textural composition of soil. (For a better understanding of textural categories, see http://soils.usda.gov/technical/manual/contents/chapter3_index.htm.)

Cleanup

Once the landscape installation is complete, site cleanup can begin. Typically, this involves removing any remaining construction debris, including temporary erosion control measures; any remaining vegetation that was removed when the site was cleared; and extra construction materials such as pavers, rock, or stone. These materials are generally transported and disposed of off-site. After the debris is removed and final touch-ups to the construction are complete, the walkways, driveways, and other hardscape areas are swept or washed to remove soil, mulch, or other

TOPSOIL

Many construction plans call for placement of topsoil after site construction is complete and prior to plant installation. But what constitutes topsoil is broadly defined. Sometimes the topsoil originally stockpiled from the site is used. This soil tends to be in fair shape and serves the necessary functions of topsoil. In other instances, topsoil is imported. Imported topsoil may be very different from the native soil on the site. Often it is a sandy loam or a compost/soil mix that is very high in organic matter. In both cases, it creates a shallow and nonfunctional growing environment. Another common practice is to use excavation spoils as topsoil. Although these spoils are a cheap alternative, they often contain subsoil, rocks, and soil parent material, none of which provides a suitable growing environment for plant roots. Ideally, the topsoil that is used has good aeration and drainage, contains adequate organic matter, and is free of weed seeds.

Figure 3-7 The soil erosion that has occurred on this construction site has ended up in the street and adjacent to the curbs. It will be hard to avoid polluting the storm sewers as this site is cleaned up.

organic matter. When the areas are cleaned using a hose or power washer, the wastewater often runs into storm sewers either on the site or adjacent to the site, or into nearby waterways (Figure 3-7). The sediment in this water can cause a significant increase in nonpoint source pollution for affected streams and rivers.

Conventional landscape construction processes do not account for the environmental impact that results from the site work. Removing native soils and existing vegetation significantly disrupts and damages the pre-existing ecosystems on the site. Often this type of damage is difficult and costly, if not impossible, to repair. Conventional cleanup strategies at the end of the project can cause further environmental damage to the site and surrounding areas. Wastewater from the cleanup phase typically ends up in streams, rivers, and storm sewers. These systems are particularly vulnerable to pollution from sediment runoff and chemical waste from the construction process. Relatively minor modifications to how the construction process unfolds can result in significant reductions in environmental damage to the site. A number of these modifications are encompassed in the term "sustainable development."

A SUSTAINABLE LANDSCAPE CONSTRUCTION PROCESS ALTERNATIVE

Low-impact development (LID), also called "sustainable development" or "green development," implements practices and strategies that allow site development while minimizing the impact on the environment. A major component of LID for landscapes is to use site-appropriate designs and environmentally sensitive construction practices that minimize the impact on the site.

Just as with the design process, the Sustainable Sites Initiative (2009) has created a matrix to evaluate sustainability of the landscape construction process. The overriding goal outlined in the matrix is to "minimize effects of construction-related activities" (Sustainable Sites Initiative 2009). Table 3-2 lists each goal and the outcome that is achieved when

TABLE 3-2 Environmentally Sensitive Construction Practices as Outlined in the Sustainable Sites Initiative (2009)

Goal	Purpose
Control and retain construction pollutants.	Prevent and minimize discharge of construction site pollutants and materials to protect receiving waters (including surface water, groundwater, and combined sewers or storm water systems), air quality, and public safety.
Restore soils disturbed during construction.	Restore soils disturbed during construction in all areas that will be revegetated (all areas that will not be built upon) to rebuild soils' ability to support healthy plants, biological communities, water storage, and infiltration.
Restore soils disturbed by previous development.	Restore soil function in areas of previously disturbed topsoils and subsoils to rebuild the site's ability to support healthy plants, biological communities, water storage, and infiltration.
Divert construction and demolition materials from disposal.	Divert construction and demolition (C&D) materials generated by site development from disposal in landfills and combustion in incinerators. Recycle and/or reuse C&D materials on-site when possible or redirect these materials back to the manufacturing process, other construction sites, or building materials reuse markets to support a net zero-waste site and minimize down-cycling of materials.
Reuse or recycle vegetation, rocks, and soil generated during construction.	Divert from disposal vegetation, soils, and mineral/rock waste generated during construction to achieve a net zero-waste site.
Minimize generation of greenhouse gas emissions and exposure to localized air pollutants during construction.	Use construction equipment that reduces emissions of localized air pollutants and greenhouse gas emissions.

the goal is met. Three of these goals are directly related to the construction process and include the following:

- Control and retain construction pollutants.
- Divert construction and demolition materials from disposal.
- Reuse or recycle vegetation, rocks, and soil generated during construction.

These three goals are described below, and all of the goals are outlined in detail in the Sustainable Sites Initiative (2009).

Control and Retain Construction Pollutants

A frequent consequence of standard construction practices is soil compaction, and compacted soils are directly related to reduced infiltration rates and subsequent increased runoff. Recently, federal and state regulations mandating management of on-site and off-site erosion during the construction phase have been implemented (National Pollutant Discharge Elimination System 2009; U.S. Environmental Protection Agency 2009).

Retaining pollutants and sediments on-site prevents off-site contamination of waterways used for drinking water and recreation such as swimming and fishing. Creating and implementing an erosion, sedimentation, and pollutant control plan, commonly referred to as a Stormwater Pollution Prevention Plan (SWPPP) or an Erosion and Sedimentation Control (ESC) Plan, can provide the framework to accomplish this goal. Examples of strategies often outlined in the plan include the following:

- Prevent the loss of soil during construction by storm water runoff or wind erosion by protecting stockpiled topsoil.

- Prevent runoff and infiltration of other pollutants from the construction site (i.e., concrete wash, fuels, solvents, hazardous chemical runoff, and pavement sealants) and ensure proper disposal (Sustainable Sites Initiative 2009).

Divert Construction and Demolition Materials from Disposal

Implementing sustainable design approaches can reduce waste generated from the landscape site as a result of demolition and construction processes. Retaining and reusing these materials reduces landfill disposal costs and also reduces the costs for new construction materials because fewer materials are needed.

Figure 3-8 Boulders that were uncovered during excavation on this site were used to create a series of retaining walls.

Reuse or Recycle Vegetation, Rocks, and Soil Generated during Construction

During the typical landscape construction process, vegetation, boulders, and, in some cases, soil are removed and disposed of off-site after the clearing and grading phases have been completed. A sustainable construction approach involves incorporating these existing resources in the landscape design and using them during the construction phase. For example, boulders from the site can be used to create retaining walls or to add aesthetic interest to the design (Figure 3-8). Soil that was removed due to grading can be used on a different location at the site. If vegetation must be removed during site clearing, it should be stockpiled as mulch or composted on-site. Compost can be used as an organic amendment to the soil, and mulch can be applied to new planting beds or used as an erosion protection measure. By using these strategies, less demolition and construction debris will end up in landfills or incinerators, thereby reducing the waste stream and enhancing the sustainability of the construction process.

Preserving and Incorporating Existing Vegetation

In addition to managing soil during the construction process, LID also includes preserving and incorporating existing vegetation when possible. Wooded building sites often command a premium purchase price. Yet all too frequently, the existing trees and shrubs that make the site attractive and valuable are damaged during the construction process. Construction damage to existing plants occurs from physical injury or changes to the environment around the plants. Examples of physical injury include broken limbs, gouged trunks or root collars, and severed roots. Environmental changes include increased light exposure, soil compaction, decreased root zone aeration due to excessive fill soil depth, and changes in drainage patterns that result in a significant increase or decrease in soil moisture and oxygen available to the roots. Not all species are equally sensitive to soil-related construction injury, and younger, smaller trees can withstand more root injury than large mature trees. Table 3-3 lists tree species that are tolerant to some construction damage. Conifers, oaks, redbud, and sugar maple are sensitive to soil condition changes, whereas other species such as poplar, willow, basswood, and river birch tend to tolerate these changes (Elmendorf, Gerhold, and Kuhns 2005). In general, many shrubs can withstand construction damage, because they are multistemmed, smaller than trees, and able to regenerate new root systems rapidly.

Arborists and skilled landscape contractors should work collaboratively with general contractors during initial site development to implement environmentally sensitive construction protocols.

TABLE 3-3 Common Landscape Tree Species and Their Relative Tolerance to Construction Damage

Scientific Name	Common Name	Root Severance	Soil Compaction and Flooding
Evergreen Trees			
Abies balsamea	Balsam fir	Tolerant	Tolerant
Abies concolor	White fir	Tolerant	Sensitive
Juniperus viginiana	Eastern red cedar	Tolerant	Sensitive
Picea abies	Norway spruce	Tolerant	Tolerant
Picea mariana	Black spruce	Tolerant	Tolerant
Picea pungens	Colorado spruce	Intermediate	Tolerant
Pinus banksiana	Jack pine	Tolerant	Sensitive
Pinus resinosa	Red pine	Tolerant	Sensitive
Pinus strobus	White pine	Tolerant	Sensitive
Pinus sylvestris	Scotch pine	Tolerant	Sensitive
Thuja spp.	Arborvitae	Tolerant	Tolerant
Tsuga canadensis	Eastern hemlock	Sensitive	Sensitive
Deciduous Trees			
Acer rubrum	Red maple	Tolerant	Tolerant
Acer saccharinum	Silver maple	Tolerant	Tolerant
Acer saccharum	Sugar maple	Tolerant	Sensitive
Amelanchier alnifolia	Serviceberry	Intermediate	Intermediate
Betula nigra	River birch	Tolerant	Tolerant
Betula papyrifera	Paper birch	Intermediate	Sensitive
Carpinus caroliniana	Ironwood	Sensitive	Sensitive

(*Continued*)

TABLE 3-3 (Continued)

Scientific Name	Common Name	Root Severance	Soil Compaction and Flooding
Celtis occidentalis	Hackberry	Tolerant	Intermediate
Cercis canadensis	Eastern redbud	Intermediate	Intermediate
Cornus spp.	Dogwood	Intermediate	Intermediate
Crataegus spp.	Hawthorn	Tolerant	Tolerant
Fagus grandifolia	American beech	Sensitive	Sensitive
Fraxinus nigra	Black ash	Tolerant	Tolerant
Ginkgo biloba	Ginkgo	Tolerant	Tolerant
Gleditsia triacanthos	Honey locust	Tolerant	Tolerant
Gymnocladus dioicus	Kentucky coffee tree	Intermediate	Intermediate
Liriodendron tulipifera	Tulip tree	Sensitive	Intermediate
Malus spp.	Crab apple	Tolerant	Tolerant
Nyssa sylvatica	Black gum	Tolerant	Tolerant
Prunus serotina	Black cherry	Intermediate	Sensitive
Quercus alba	White oak	Sensitive	Sensitive
Quercus bicolor	Swam white oak	Intermediate	Intermediate
Quercus macrocarpa	Bur oak	Tolerant	Tolerant
Quercus palustris	Pin oak	Sensitive	Tolerant
Quercus rubra	Red oak	Tolerant	Sensitive
Tilia americana	American basswood	Sensitive	Sensitive
Ulmus fulva	Slippery elm	Tolerant	Intermediate

For example, they can determine how the site will be cleared and what trees should be protected and preserved. These professionals prioritize which trees to retain based on the tree's location, overall health, species, and structural soundness. The next step is determining what type of protection, such as a root protection zone, is necessary to preserve the tree during the construction process (Figure 3-9). When the site allows, landscape contractors can plan construction traffic patterns that minimize root damage and soil compaction. They can also designate appropriate locations for on-site soil storage to minimize the likelihood of suffocating roots. If plant materials are damaged, qualified arborists and landscape contractors will be able to make correct pruning cuts if necessary to limbs and roots to ensure wound closure and to minimize the opportunity for disease or insect attack.

It takes three to seven years for construction damage to appear on most tree species. If property

(a)

(b)

Figure 3-9 (a) Root zone protection is essential to prevent damage to existing trees during construction. (b) In many cases, however, roots are not protected, and construction occurs adjacent to large trees, causing irreparable damage.

managers implement an annual tree care program, even trees moderately affected by construction damage often recover. Preserving existing plant material and incorporating it into newly constructed landscapes is a valuable part of sustainable design. If plants are protected appropriately and withstand minimal construction damage, the amount of new plant material required can be significantly reduced.

SUSTAINABLE IRRIGATION DESIGN AND INSTALLATION STRATEGIES

In the quest for sustainability, it may be easy to conclude that irrigation systems should be left out of the plan entirely because proper plant selection for the site should alleviate the need for supplemental water. Perhaps this would make sense in situations where natural landscapes evolve slowly over centuries, but it is shortsighted in the context of constructed landscapes. Constructed landscapes present a number of challenges to plant establishment and growth, including major soil disturbance, the fact that a majority of new plantings use large nursery-grown stock with compromised root systems, and the reality that planting is sometimes done during undesirable times of the year. The result of these challenges is drought-induced plant mortality, which delays development of the landscape and costs everyone involved time and money. Ultimately, client expectations and the designer's knowledge of plant materials and the local climate should guide the decision on whether or not irrigation should be installed.

Irrigation Design

Assuming irrigation is necessary, the goal is to produce a system that accomplishes two things. First, the system must meet the needs of the developing landscape by providing adequate moisture during the establishment phase. Second, the system must be designed for long-term efficiency and effectiveness. Chapter 2 described the importance of designing an irrigation system in parallel with the lawn and planting bed areas to accomplish these two goals.

IRRIGATION SYSTEMS: SHORT- AND LONG-TERM BENEFITS

Forgoing an irrigation system strictly on the principle that it is an unnecessary addition to the landscape is shortsighted. From a short-term perspective, a well-designed and well-managed irrigation system can provide the necessary assurance that plants will survive during the establishment phase. From a long-term perspective, an irrigation system allows for multiple options for replanting a landscape should the function of the landscape change. Retrofitting a landscape to add irrigation is more expensive than installing a system during the initial construction phase of the project.

Figure 3-10 This pop-up head is watering a shrub, ground cover, and turfgrass, all of which have different watering needs.

Creating Irrigation Zones

The size of individual irrigation zones is largely determined by the hydraulic capabilities of the local water supply or the pumping capacity of wells. When designing irrigation zones, there are two key rules to follow: minimize the number of zones and create separate lawn and shrub bed zones wherever possible. Using fewer zones minimizes the number of zone valves and reduces installation costs. A consideration with this approach, however, is that, as zones become larger, the chance of dissimilar areas being watered together increases (Figure 3-10) because those areas requiring more irrigation will determine run times and areas requiring less water will get too much.

The design of an irrigation system must take into account the current size of the plantings, the size of the plantings at maturity, and the relative location of irrigation zones. For example, a new lawn oriented in a north–south layout may be in full sun at installation. The north–south irrigation zones will ensure each end receives the same amount of water (Figure 3-11a). Such an arrangement is adequate at the outset while the surrounding landscape is still small and trees and shrubs have not matured to large canopies. However, as the trees grow and the grouping planted at the southern end of the lawn begins to provide summer shade, this portion of the lawn will require less water (Figure 3-11b). In this future scheme, when the necessary amount of water is applied to the exposed northern part of the lawn, the shaded southern end will be overwatered (likewise, if the system applies only the amount of water required by the southern end—the northern end of the lawn will be too dry). Had the irrigation zones been arranged differently during the design phase (i.e., east–west orientation), this variation in the future water requirements of the different turf areas would have been addressed (Figure 3-11c).

Creating separate zones for planting beds and lawns makes sense only if precipitation rates are considered and run times are adjusted to deliver the appropriate amount of water to the ornamental plants and the lawn.

Irrigating at the Plant and Hardscape Interface

Common sense suggests that any irrigation water that goes beyond the boundary of the lawn or planting bed is wasteful and inefficient. In egregious cases of water overspray, this is true. But, in reality,

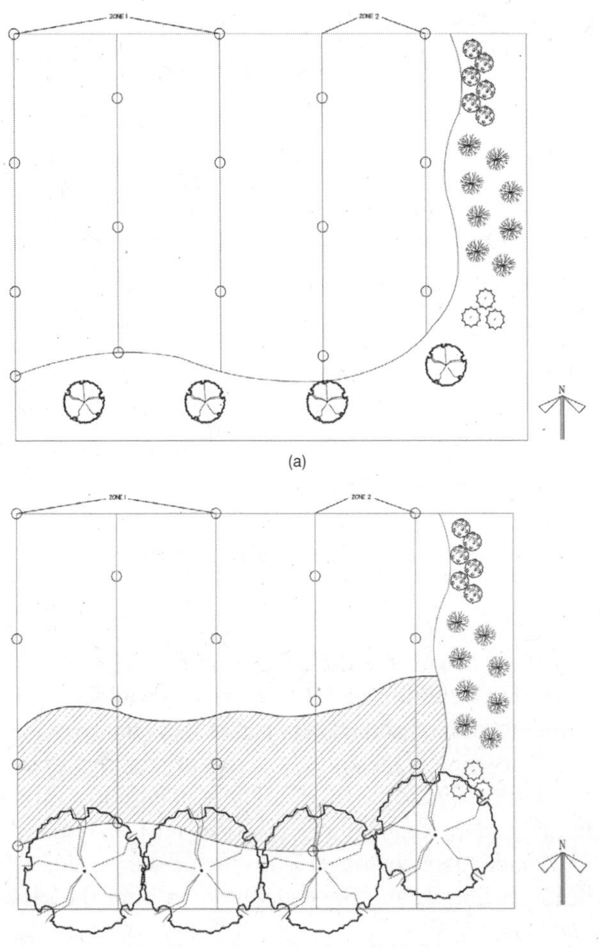

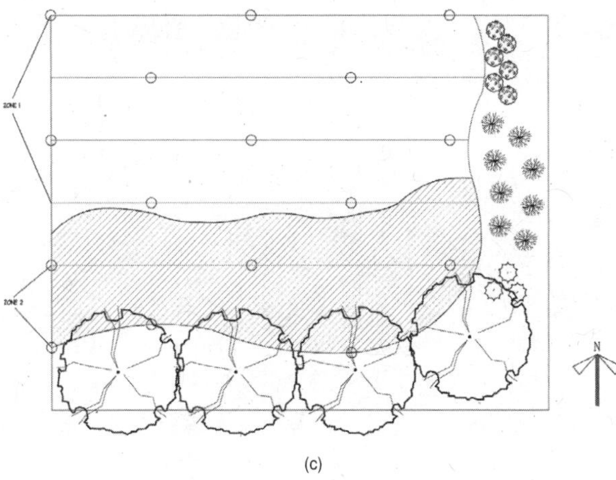

Figure 3-11 (a) When the landscape is immature and the tree canopies are small, the irrigation zoning shown here will work fine. (b) As the landscape matures and the canopy size increases, however, the current zoning will be ineffective. The turf shaded by the trees will be overwatered compared to the turf in full sun. (c) This is an example of an irrigation system that is zoned correctly to account for the maturing landscape and increased canopy size, which will shade the lawn.

the only way to water edges is to apply water to an area slightly larger than the target area. Some water needs to spray onto sidewalks or other hardscapes in order to get enough water on the lawn or adjacent bed. In large lawn areas crisscrossed by sidewalks, it makes more sense to irrigate without respect to the hardscape so a more uniform distribution of water is achieved across the entire area.

Irrigation Installation

The irrigation installation process is largely governed by local regulatory codes, but there are several practical issues that should be negotiated with designers or used by installers. Examples of these include the height of the rotor head relative to the lawn surface (stem length), installing an appropriate system for the planting beds, the head spacing, and the nozzle size. All of these have a major impact on how well the irrigation system functions.

Height of the Rotor Head Relative to the Lawn Surface (Stem Length)

Pop-up rotor heads are the irrigation method of choice for irrigating lawns. Part of this system includes a stem at the base of the head (Figure 3-12),

Figure 3-12 Pop-up rotor heads on stems of different lengths allow for effective and efficient irrigation.

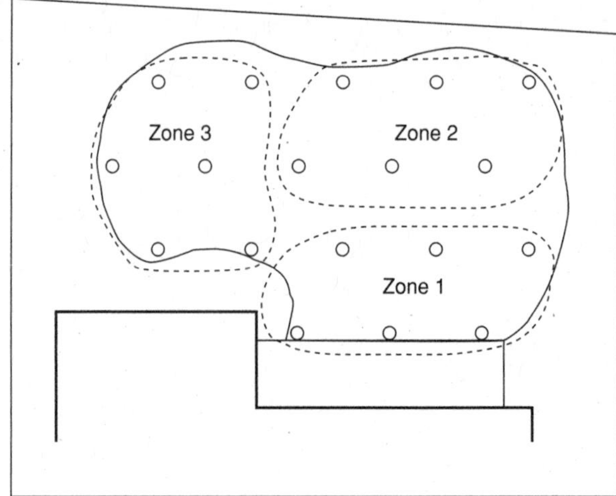

Figure 3-13 This well-designed irrigation system has multiple zones with proper head spacing in each zone to achieve optimum coverage.

which varies in length. In most instances, a longer [6 inches (15 cm)] pop-up stem is a better choice than a shorter [4 inches (10 cm)] stem. Longer stems are less likely to be obscured by grass as the system settles over time and will also compensate for the eventual buildup of thatch, allowing the head to rise high enough to ensure uniform distribution.

Installing an Appropriate System for Planting Beds

Planting beds can create a unique challenge when selecting an irrigation system. Because the perennials, shrubs, and trees in these beds will grow and mature over time, both the initial size and the mature size need to be considered when selecting and installing the system. Depending on the situation, tall pop-up heads or tall fixed heads will be most effective in bed interiors. Pop-up and fixed heads should be fitted with high-arc nozzles designed to shoot over shrubs where necessary. When berms or slopes are being irrigated, low-precipitation-rate stream rotor nozzles are a good choice and will reduce runoff potential.

Head Spacing

After initial placement of the heads, it is important to remeasure the distance between heads to ensure that the spacing is correct and optimum coverage is achieved. Where the dimensions of the area do not allow for optimum placement, heads should be positioned so the distance between them is uniform instead of some being too close and others being too far apart (Figure 3-13). Faulty measurement and poor head placement will result in uneven spacing and inadequate coverage. It is much easier to adjust head spacing during construction than after the system is installed.

Nozzle Size

Like head spacing, another critical irrigation system design consideration is nozzle size. In zones with both full- and partial-circle heads, the only way to achieve matched precipitation for the zone is to use different-sized nozzles. For instance, if a full-circle head delivers 4 gallons/minute (gpm) (16 liters/minute), half-circle heads should deliver 2 gpm (8 lpm), and quarter-circle heads should deliver 1 gpm (4 lpm). There is a tendency among some installers to use prenozzled heads. This often results in all irrigation heads, whether full- or part-circle, applying the same amount of water and leads to poor application uniformity.

SUSTAINABLE HARDSCAPE MATERIALS

Most landscapes include a combination of hardscapes (entrance areas, driveways, walkways, and outdoor seating areas), turf areas, and ornamental plants. In commercial and public spaces, hardscapes can be a significant part of the overall landscape. The diverse products available on the market today make it possible to select from a wide variety of hardscape materials, many of which will enhance the overall sustainability of the landscape. For example, permeable pavements create more efficient land use by eliminating the need for retention ponds, swales, and other storm water management devices. As a result, these products have the ability to lower overall project costs.

Figure 3-14 Limestone salvaged from a demolished retaining wall was used to create a functional patio for this seating area.

Reduce, Reuse, Recycle

Sustainability can be achieved by using fewer virgin materials in the landscape, reusing existing materials when possible, and selecting recycled products. Recycling existing materials and using products created from recycled materials also result in using fewer virgin materials.

It is possible to reuse existing materials such as wood, glass, brick, and concrete in landscapes without the materials first going through the resource-intensive industrial recycling process. Examples include reusing limestone boulders or slabs for retaining walls; using broken pieces of concrete for an outdoor seating area or walkway; or using crushed, tumbled glass as an alternative material in asphalt, concrete, or other paving mixes or as an inorganic mulch (Thompson and Sorvig 2008) (Figure 3-14). Another example of reusing existing materials is the practice of using some types of construction debris to create ballast for berms or other artificial landforms on the site.

In other cases, new hardscape products are made when materials do go through an industrial recycling process. Composite wood products, manufactured by combining recycled plastics with wood by-products, are an example of this type of hardscape material (Figure 3-15). Consulting local, regional, and national organizations affiliated with the recycling industry can be a good way to learn about recycled products available in your area.

Figure 3-15 Composite wood products are available in a range of colors, textures, and dimensional sizes.

Environmental Impact after Installation

Hardscape materials vary in their effect on the environment. For example, concrete prevents water from soaking into the soil, thus increasing runoff, which can carry contaminants into streams and other water sources. Porous materials such as permeable interlocking concrete pavers, porous asphalt, and pervious concrete allow water to soak into the soil. Limestone is a material that will slowly break down over time and alter the pH of the adjacent soil. Chemically treated wood can be used for a number of landscape applications, but there is significant concern about the leaching properties of some of these products. Much of this concern is unfounded, yet public perception persists that these products will release harmful amounts of chemical preservatives into the soil (American Wood Preservers Institute 2004). New wood-based products have come on the market, which use more environmentally sensitive chemicals to preserve the wood or use no chemical preservatives at all.

TREATED WOOD

After being used for more than 70 years as a wood preservative, chromated copper arsenate (CCA) was removed from the nonindustrial wood preservative market on December 31, 2003. CCA is still used for products with an industrial end use such as highway construction, utility poles, and pilings (American Wood Preservers Institute 2004). Removal of CCA from the market was due in part to new policy standards and a safety review of potential health hazards from arsenic. In place of CCA, three new generations of wood-preserving products have come on the market: ammoniacal copper quat (ACQ), copper boron azole (CBA), and copper azole (CA-B). These products are marketed as ACQ Preserve, NatureWood, and Wolmanized Natural Select wood (American Wood Preservers Institute 2004). As with CCA, the new preservatives have gone through rigorous health and safety testing and have been approved for use by the U.S. Environmental Protection Agency (American Wood Preservers Institute 2004; Wilson 2002). These wood preservative products can extend the useful life of natural wood products from just a few years to more than 20 years.

EVALUATING HARDSCAPE SUSTAINABILITY

Before selecting any hardscape material, evaluate it on a variety of criteria, including:

- What virgin materials were used in manufacturing the product?
- Does the product incorporate recycled or reused materials?
- Is the surface water permeable?
- Is the material aesthetically pleasing and appropriate for the landscape design?
- Does the product have adequate structural strength for its intended use?
- How long will the product last?
- How much maintenance will the product require based on the environment where it will be installed?
- What are the initial product and installation costs?
- What tools and additional materials are needed for installation?
- Is the product readily available in your area?
- Is the product allowed for use in your area by regulatory (municipal) codes?

Maintenance Requirements

The long-term maintenance costs of some hardscape materials can be significant. Examples of maintenance include power washing composite wood, occasional vacuuming of pervious concrete, resanding concrete paver joints, resetting pavers due to settling, and reseeding turf blocks. Maintenance needs vary by product and the environment where it is used. For specific information, consult a landscape construction reference (see the Suggested Reading at the end of this chapter) or a local landscape contractor who has experience with the specific material.

Sustainable Hardscape Products for Entrance Areas, Driveways, Walkways, and Outdoor Seating Areas

Because hardscapes can account for a significant portion of commercial landscapes, it is important to choose materials that can enhance the overall sustainability of the site. The combination of increased land prices and the need to meet new storm water management requirements have led to interest in using materials other than impervious materials such as concrete (Figure 3-16).

Impervious hardscapes have a significant effect on the need for storm water management strategies. If storm water is not managed on-site, then it becomes an off-site issue that still needs to be

Figure 3-16 This public fountain in Chicago, Illinois, was surrounded with permeable interlocking concrete pavers. The result is a beautiful outdoor space and a large hardscape area that does not have runoff.
Courtesy of Unilock, Inc.

DISCUSSION POINTS

A 12-acre (5 ha) commercial project, which included 7 acres (3 ha) of parking, was recently developed. The development plan originally called for 1-½ acres (0.5 ha) to be set aside as a storm water detention basin. The developer opted to use pervious concrete instead of standard concrete. As a result, the developer was able to eliminate the storm water retention pond, which resulted in an overall net savings of $400,000. Why was the developer able to eliminate the storm water retention pond? What could have accounted for the net savings?

addressed. One way to manage storm water on-site is to use permeable pavements. Significant research has demonstrated the ability of permeable pavements to substantially reduce urban runoff (Interlocking Concrete Pavement Institute 2008; D. A. Smith, pers. comm.). Further, permeable pavements are recognized as a best management practice (BMP) by the U.S. Environmental Protection Agency and many local and regional storm water management agencies (Interlocking Concrete Pavement Institute 2008). Low-impact development (LID), which was discussed earlier in this chapter, includes permeable pavements as a cornerstone of its regulations, and the Leadership in Energy and Environmental Design (LEED) program offers credit for site designs that include permeable pavements (Burak and Smith 2008; U.S. Green Building Council 2009).

Permeable pavements are characterized by having high initial surface infiltration rates. These surfaces can immediately infiltrate and store rainfall and, in many cases, runoff is completely eliminated. If contaminants (oil, landscape chemicals, etc.) are on the surface of these paving materials at the time of a rainfall event, the contaminants are moved along with the rainfall through the stone subbase where they are then subjected to the natural processes that cleanse water (Bean et al. 2004; D. A. Smith, pers. comm.). When these products are used around or adjacent to plantings, they will allow water and oxygen to infiltrate into the soil, which is necessary for plant growth and development.

In commercial landscape situations, the primary technologies used to make vehicular and pedestrian pavement permeable are pervious concrete, porous asphalt, and permeable interlocking concrete pavement (Interlocking Concrete Pavement Institute 2008). Each technology has advantages and disadvantages, but all are viable alternatives to impervious hardscapes, which can result in storm water runoff. Table 3-4 compares these three products in regard to color choices, installation issues, surface cleaning requirements, winter durability, ease and effectiveness of repairs, the recycled content included in the products and if the materials themselves can be reused, and the product costs.

Pervious Concrete

Although pervious concrete has been used throughout Europe for decades, it has only been used in the United States in the past decade. It is a durable, high-porosity concrete that allows water and air to pass through it (Figure 3-17). The products function by moving water through the concrete to a 10 to 12 inch (25 to 30 cm) thick subgrade aggregate base, which holds the water until it can soak into the soil or flow to the sides (or into tiling) and into a storm water system (Figure 3-18). Pervious concrete is produced by mixing carefully controlled amounts of water and cementitious materials to create a paste, which is then mixed with aggregate particles, resulting in a thick coating around the individual particles. This results in a series of interconnected voids that allow water to drain quickly (National Ready Mixed Concrete Association 2009).

Porous Asphalt Pavement

Porous asphalt pavements are fast and easy to construct. With the proper information, most asphalt manufacturers can easily prepare the mix, and general paving contractors can install it (Asphalt

TABLE 3-4 Comparison of Characteristics of Pervious Concrete Pavement, Permeable Interlocking Concrete Pavement, and Porous Asphalt

	Color	Installation	Maintenance: Surface Cleaning	Maintenance: Winter Durability	Maintenance: Repairs	Recycled Content and Reuse	Cost
Pervious concrete pavement	Limited range of colors and textures	Cast in place; requires formwork; requires seven-day curing period	Vacuum-sweep and pressure-wash to remove sediment and surface debris	Deicing chemicals not recommended; saturation when frozen may damage concrete; snow melts and immediately drains, reducing ice hazard	Damaged or highly clogged areas can be cut out and replaced; repaired area needs to cure before use; repaired area will not match original material	Generally not manufactured with recycled aggregate or cement substitutes; concrete can be crushed and recycled	Competitive with permeable interlocking concrete pavement
Permeable interlocking concrete pavement	Wide range of colors and textures	Manufactured units of uniform size; no formwork required; can be mechanically installed; can be used immediately after installation	Vacuum-sweep to remove sediment and surface debris	Deicing salt resistant; saturation when frozen will not damage pavement; snow melts and immediately drains, reducing ice hazard	Units and aggregate can be removed, repaired, and replaced; repaired area will match surrounding area	Manufactured units can accommodate cement substitutes (e.g., fly ash, slag, etc.); pavers can be crushed and recycled	Competitive with pervious concrete pavement and porous asphalt; life cycle costs may be lower than these two products in some markets
Porous asphalt	Black or shades of gray	Requires no formwork; temperature of the mix is critical to project success; requires 24-hour curing period	Vacuum-sweep and pressure-wash to remove sediment and surface debris	Liquid deicing materials recommended; saturation when frozen may damage asphalt; snow melts and immediately drains, reducing ice hazard	Limited repair potential; can patch with impervious material; repair will not match original area	Generally not manufactured with recycled asphalt or recycled aggregate; pavement can be recycled	Less expensive than permeable interlocking concrete and pervious concrete pavement

Source: Table adapted from Interlocking Concrete Pavement Institute (2008).

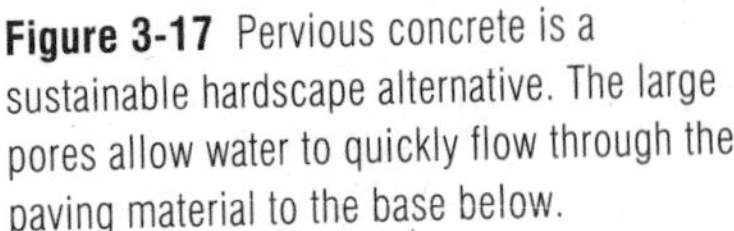

Figure 3-17 Pervious concrete is a sustainable hardscape alternative. The large pores allow water to quickly flow through the paving material to the base below.

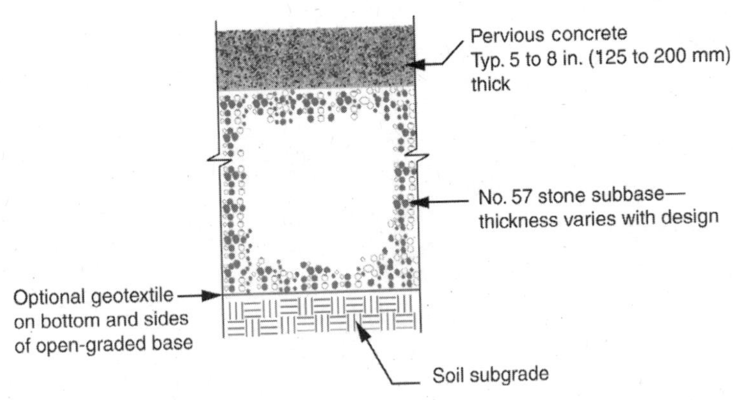

Figure 3-18 Cross section of a pervious concrete installation.

Courtesy of Interlocking Concrete Pavement Institute.

Pavement Alliance 2009). Similar to pervious concrete, water drains through the porous asphalt and into the stone subbase and then infiltrates into the soil. In contrast to pervious concrete, however, the stone subbase for porous asphalt is often 18 to 36 inches (45 to 90 cm) deep (Figure 3-19).

Permeable Interlocking Concrete Pavement

Permeable interlocking concrete pavement (PICP) is similar to both pervious concrete and porous asphalt in infiltration rate, but differs in that the pavement surface is composed of concrete pavers separated by ⅛ to ½ inch (0.3 to 1.25 cm) wide joints filled

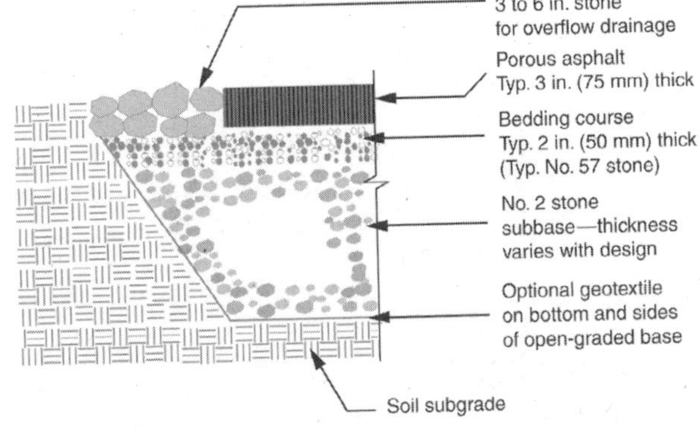

Figure 3-19 Cross section of a porous asphalt installation. Courtesy of Interlocking Concrete Pavement Institute.

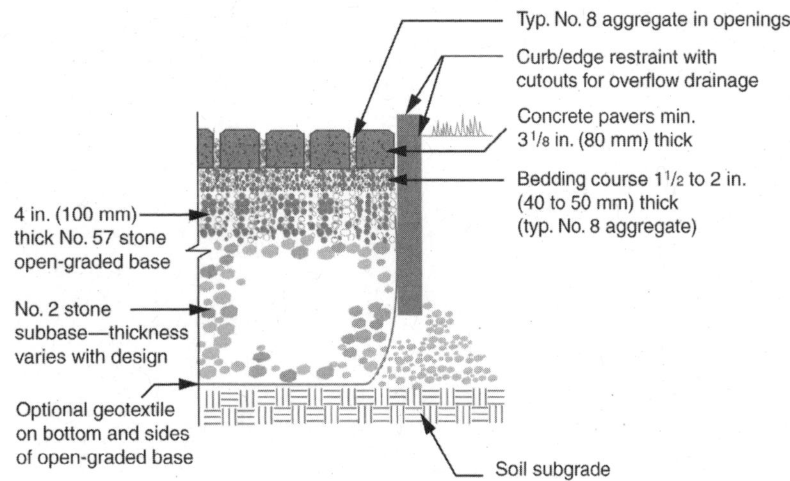

Figure 3-20 Cross section of a permeable interlocking concrete pavement installation. Courtesy of Interlocking Concrete Pavement Institute.

with aggregate (Figure 3-20). The pavers themselves are not pervious, but the joints between the pavers are, which accounts for the high infiltration rates. The pavers are installed on top of a 1½ to 2 inch (4 to 5 cm) thick bedding course of small aggregate, which sits on top of a stone subbase that is 8 to 12 inches (20 to 30 cm) thick. This stone subbase serves as a reservoir for water that has filtered through the aggregate-filled joints.

Other Sustainable Hardscape Products

In addition to the hardscape materials described earlier for entrances, walkways, driveways, and parking lots, other sustainable hardscape materials are available for other landscape uses. One such product is composite wood. Composite wood is made from a combination of recycled plastic, wood products, and glue (resin) (Color Plate 3-3). Occasionally, a small amount of virgin material, compared to the volume of recycled plastic and wood, is added to increase strength and wear resistance. The plastic and wood combination resists ultraviolet light (sunlight) damage and does not warp, bow, or fade over time and is moisture and insect resistant. It also does not require sealing, painting, or staining.

Composite wood is available in the same sizes as other dimensional lumber (i.e., 1 × 4, 2 × 4, etc.). It is also milled into prefabricated decorative elements such as balusters, handrails, rail posts, and post caps and is available in a range of colors and textures. This product can be used for outdoor seating such as benches or retaining wall caps and for large planters. Although the initial cost of composite wood products is slightly higher than that of products made from wood, the long-term cost savings can be substantial. The composite products do not require frequent maintenance such as painting or staining, and most products have a 25-year replacement warranty for cracking, warping, and splintering.

SUMMARY

Landscape construction is a multiphase process, and successful installation projects benefit from having good communication between the designer and the landscape contractor. This chapter compared the traditional landscape construction process to a low-impact development (LID) alternative that focuses on maintaining as much of the initial site integrity as possible with a specific focus on soils and existing vegetation. Additional ways to enhance the sustainability of a construction project discussed in this chapter include designing and installing an efficient irrigation system for lawns and planting beds, managing storm water runoff by choosing permeable pavement options over traditional impervious products, and selecting site amenities made from recycled materials.

STUDY QUESTIONS

1. Describe site grading, including the sequential steps, end result, and ways to make it a more sustainable process.
2. Define "rough grade."
3. Define "finish grade."
4. List the acceptable slope percentages for the following landscape features:
   a. Major walkway
   b. Parking area
   c. Lawn (mowed)
   d. Unmowed bank
5. Describe the impacts of soil compaction on plant establishment and growth.
6. List and describe three ways to make site development more sustainable.
7. Describe the benefits and drawbacks of incorporating existing site vegetation into a design.
8. List four strategies that can be used to prevent construction damage to existing site vegetation.
9. Describe the concept of irrigation zones. Why are they important? How can their design make a landscape more sustainable?
10. Describe treated wood and the controversy associated with its use.
11. What types of questions should be asked when evaluating the sustainability of a hardscape material?
12. What is permeable pavement?
13. Define and differentiate:
    a. Pervious concrete
    b. Porous asphalt
    c. Permeable interlocking concrete pavement

SUGGESTED READING

Sauter, D. 2005. *Landscape construction.* 2nd ed. Clifton Park, NY: Thompson Delmar.

chapter 4

Retrofitting Existing Landscapes for Sustainability

INTRODUCTION

By their very nature, landscapes evolve over time. As a result, many landscapes grow and mature into a space different from that originally intended or are no longer maintained as originally planned. When this happens, the landscape should be redesigned to integrate resource efficiency (sustainability), site functionality, and aesthetics. Through careful planning and execution, existing landscapes can be retrofitted to improve sustainability. The goal of this modification is to minimize the landscape's environmental impact and maximize the value received from the dollars expended. This chapter will focus on design and management strategies and will explore options to change existing landscapes so they are more sustainable. In large measure, this chapter is about taking a critical look at existing landscapes and finding ways to eliminate problem areas to make the site more sustainable. Specific landscape design, installation, and management strategies are described in the other chapters of this text.

This chapter will discuss the following topics:

Site analysis for retrofitting

Identifying opportunities to improve landscape sustainability

SITE ANALYSIS FOR RETROFITTING

Site analysis of an existing landscape is different from site analysis for a new landscape design. However, one common element between the two is the need to understand the design intent. Working with the original landscape designer for the site can be a valuable first step in analyzing the existing landscape. The other specific elements to evaluate during the site analysis can be summed up by addressing three main questions:

Does the landscape design still work aesthetically?

Are there landscape maintenance issues?

Are there problems with the infrastructure elements (sidewalks, driveways, parking areas, lighting elements, etc.)?

Does the Landscape Design Still Work Aesthetically?

Because ornamental plants and lawns account for a significant portion of landscapes, it is important to determine how well the plants are functioning in the existing landscape. What follows is a list of specific plant-related questions that should be asked to determine if the design needs to be modified. Each question is followed by possible reasons why the issue developed and potential retrofit solutions.

Are Key Plants Serving Their Purpose in the Landscape?

Plants have a number of functional and aesthetic roles in the landscape. Functional roles include defining spaces, framing desirable views or screening undesirable views, impacting circulation patterns, controlling erosion, and deflecting light. When plants are used for functional purposes such as screening or hedging, it is important to allow the plants to mature into those functional roles. Plants that are serving a purely aesthetic role should be allowed to mature into their natural size and form. Sometimes careless and unnecessary pruning leads to oddly shaped and grotesquely distorted plant forms that do not enhance the aesthetic of the planting composition (Figure 4-1a).

Solution

Appropriate plant selection combined with appropriate management strategies allows plants to fulfill their intended functional or aesthetic purpose in the landscape. In the example shown in Figure 4-1a of a parking lot planting, the overall aesthetic of the design would be greatly enhanced if the shrubs were allowed to develop into their natural form (Figure 4-1b). The planting composition would be improved further by including ground covers to reduce the inputs (labor and/or chemicals) needed for weed control.

Are Plant Sizes in the Right Proportion to Each Other?

Plants have variable growth rates, and, over time, these differences may become quite pronounced. One way to alleviate this problem initially is to combine larger sizes [5-gallon (20 l)] container or balled-and-burlapped stock of slow-growing plants with smaller sizes [4-inch or 1-gallon (10 cm or 4 l) container] of fast-growing plants. This should help the planting composition stay in the correct proportion throughout the early years of the landscape's life span.

Solution

If, over time, the proportions have changed significantly, and some plants are just too large relative to others, plants can be selectively replaced. This is a

(a)

(b)

Figure 4-1 (a) These shrubs have been sheared into unnatural plant forms that detract from the aesthetic of this planting and result in a lot of bare ground suitable for weed germination. (b) Allowing the plants to develop into their natural form and adding ground cover to the bed will make the design more attractive and reduce the need for herbicides and labor to control weeds.

more sustainable option to replacing the entire landscape. It may also be a better long-term solution than having to constantly prune large plants to keep them in scale. This type of pruning is not sustainable as it requires substantial labor inputs and it creates a large amount of green waste.

Has There Been Significant Attrition, Inappropriate Additions, or Invasion of Volunteer Plants over Time? Does Order to the Overall Composition Need to Be Restored?

As microclimates on a site change due to a maturing landscape, so, too, will the plant species that are best suited to the site. Loss of original plants due to attrition can be a major problem in older landscapes. In addition to these losses, the original planting composition can change significantly because new plants are added or volunteer plants have colonized the site. All three of these combine to create a very different-looking design than what was originally intended.

Solution

The landscape may require major redesign and the inclusion of a very different plant palette than that of the original design. The new plants should be selected based on the current site conditions with an eye toward additional microclimate changes that are expected due to continued growth and development of the landscape.

Are There Too Many or Too Few Annual Flower Beds?

Flower beds filled with annuals are a beautiful addition to the landscape. They are a great way to accentuate a driveway or a building entrance. But these plantings are resource (labor, plants, water, and fertilizer) intensive. Thoughtful design and incorporation of these beds in key locations can be an effective way to visually enhance the landscape.

Solution

Consider how to maximize the impact gained from these planting beds. Locate them only in high-visibility areas; select plants that thrive with minimal inputs of water, fertilizer, and deadheading; and use mass plantings to maximize visual impact (Color Plate 4-1).

Are Lawns Used Inappropriately Such as on Steep Slopes, Areas That Are Difficult to Mow, or Areas with Poor Drainage?

Often lawn areas are used as "filler" in commercial designs. They are relatively inexpensive to install, grow in quickly, and give an instant visual appeal. Unfortunately, it seems that little thought is given to the long-term maintenance needs of lawns, including watering, fertilizing, and mowing. Odd-shaped lawn areas make it difficult to do these tasks.

Solution

In some cases, a similar design aesthetic can be achieved by substituting ground covers for lawn areas (Figure 4-2). Consider replacing narrow medians, parking lot strips, and other areas that do not have high foot traffic with a low-growing ground cover such as common periwinkle (*Vinca minor*) in full-sun areas or bugleweed (*Ajuga reptans*) in shady locations. Once established, the ground covers will

Figure 4-2 Japanese pachysandra (*Pachysandra terminalis*) makes a dense ground cover in this narrow planting bed. It is a sustainable alternative to turf, which would be hard to mow and difficult to water effectively because of the shape and slope on the site.

require fewer inputs of water, fertilizer, and labor, making them an attractive and sustainable choice.

Are There Landscape Maintenance Issues?

Landscape management practices must evolve as the landscape evolves. Yet, in many cases, these practices don't change much from year to year. Ultimately, although the landscape has changed, the maintenance strategies have not. It is important for landscape managers to evaluate their maintenance program at least annually, if not more frequently, depending on the growing climate. Following are a series of landscape maintenance questions to ask when evaluating sustainability, along with reasons the maintenance problems may have developed and potential solutions.

Are the Plants Vigorous and Healthy?

Not matching plants to the growing conditions of the landscape site can lead to reduced plant vigor and poor health. These problems can be exacerbated as a result of changing microclimates (sun exposure, moisture availability, reduced air circulation) on the site over time (Figure 4-3a).

Solution

A retrofit option includes removing plants that are not performing well and replacing them with species better adapted to the site. For example, a rhododendron (*Rhododendron* spp.) growing in a relatively high pH, full-sun parking lot planting island will never thrive (Figure 4-4). It should be replaced with a tough shrub able to handle the soil conditions as well as the high levels of reflected light and heat. In other

(a)

(b)

Figure 4-3 (a) As the evergreen tree on this site has developed, the shade it creates has caused the lawn under it to thin out. (b) A sustainable design alternative is to modify the existing planting bed and replace the turf with a shade-tolerant ground cover.

Figure 4-4 Most rhododendrons (*Rhododendron* spp.) are not well suited to the harsh growing conditions of parking lot planting islands. This one should be replaced with a species that is better adapted to the site conditions.

Figure 4-5 The extensive inputs required to edge the unique shape of this hardscape do not reflect sustainable practices.

cases, the retrofit may require a major redesign of the landscape. Lawn and bed areas may need to change in size and shape to accommodate new species added to the design or to account for new microclimates that have developed since the original design was installed (Figure 4-3b).

Do Odd-Shaped Lawns and Awkward Bed Lines Need to Be Streamlined to Make Maintenance Easier?

The designer's intent to develop a visually pleasing landscape can result in difficult maintenance situations. Just because something looks good on paper, doesn't necessarily mean it can be maintained in an efficient and cost-effective way (Figure 4-5). Balancing aesthetic goals with maintenance realities will result in a more sustainable landscape and should be a primary consideration during the design phase.

Solution

Some maintenance problems will be easier to address than others. The hardscapes in Figure 4-5 will make the design difficult to retrofit. One option is to replace the turf with a slow-growing ground cover that will only need edging once or twice a growing season, rather than the biweekly edging that the lawn requires. Figure 4-6 illustrates a design/maintenance problem that can easily be alleviated by extending the mow strip around the base of the wall to the sidewalk. It may not be the most attractive solution, but it works.

Figure 4-6 This maintenance problem is easily fixed by enlarging the unmowed area adjacent to the wall.

Is the Current Maintenance Program Appropriate for All Parts of the Landscape?

All areas of a landscape do not need to be maintained at the same level. Obviously, high-visibility areas will need more inputs, but in other areas, a lower visual quality of the landscape may be acceptable. Maintenance contractors should work closely with property managers and owners to determine their goals for the landscape.

Solution

Providing property managers and owners with landscape management alternatives, such as less frequent lawn mowing, irrigation, or pruning to allow plants to develop into their natural shape, is an important role for landscape managers. Explaining how these changes can enhance the site's sustainability and translate into cost savings will be appreciated by most clients.

Are There Opportunities to Replace High-Maintenance Plants with Lower-Maintenance Plants?

High-maintenance plants can require significant amounts of water, fertilizer, and labor. Sometimes species are considered high maintenance because they are susceptible to disease and insect infestations. These infestations must be managed or the plants will perform poorly or even die. Hybrid tea roses are a prime example of such plants. Landscapes that have even just a few of these high-maintenance species can require a lot more inputs than landscapes that only contain low-maintenance species.

Solution

This solution is straightforward: replace high-maintenance species with low-maintenance species. For example, hybrid tea roses can be replaced with low-maintenance, disease-resistant shrub roses such as Carefree Wonder (*Rosa* 'MEIpitac') or Knock Out (*Rosa* 'RADrazz') (Color Plate 4-2). Both provide great color throughout the summer, and both require minimal inputs.

Have Pruning Practices Improved or Detracted from the Landscape's Appearance?

Allowing plants to develop into their natural form greatly enhances the landscape's aesthetic. The landscape design and subsequent maintenance program should allow for this to occur. When the plants selected are too large, they will require constant pruning to keep them in bounds. Often this indiscriminate pruning results in ugly and misshapen specimens. Sometimes regular pruning isn't done because the plants are too large for the site but rather to shape the plants into neat and tidy looking forms (Figure 4-7). In either case, this type of pruning detracts from the landscape's appearance.

Solution

Replace plants that have been severely pruned to the point of deformity with other species that will work in that location. Consider the role of the plants in the design, functional or aesthetic, and select them based on this. Choose species that are slow growing and space them according to their mature height and spread.

Figure 4-7 The small shrubs under this bank of windows should be allowed to mature into a natural hedge.

Are There Competition Problems between Shrubs and Ground Covers?

Shrubs and ground covers growing in a planting bed are competing for the same water and fertilizer resources. Because many ground covers are fast growing, they can quickly cover the soil and outcompete shrubs that may be slower to establish. If this competition isn't managed, especially during the establishment phase, the shrubs may struggle to grow.

SOLUTION

Removing an area of ground cover adjacent to the shrub trunk and extending it to the shrub's drip line will allow the shrub roots to effectively absorb water and nutrients without competing with the ground cover (Figure 4-8). Landscape managers may need to manage this competition annually depending on the growth rate of the ground cover.

Does the Landscape Require Excessive Use of Herbicides to Manage Weeds?

A relatively dense canopy of plants prevents light from reaching the soil, thereby limiting the germination potential for many weed species. Landscape designs that are not planted densely enough to provide significant coverage of plant material often result in major weed problems. The exposed soil, or mulch, is a prime location for weed seeds to germinate and spread (Figure 4-9a). In established beds, the loss of plants through attrition can result in vast expanses of mulch with a few shrubs. The result is the same as an underplanted bed: the area becomes quickly infested with weeds. In both cases, excessive herbicides and/or hand labor are required to manage the weed population. Neither of these options is sustainable over the long term.

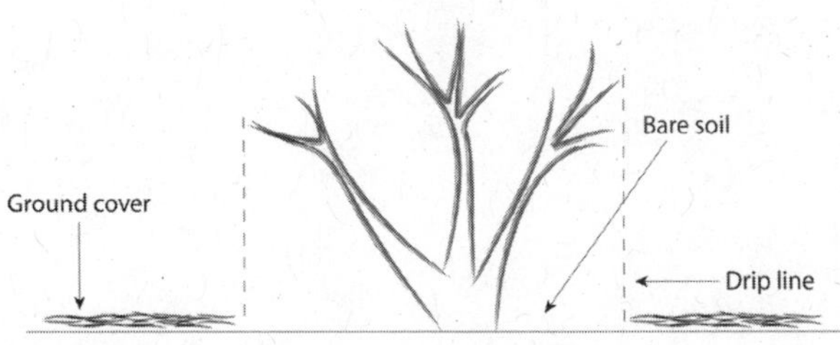

Figure 4-8 This illustration shows how an open area can be created by removing ground cover from the base of a shrub to its drip line. This will eliminate competition.

SOLUTION

Landscapes that have adequate canopy density generally have fewer weed problems and require fewer herbicides (Figure 4-9b). This density can be created by arranging plants so they overlap just slightly at maturity. It can also be achieved by using ground covers. Once established, ground covers are often able to outcompete many weeds. They also make it difficult for weed seeds to reach the soil surface, which prevents them from germinating.

Does the Site Generate Significant Landscape Waste? If So, How Is Landscape Waste Managed?

Excessive pruning due to poor plant selection can result in a significant amount of green waste. Coupled with high irrigation and fertilizer applications, this can have a dramatic impact on the amount of landscape waste generated at the site. Often this waste must be managed by removing it from the site. Although historically the waste would end up in landfills, much of it now goes to municipal or private composting facilities. The end product created from the composting process is then sold back to landscape companies to be reapplied to the landscape.

SOLUTION

Replacing plants that require excessive pruning with species that are better suited is a good first step. Table 4-1 provides examples of dwarf, compact, or slow-growing cultivars of some common landscape plants. A second strategy is to limit irrigation and fertilizer applications to the minimum point needed to maintain an acceptable level of plant quality. Combining the plant replacement strategy with the reduced irrigation and fertilizer concept should result in selecting low-input species that generate minimal landscape waste.

(a)

(b)

Figure 4-9 (a) The open ground in this bed makes it easy for weed seeds to germinate. (b) In contrast, the ground in this planting is covered by ground cover and shrubs, which prevent weed growth.

TABLE 4-1 Examples of Dwarf, Compact, or Slow-Growing Cultivars of Some Common Ornamental Plant Species

Plant Species and Cultivar	Height (feet)	Spread (feet)
Deciduous Trees		
Malus spp.		
'Lanzam' (Lancelot)	8–10	8
'Louisa'	15	15
'Select A' (Firebird)	5	8
'Snowdrift'	15–20	20–25
'Tina'	5	10
Evergreen Shrubs		
Buxus microphylla		
var. *koreana* × *sempervirens* 'Glencoe' (Chicagoland Green)	2–3	2–3
var. *koreana* × *sempervirens* 'Green Velvet'	2–3	3
Juniperus chinensis		
'Kallays Compacta'	2–3	6
'Saybrook Gold'	2–3	6
Juniperus communis var. *depressa*	2–5	8–12
'AmiDak' (Blueberry Delight)	1	4–5
Juniperus procumbens		
'Nana'	6–10	3–5
Picea abies		
'Little Gem'	2–3	2–3
'Nidiformis'	3	2–3
Picea glauca		
'Conica'	5	2–3
Pinus mugo	3–5	3–6
Pinus strobus		
'Blue Shag'	3–5	3–5
'Nana'	4	7
Taxus × media		
'Tauntonii'	3–4	4–6
Thuja occidentalis		
'Hetz Midget'	2	2–3
'Holmstrup'	4	2
'Rheingold'	4–5	3–4

Plant Species and Cultivar	Height (feet)	Spread (feet)
Deciduous Shrubs		
Acer tataricum ssp. *ginnala*		
'Bailey Compact'	10–12	10–12
'Emerald Elf'	5–6	5–6
Berberis thunbergii		
var. *atropurpurea* 'Bailone' (Ruby Carousel)	3–4	3
var. *atropurpurea* 'Bailtwo' (Burgundy Carousel)	3	4–5
Caragana frutex		
'Globosa'	2–3	2–3
Cornus alba		
'Bailhalo' (Ivory Halo)	5–6	5–6
Deutzia gracilis		
'Nikko'	2	5
Euonymus alatus		
'Compactus'	6–8	6–8
'Rudy Haag'	4–5	4–5
Ilex verticillata		
'Afterglow'	4–6	4–6
Lonicera tatarica		
'Honeyrose'	10	8–10
Lonicera xylosteum		
'Miniglobe'	3–4	3–4
Physocarpus opulifolius		
'Dart's Gold'	4–5	4–5
Rhamnus frangula		
'Columnaris'	12	3
Ribes alpinum		
'Green Mound'	2–3	2–3
Spiraea × *bumalda*		
'Anthony Waterer'	3–4	4–5
Stephanandra incisa		
'Crispa'	1–3	3–6
Syringa × *'Bailsugar'*	4–5	4–5
Syringa meyeri		
'Palibin'	4–5	5–7
Syringa patula		
'Miss Kim'	4–8	4–8
Viburnum dentatum		
'Christom' (Blue Muffin)	5–7	4–6
'Synnestvedt' (Chicago Lustre)	10	10

Is the Irrigation System Functional and Updated with Current Controllers and Heads?

Inefficient irrigation systems result in a number of landscape maintenance problems, including a reduced aesthetic and poor plant performance from either overwatering or underwatering.

SOLUTION

Annual maintenance of the irrigation system will ensure the system is fully functional. Updating the system with current equipment and technology will further enhance its effectiveness. See Chapters 8 and 9 for more information on irrigation system management.

Are There Problems with Infrastructure Elements (Sidewalks, Driveways, Parking Areas, Lighting Elements, etc.)?

The infrastructure of a landscape, including hardscapes, lighting, and other site amenities, are essential to the functionality of the landscape. If walkways and driveways are in poor repair or are not functional, circulation and access on the site will be limited. When lighting components are obscured because of plant growth, their functionality is lost. Although these elements tend to be more expensive to retrofit than some of the other examples discussed previously, their impact on the landscape is substantial. Following are a few questions related to landscape infrastructure elements, along with reasons why the problems may have developed and potential solutions.

Are Sidewalks and Other Hard-Surface Features in Working Order?

The functionality of sidewalks, driveways, parking lots, and other hardscapes can decline over time. Often this decline is due to wear and tear, harsh weather conditions impacting the material, or improper installation. Ensuring a uniformly level walking surface is important for both accessibility and safety. Parking areas should be easy to access without interference from plant materials in island beds.

Solution

Damaged hardscapes should be replaced. Particular attention should be given to walkways and other areas in the landscape that have significant pedestrian traffic (Figure 4-10). Replacing damaged materials with more durable and sustainable products where appropriate and ensuring the materials are installed properly will reduce the need for future repairs.

Figure 4-10 Concrete unit pavers are easy to install, fix, and replace if necessary.

Have Access and Circulation Declined over Time?

Maturing trees and shrubs can significantly reduce access and circulation patterns on a site (Figure 4-11). Accounting for mature size is essential when selecting plants for a design, particularly those that will be adjacent to walkways, driveways, parking lots, and buildings.

Figure 4-11 Evergreens planted on this site are adjacent to the sidewalk and are already maturing to the point where they are impeding circulation.

Solution

Although selective pruning may restore accessibility and circulation in some cases, in other situations the plants may need to be removed and replaced with more appropriately sized species. Generally, removing and replacing plants is a cheaper alternative to altering a hardscape.

Can Impervious Surfaces Be Converted to Permeable Surfaces?

Managing storm water on-site continues to be an important design and management component of many landscapes. For commercial sites, this is a particular challenge because the large hardscape areas are often constructed from mostly impervious materials. Finding ways to contain the water on-site, rather than moving it off-site, is a key component of the Sustainable Sites Initiative (2009).

SOLUTION

Chapter 3 describes a number of permeable hardscape alternatives, including pervious concrete, porous asphalt, and permeable interlocking concrete pavement. Retrofitting hardscape areas by replacing existing nonpermeable surfaces with one of these permeable alternatives can greatly reduce storm water runoff and significantly enhance the site's sustainability (Figure 4-12).

Figure 4-12 This parking lot area at Morton Arboretum was converted to permeable interlocking concrete pavement to eliminate storm water runoff.

Courtesy of Unilock, Inc.

Are Lighting Elements Functioning at Their Optimum Level?

Loss of functional lighting on a site can be a result of poor design, maturing plants, and poor product quality. Poor design results in lights being placed too close to trees or in turf areas where it is difficult to mow around them (Figures 4-13 and 4-14). As the trees mature, they will partly or completely obscure the lighting element. Designers must account for this tree growth, and installation contractors must work with designers during the installation phase when there is an obvious placement conflict between these two elements. Installing inferior lighting products can also reduce their functionality over the long term.

SOLUTION

Some landscape architecture companies specialize in outdoor lighting design. If this phase of a project is contracted out, then it must be reviewed in the

Figure 4-13 Clearly, the light (on the right) is too close to the tree to be functional. This layout should never have been installed.

Figure 4-14 Uplighting is an effective way to highlight certain plants, but the location of these lights in lawn areas makes maintenance difficult and time consuming.

context of the entire landscape design before it is installed. Once a lighting system is installed, it can be costly to retrofit. Examples of retrofitting might include either removing a plant that is obscuring a light (easy enough to do for small shrubs) or removing the lighting element and relocating it (which might be a better alternative when large trees are involved). Lights that are placed in lawn areas should have mow circles installed around them to protect the fixtures. Poor-quality lighting elements should be replaced with high-quality sustainable products.

IDENTIFYING OPPORTUNITIES TO IMPROVE LANDSCAPE SUSTAINABILITY

The property manager and landscape maintenance contractor are important resources to consult when retrofitting an existing landscape. Their familiarity with the property will provide important information regarding problem areas such as sections of a walkway that have standing water after a rain or steep slopes that are difficult and dangerous to mow. These professionals can provide further information on areas of poor site functionality due to things like inadequately sized entrances or overgrown plant materials. Their input can also highlight aesthetic features of the landscape that should be maintained or accentuated, like views from inside the office building that are particularly attractive. All of this information can then be used to address problems on the site and create a landscape that is sustainable as well as aesthetically pleasing.

Once the retrofitting needs have been determined, the first step is to prioritize which areas to address. First on the list are problem areas, followed by high-visibility areas such as entrances, areas used by employees, and distant areas of the landscape that are not regularly used. After the areas have been prioritized, the next step is to determine the types of retrofitting that needs to be done. In the case of many mature landscapes, addressing five main issues can increase sustainability. These issues include:

- Eliminating problem areas
- Improving access and circulation
- Improving maintenance efficiencies
- Improving irrigation effectiveness
- Managing water on-site

Eliminating Problem Areas

Many landscape issues can fit into the category of "problem area" when a landscape is being evaluated for ways to improve sustainability. Some examples, such as walkway sections with standing water, steep slopes where the lawn is dangerous or hard to mow, or poor site functionality, have already been listed. Each landscape will have its own unique set of problem areas. Walking the site, completing a site analysis, and conducting detailed interviews with the property manager and landscape maintenance contractor are the best place to start when determining what areas need to be fixed. Often these problem areas are related to a few specific issues such as ineffective access and circulation, maintenance inefficiencies, and irrigation inefficiencies.

Improving Access and Circulation

Landscape functionality requires having appropriately sized spaces for both foot and vehicular traffic and the ability to easily gain access to these areas. As the landscape grows and matures, it may become difficult to access spaces (i.e., entrances, driveways, and sidewalks) within the landscape and to move within those spaces due to overgrown plants. In other cases, the hardscape materials in that area may have failed completely or be in disrepair.

In cases where access and circulation are limited because plant material has outgrown the allotted space, judicious pruning may alleviate the problem. Pruning should be limited to that which maintains natural growth patterns. Hedging, topping, and shearing of landscape plants to keep them at a desired size and shape encourages excessive new growth and generates considerable landscape waste. If substantial and regular (monthly, bimonthly, or even annual) pruning is required, a better alternative is to remove the plant and replace it with a more suitable alternative. In some cases, that alternative may be a dwarf or compact cultivar of the species, while, in other cases, a completely different species may be a better choice (Table 4-1).

Hardscapes used for driveways, walkways, and parking lots may fail and need repair after years of use. In addition to replacing the materials used in the driveway, walkway, or parking lot, these areas may need to be redesigned to account for increased traffic load or even different-sized vehicles than the spaces were originally designed to accommodate. Chapter 3 describes a number of sustainable hardscape material options. The combination of redesigning the area to make it more functional and using sustainable hardscapes will have a positive impact on the functionality and sustainability of the site.

Improving Maintenance Efficiencies

Maintaining a landscape consists of balancing three related goals: keeping the living part of the landscape healthy, keeping the constructed parts in good repair, and balancing the first two goals against human uses of the space (Thompson and Sorvig 2008). Regular and appropriate maintenance is a critical factor in the long-term success of a landscape and is described in detail in Chapters 8 and 9. When maintenance efficiencies are evaluated when retrofitting a landscape, the focus should be on design modifications, paying particular attention to the size and shape of planting beds and lawns. The ornamental plant materials on the site should also be evaluated regarding their suitability to the site and the overall design.

Good Design Results in Easier Maintenance

Good design is the first place to start with improving maintenance efficiencies. Retrofitting a landscape to improve sustainability provides a great opportunity to analyze the existing design and make necessary modifications. These design changes should focus on creating maintainable spaces. An obvious place to start is designing bed and lawn shapes to facilitate easy mowing and edging and to minimize obstacles that increase hand work (Figure 4-15).

As part of this redesign, it is important to consider the type of equipment used to maintain the site. Examples include adequately sized gates that allow equipment to pass through, turf areas that allow mowers to turn easily, and hedges that can be trimmed without needing to reach over a fence or other obstacle. Consulting with the landscape maintenance contractor will provide essential information on the types of equipment that are used on the site and any current maintenance problems he or she is facing. Once equipment needs are addressed in

Figure 4-15 In this design, extending the planting bed to the sidewalk is a good design alternative and would eliminate the odd-shaped lawn area and the need to mow around the fire hydrant.

the design, the focus can shift to the plants and the aesthetics associated with their arrangement.

Modifying Planting Beds

When a landscape designer does not account for the changes in size and shape of maturing trees, shrubs, and ground covers, the design often fails. Sometimes selective removal of a few plants can rectify the problem, but other times the entire planting may need to be removed and the area redesigned and then replanted. The redesign process should account for both the types of plants to be included and the type of irrigation system to be used. Both of these may have a significant impact on the size and shape of the new planting bed.

Completely redesigning existing planting beds provides another opportunity to improve the site's sustainability. Sustainable landscape plantings should be composed mainly of low-input plants such as native or site-adapted species. Proper plant selection, as described in Chapter 2, has a major impact on the amount of resources needed to maintain the plants. Appropriate plant selection coupled with integrated pest management (IPM) strategies reduces the need for insecticide, herbicide, and fungicide applications and supports minimal use of fertilizers.

Figure 4-16 shows two alternative landscape designs. Figure 4-16a was not designed with sustainability in mind. The layout would be difficult to maintain because of overplanted shrub beds and odd-shaped lawn areas that are hard to access. The design also includes many high-input species that need regular applications of fertilizers or pesticides to maintain their appearance. Figure 4-16b was designed with sustainability in mind, which is reflected in the overall site layout, how the plants are arranged in the beds, and the inclusion of low-input and disease- and insect-resistant species.

In cases where major renovations are required, soil testing and improvement prior to planting should be done. Based on the soil test, necessary modifications can be made to the planting area, which should ensure the long-term success of the plantings. For example, incorporating organic matter before planting can improve otherwise poor soils into a growing medium that supports healthy plant growth while reducing water and fertilizer requirements (Figure 4-17). Once the soil has been improved, attention can then be focused on the functionality and aesthetic roles of the planting beds.

Modifying Lawn Areas

Before replanting lawns, the functionality of that area within the landscape should be evaluated, as should the existing irrigation system and potential turfgrass cultivars. If the lawn plays an important design role in the landscape, then it may warrant inclusion in its previous size and shape. However, if it was used as more of a "filler" in the overall design concept, then the space should be redesigned to fill a more functional need. Examples of functional roles include a collection space for on-site storm water management, an outdoor gathering space for building occupants, an open vista to the rest of the landscape, or a natural area attractive to wildlife. In some cases,

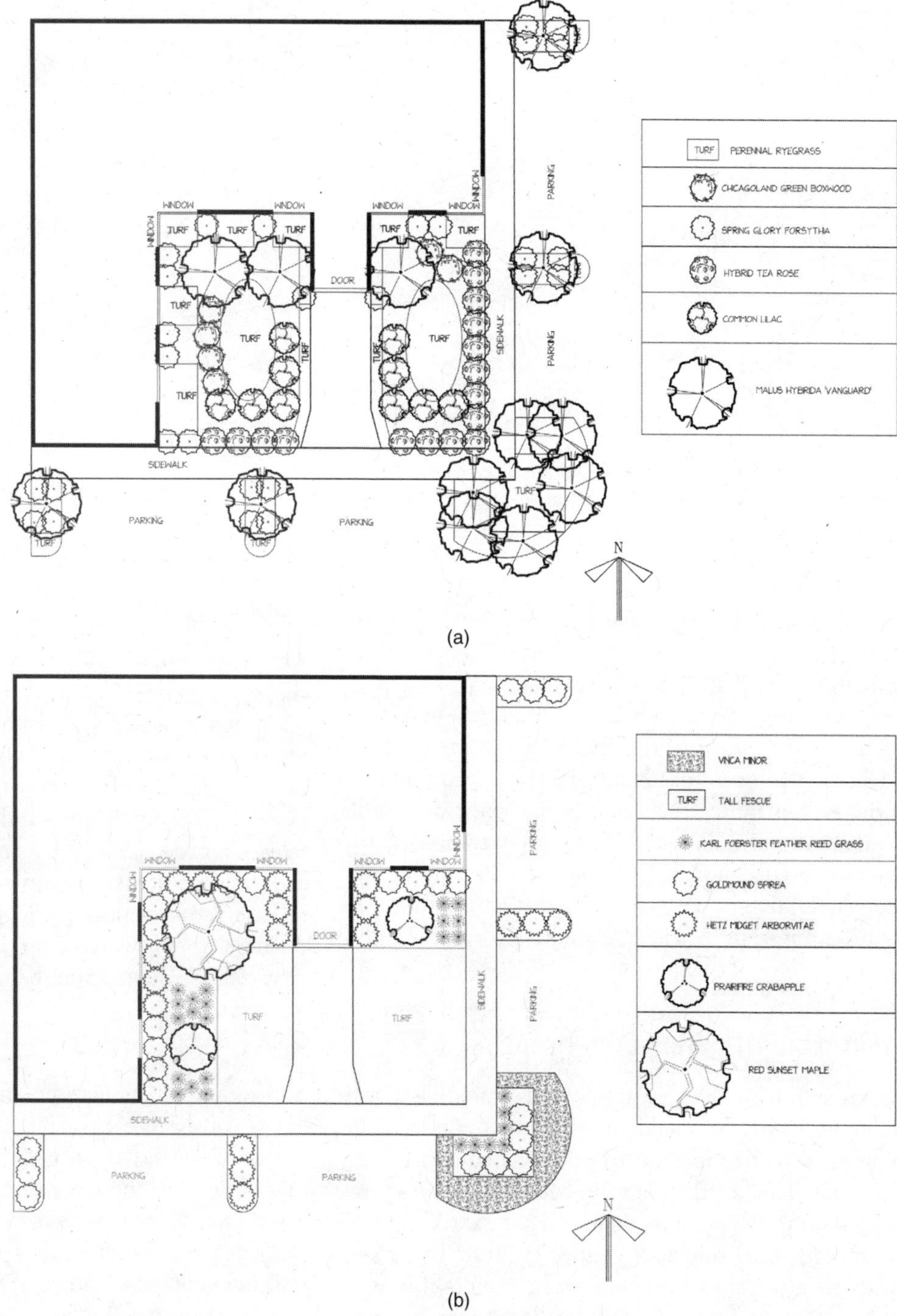

Figure 4-16 (a) This landscape design is an example of a high-maintenance, low-sustainability landscape. (b) The increase in sustainability comes from redesigning the planting beds and lawn areas and selecting low-input plant species.

Figure 4-17 This planting bed was renovated and new organic matter added and incorporated into the soil. The site is now ready to plant.

Figure 4-18 Low-volume drip irrigation systems are an effective way to irrigate planting beds.

a new design element could be added to the site by converting irrigated lawns to meadow areas or tree groves (Color Plate 4-3).

Sometimes lawns are not maintained in a sustainable way because the shape of the area makes it difficult to operate standard landscape equipment. Prior to replanting, the shape of the space should be evaluated and redesigned if necessary to accommodate standard mowing equipment. Consulting the current landscape maintenance contractor about this issue can lead to beneficial changes that improve the sustainability of the lawn area.

Improving Irrigation Effectiveness

In tandem with changes to the landscape design, the irrigation system should be evaluated. The system will need to be modified to address changes to the size and shape of the planting beds and lawn areas, as well as the new plants themselves. A retrofit of the system might also include connecting it to a weather station–based controller and using nonpotable water sources. Both of these will further the landscape's sustainability.

Planting Beds

The shape and size of a planting bed directly impacts the type of irrigation system that should be used. Although standard pop-up heads can be used, other alternatives are to use low-volume heads, which deliver significantly less water to the planting area than traditional heads, and low-volume drip systems (Figure 4-18). And, as mentioned in Chapter 2, grouping plants within a planting bed based on water use requirements prevents low-water-use plants from being overwatered, and their neighboring higher-water-use plants from being underwatered.

Lawns

Improving the irrigation effectiveness of lawn areas involves two choices: redesigning the size and shape of the lawn area to fit the irrigation system or redesigning the irrigation system to fit the lawn area. Another option is to remove lawns from areas that are difficult to irrigate with sprinklers such as parking strips and other areas bordering hard surfaces (Figure 4-19). The lawn in these areas can be replaced with other plants such as ground covers and

Figure 4-19 This small planting bed filled with mowing obstacles should have been planted with a ground cover.

low-growing shrubs that can be watered effectively with drip systems. This will reduce water waste due to sprinkler overthrow. Chapter 9 describes numerous strategies to ensure irrigation systems effectively water lawn areas, including design strategies, components, and maintenance programs.

Connecting the Irrigation Controller to a Weather Station

Overwatering is something property managers try to avoid. Increasing water scarcity in recent years, together with extended droughts in some regions of the United States, has made efficient water management essential. The best way to apply the correct amount of water to a landscape is to tie the irrigation system to the local weather conditions through a "smart controller." Smart controllers work by delivering the right amount of water to plants at the right time, thereby creating healthier growing conditions. The end result is efficient water management combined with improved plant performance.

Many irrigation companies manufacture some type of smart controller. Most also manufacture some type of weather station that can be connected to virtually any existing irrigation controller. The companies also provide the software necessary for an existing controller to access a weather station unit. Retrofitting an irrigation system with a smart controller is a relatively inexpensive investment that will yield significant savings in irrigation water use.

Irrigating with Nonpotable Water Sources

Potable water is water that is safe to drink. Because potable water is a valuable natural resource, finding alternative water sources for landscape irrigation is an important step toward achieving a more sustainable landscape. Irrigation alternatives to potable water include recycled gray water; captured rainwater, including water from rooftops (Figure 4-20); storm

Figure 4-20 A rain barrel attached to a downspout is an effective way to capture rainwater so it can be used for irrigation. This concept is applicable to commercial buildings and landscapes as well.

water basins; air conditioner condensate; or any other source of water that is treated and conveyed by a public agency specifically for nonpotable uses. Gray water is wastewater generated from domestic activities such as dish washing, laundry, and bathing. Gray water comprises 50 to 80 percent of wastewater generated from residential sanitation equipment except for toilets (Wikipedia 2010a). In some urban areas, gray water is collected from commercial buildings and repurposed for other uses on-site such as irrigation or ornamental water features. The Sustainable Sites Initiative (2009) lists a 50 percent reduction in potable water used for irrigation as a prerequisite in the site design section in order to achieve a sustainable landscape.

Managing Water On-Site

Many cities in the United States were built years before passage of the Clean Water Act in 1972. As a result, systems are in place that treat rainfall as wastewater to be disposed of rather than as a resource to be captured and reused. This is an unfortunate approach, since water is a precious commodity. In the United States alone, demand for water has increased by over 200 percent since 1950 (U.S. Environmental Protection Agency 2007a). Part of this increase is due to landscape irrigation, which accounts for more than a third of residential water use [or more than 7 billion gallons per day nationwide (26.5 billion liters)] (U.S. Environmental Protection Agency 2007b). A sustainable approach is to find ways to capture the water on-site and then reuse it for other purposes such as irrigation, or allow it to filtrate into the groundwater and provide recharge to the natural hydrologic cycle (Figure 4-21).

In 2000, the European Union adopted the Water Framework Directive, which commits European

Figure 4-21 Interest in rain gardens continues as municipalities, landscape managers, and others look for sustainable ways to manage storm water. This rain garden is an effective way to prevent runoff into the nearby river.

Figure 4-22 The concept for this bioswale is good. However, the block retaining wall makes it difficult to maintain. A better alternative is to remove the wall and plant the area with species that can handle periodic flooding.

Union member states to take steps to improve and preserve water quality for all water bodies by 2015 (Wikipedia 2010b). Over time, this legislation will likely achieve results similar to those gained from the Clean Water Act in the United States.

When retrofitting an existing landscape, aboveground retention ponds or bioswales can be created to capture and hold the water from a heavy rain event until it is reused or has time to filter into the soil (Figure 4-22). Another option is to install belowground cisterns. Water can be captured from impermeable surfaces such as rooftops and then funneled via a gravity-fed system to the cistern. In both of these cases, the water can then be redistributed throughout the landscape for irrigation when necessary.

SUMMARY

Evaluating existing landscapes to determine their overall sustainability is an important role for landscape managers. The evaluation should determine ways to improve the efficiency of the resources used to maintain the space, as well as to improve the overall site functionality and aesthetics. To frame this evaluation, three questions should be asked: Does the landscape design still work aesthetically? Are there landscape maintenance issues? Are there problems with the infrastructure elements? Based on the answers to these questions, the retrofitting priorities can be established and should start with addressing problem areas first. Much of the retrofitting will focus on redesigning areas to improve access and circulation and redesigning planting beds and lawn areas to make irrigation and maintenance more efficient. The equipment used to maintain the landscape should be considered when redesigning the site. Both the planting beds and the lawn areas should be modified to accommodate the irrigation needs of the landscape. The irrigation system should be updated to improve efficiency. As part of planting bed renovation, site-appropriate plants should be selected. Finally, addressing water management on the site will lead to successful retrofits that enhance the overall sustainability of the landscape site.

STUDY QUESTIONS

1. Describe the concept of retrofitting an existing landscape to improve sustainability.
2. List 10 examples of landscape issues or situations that would benefit from retrofitting. For each of these, outline a process that could be followed to accomplish a successful retrofit.
3. Describe four strategies to retrofit a lawn area to make it more sustainable.
4. Describe four strategies to retrofit a planting bed to make it more sustainable.
5. What is the recommended process for prioritizing landscape areas to retrofit?
6. Assume you have been hired as the new maintenance contractor for a 15-acre (6 ha) corporate park. The company CEO wants to improve the site's sustainability and has asked you to develop a proposal to accomplish this. Describe how you would develop the proposal and what it would include.

Color Plate 2-1 This irrigation system was poorly designed, as evidenced by the variation in turf color. The darker areas are receiving adequate water, while the lighter circles are not.

a.

b.

Color Plate 2-2 Seasonal color showing (a) a spring display and (b) a summer display. This relatively small area of color greatly enhances the aesthetic of the landscape. *Courtesy Bob Grover, Pacific Landscape Management.*

Color Plate 2-3 Ground cover on this slope is a good alternative to turf, and, once it is established, will be an attractive addition to the landscape.

Color Plate 2-4 The alkaline pH of the soil on this site has resulted in a number of chlorotic (yellowish foliage) plants.

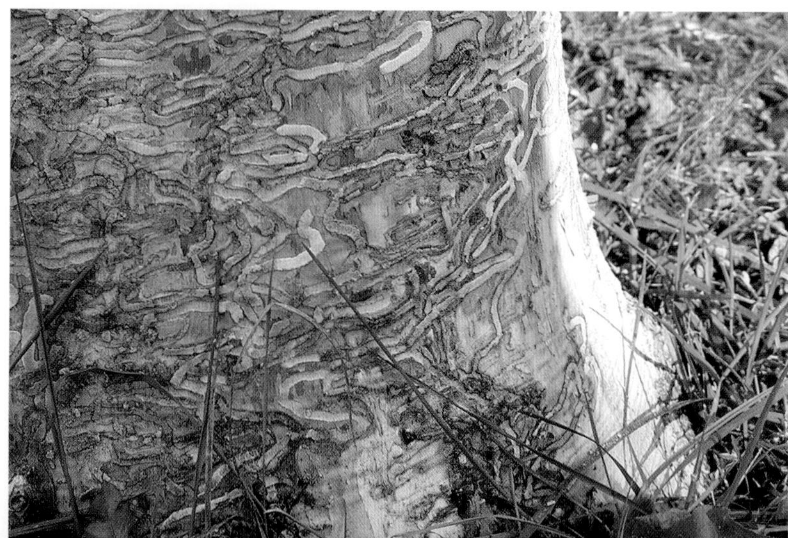

Color Plate 2-5 The galleries (curving lines) left by the emerald ash borer (*Agrilus planipennis*) are evidence that this insect killed the tree. The insect bores beneath the bark and disrupts the tree's vascular tissue, ultimately killing it. *Courtesy Mark Shour, Iowa State University.*

Color Plate 3-1 Poor-quality subsoil often ends up layered over the original topsoil, creating a poor rooting medium for newly installed plants. *Courtesy Neil Bell.*

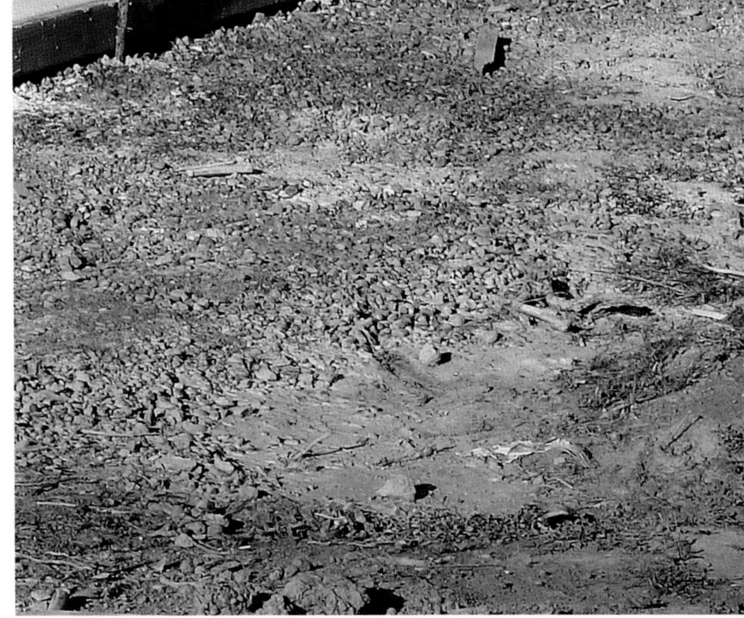

Color Plate 3-2 Compacted soils lose structure and fine particles migrate to the surface, resulting in surface crusting and decreased infiltration.

Color Plate 3-3 A composite wood material was used to build these steps. The product looks like wood but has a longer life span and requires less maintenance than wood.

a.

Color Plate 4-1 The entry to this building was redesigned to improve the curb appeal and develop attractive but low-input plantings that include annual color: (a) before and (b) after.

b.

Color Plate 4-2 Hardy shrub roses like Knock Out are a great way to get summer-long color without the maintenance input required of hybrid tea roses.

◀ Color Plate 4-3 An area that was once a large lawn was converted to a native prairie. This space now reflects the regional midwestern landscape. *Photo of Song of the Lark Meadow at Lauritzen Gardens, Omaha, Nebraska.*

▼ Color Plate 5-1 These naturalistic landscapes in (a) a public park and (b) a golf course were created to replicate the native landscapes of the two areas. *Part (b) courtesy Rick Martinson, WinterCreek Restoration, Bend, Oregon.*

a.

b.

Color Plate 5-2 As a result of the growth of these trees, the area underneath has become extremely shady, and the turfgrass planted originally struggles to survive.

a.

b.

Color Plate 8-1 (a) Container plants planted without feathering or butterflying the roots often respond to nitrogen fertilizer at planting: unfertilized on left; fertilized on right. (b) When roots are placed in contact with the soil, the fertilizer has less effect: unfertilized on left; fertilized on right.

a.

b.

Color Plate 8-2 Transplanted trees often struggle for several years due to nitrogen deficiency and do not grow and develop rapidly.

Color Plate 8-3 (a) Notice the early fall color in this unfertilized tree. (b) Notice the delayed fall color in this fertilized tree.

▲ **Color Plate 8-4** Determinate-growth trees normally produce one flush of growth each year. In this example, we see increased color (leaves on the right) but no measurable growth during the first year of fertilizer applications compared to no fertilizer.

▶ **Color Plate 8-5** Repeated shearing results in a proliferation of shoots and very dense tight foliage at the outer margin of the plant, causing interior shoots to die due to lack of light. If you cut into the dead zone of conifers, no new shoots will develop to fill in the hole.

a.

b.

Color Plate 8-6 (a) *Bumald spirea* (*Spiraea* × *bumalda*) flowers in summer on new growth so it can be pruned hard in spring and still produce a full flower crop. (b) The plant on the left was pruned to 18 inches (45 cm) in late winter, while the one on the right was pruned to the ground.

Color Plate 8-7 This bed was once filled with plants that may have died from various causes, such as a basic lack of adaptation, drainage issues, or exposure to extreme weather.

Color Plate 8-8 Allowing leaves to accumulate as they fall in beds facilitates organic matter recycling and even returns potassium and phosphorus to the soil.

a.

b.

Color Plate 8-9 For at least part of the leaf-drop season, leaves can be mulched into lawns and left to decompose. (a) Early leaf drop when leaves can be mulch mowed. (b) Lawn appearance after mulch mowing.

Color Plate 9-1 This grass-dicot mixture contains English daisy (*Bellis perennis*) and several other dicots. English daisy flowers in spring from March to early May in this climate.

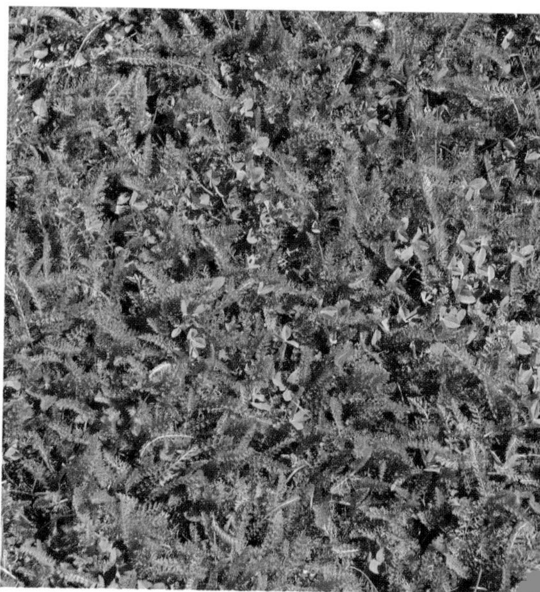

Color Plate 9-2 Common yarrow (*Achillea millefolium*) and clover (*Trifolium* spp.) are compatible with grasses and are very drought tolerant. This site has not received water for over three weeks.

Color Plate 9-3 Numerous plants are potential candidates for grass-dicot mixtures. (a) Buttercup (*Ranunculus* spp.) and English daisy (*Bellis* spp.) in a naturalized lawn. (b) Speedwell (*Veronica* spp.) with attractive blue flowers. (c) Lady's bedstraw (*Galium verum*) looks much like a grass lawn when viewed from a distance. (d) Clover (*Trifolium* spp.) is attractive and fixes atmospheric nitrogen.

a.

b.

Color Plate 9-4 There can be more than one acceptable standard for lawns: (a) no irrigation leads to dormancy, (b) modest irrigation produces turf with some browning, and (c) regular irrigation produces lush green turf.

c.

a.

b.

c.

Color Plate 10-1 An IPM plan should identify and correct problem situations, such as plantings in (a) severe sites; (b) low, wet areas; or (c) deep shade.

Color Plate 10-2 European crane fly (*Tipula paludosa* Meigen) adults mate shortly after hatching. The male is on the left, and the female is on the right.

Color Plate 10-3 Shortly after mating, gravid females deposit eggs in the thatch at the soil surface, as shown in this photo.

Color Plate 10-4 European crane fly larvae develop through four instar stages. The third instar, shown here, are voracious feeders on the roots and foliage of most grasses.

Color Plate 10-5 Larvae spend their entire life in a zone between 0 and 3 inches (0 and 7.5 cm) below the soil surface. They normally surface only at night to feed on grass leaves.

Color Plate 10-6 European crane fly damage is visible in spring and appears most often as moderate to severe thinning, as shown here.

a.

b.

Color Plate 10-7 (a) Stopping herbicide use on conventional beds results in severe weed encroachment. (b) New plantings are prone to weed encroachment.

a.

b.

Color Plate 10-8 (a) A bed with a geotextile fabric covered by 3 inches (7.5 cm) of mulch. (b) Winter annual weeds germinated in the mulch, resulting in severe weed encroachment by early spring.

Color Plate 10-9 Weeds growing in mulch above weed fabrics may penetrate the fabric and grow into the soil below, negating any benefit from the fabric.

Color Plate 10-10 Gravel and crumb rubber placed over fabric provide excellent weed control for several years after installation. As debris collects in the gravel, weed seeds will eventually grow in the gravel mulch, too.

Color Plate 10-11 In the lower portion of this photo, oxadiazon activity is diminished when mulch is placed over it after application (left). Oxadiazon is very effective on bare soil (right).

chapter 5

Ecosystem Development and Management in the Context of Sustainable Landscapes

INTRODUCTION

Ecological landscape design focuses on the development of landscapes as ecosystems. An ecosystem is a complex set of relationships among the living resources, habitats, and residents of an area (U.S. Forest Service 2010). It includes plants and animals, environmental elements such as water and soil, and people. Though ecosystems vary in size, all share the common feature that each element that contributes to the ecosystem is a self-contained, functioning unit. If one part of the ecosystem is damaged or disappears, it has an impact on everything else. Ecosystems are critical to human well-being, including our health, prosperity, security, and social and cultural identity (Millennium Ecosystem Assessment 2007).

A healthy ecosystem is sustainable, and all of the system elements live in balance, or in a state of natural equilibrium (U.S. Forest Service 2010). A sustainable ecosystem also includes biodiversity. Ahern, Leduc, and York (2006) suggest the National Biological Information Infrastructure (NBII) definition of biodiversity is inclusive of many concepts agreed on by governmental, nongovernmental, academic, and industry stakeholders. This multidisciplinary organization defines biodiversity as "the sum total of the variety of life and its interactions and can be subdivided into (1) genetic diversity, (2) species diversity, and (3) ecological or ecosystem diversity."

By taking into account the complex and interrelated features that constitute an ecosystem, ecological landscape design considers landscapes as ecosystems. This design approach addresses how to establish a new planting as well as what happens to

THE CLIMAX STAGE OF AN ECOSYSTEM

Ecosystems evolve over time by passing through a serial progression of phases. Ecologists originally believed that a climax phase was the end point of this progression and was a long-term steady state of the landscape. However, more recent research has shown that the climax phase is neither completely stable nor necessarily long term and self-perpetuating. Today, ecologists realize that the periodic disturbance of natural events such as fire, flooding, and damage by insects plays a critical role in maintaining the diversity of species and habitats in a region. These events are now considered essential to creating ecosystems in different succession stages, which include different vegetation types and result in different habitats. For more information on ecosystem progression, see Lee (2009).

the landscape over time as it matures and how environmental factors affect its growth, development, and function.

This chapter will discuss the following:

- Sustainable landscapes and ecosystem services
- Historical review of ecological design
- How landscapes function as ecosystems
- Considerations in designing a new landscape ecosystem
- Establishment strategies for a new landscape ecosystem
- Management strategies for a landscape ecosystem

SUSTAINABLE LANDSCAPES AND ECOSYSTEM SERVICES

In the context of creating a sustainable landscape, where a landscape is representative of an ecosystem, it is important for the landscape designer, landscape contractor, and landscape manager to work toward a holistic approach to the landscape's function. This approach will require selecting plant material for more than just functional (i.e., screening and recreation) or aesthetic purposes. The ability of these plants to provide ecosystem services, such as air and water cleansing, pollination, and habitat, is equally important.

Ecosystem services are goods and services of direct or indirect benefit to humans that are produced by ecosystem processes involving the interaction of living elements and nonliving elements (Sustainable Sites Initiative 2009a). A less cumbersome way to describe ecosystem services is to imagine how our lives are improved as a result of what happens in the ecosystem. For example, carefully managing a wetland area and keeping it intact allows the plants to filter out excess nitrogen from fertilizer that ended up in the street when it was improperly applied to a landscape and then carried via storm water to the wetland area. The result is clean water entering into an adjacent stream or percolating down into the water table. Because the nitrogen has been removed, the water is now of a higher quality and may be suitable for drinking water or as a suitable habitat for fish. This is just one of the many examples of ecosystem services described in the Sustainable Sites Initiative (2009a).

Table 5-1 describes the 12 broad classifications of ecosystem services defined by the Sustainable Sites Initiative (2009a). For a detailed description of these ecosystem services and additional background information about how these services were selected and the value of sustainable landscapes, refer to the "Case for Sustainable Landscapes" (Sustainable Sites Initiative 2009b). This publication provides a thorough discussion of each ecosystem service; their interrelatedness; and their impacts on local, regional, and global scales.

Along with identifying these 12 key ecosystem services, the Sustainable Sites Initiative (2009a) has also developed a detailed evaluation matrix that measures how the multiple steps in the landscape design, construction, and operations and maintenance processes can be measured against their capacity to achieve one or more of the ecosystem services. The Sustainable Sites Initiative's goal in identifying ecosystem services and developing the evaluation matrix is to help landscape professionals develop sustainable sites. According to its work, "a sustainable site protects, restores and enhances ecosystem services wherever possible through sustainable land development and management practices" (Sustainable Sites Initiative 2009a).

HISTORICAL REVIEW OF ECOLOGICAL DESIGN

Since the 1960s, ecology has increasingly influenced the design professions, resulting in a more inclusive outlook on nature, the environment, and the landscape. Makhzoumi and Pungetti (1999) argue that

TABLE 5-1 Twelve Ecosystem Services Described by the Sustainable Sites Initiative

Ecosystem Service	Description
Global climate regulation	Maintaining balance of atmospheric gases at historic levels, creating breathable air, and sequestering greenhouse gases
Local climate regulation	Regulating local temperature, precipitation, and humidity through shading, evapotranspiration, and windbreaks
Air and water cleansing	Removing and reducing pollutants in air and water
Water supply and regulation	Storing and providing water within watersheds and aquifers
Erosion and sediment control	Retaining soil within an ecosystem and preventing damage from erosion and siltation
Hazard mitigation	Reducing vulnerability to damage from flooding, storm surge, wildfire, and drought
Pollination	Providing pollinator species for reproduction of crops and other plants
Habitat functions	Providing refuge and reproduction habitat to plants and animals, thereby contributing to conservation of biological and genetic diversity and evolutionary processes
Waste decomposition and treatment	Breaking down waste and cycling nutrients
Human health and well-being benefits	Enhancing physical, mental, and social well-being as a result of interaction with nature
Food and renewable nonfood products	Producing food, fuel, energy, medicine, or other products for human use
Cultural benefits	Enhancing cultural, educational, aesthetic, and spiritual experiences as a result of interaction with nature

Source: Adapted from Sustainable Sites Initiative (2009a).

the launch of ecological design came as a result of dissatisfaction with traditional design approaches:

> Enthusiasm for ecological landscapes was prompted by the failure of contemporary landscape architecture to find a convincing theoretical and practical basis for dealing with urban landscape problems. Some argue the urban landscape has an aesthetic viewpoint that reduces nature through impoverished artificial landscapes that are not sustainable. (Makhzoumi and Pungetti 1999)

In the context of a sustainable landscape, one interpretation of this statement is that the public finally tired of the preponderance of generic, artificial-looking landscapes packed with sheared shrubs and large expanses of bark mulch (Figure 5-1). They wanted something different—something that looked more natural, reflected the local native landscape, and did not require a lot of weekly maintenance. Because of this demand for a different type of landscape, designers began to modify how they approached the design process.

The result of this critical review of existing landscape design and development practices over the past two decades is an improved approach to landscaping. Many in the landscape design professions now take a comprehensive systems approach. In terms of problem solving and design, a systems approach takes into account how one change will influence every other part of the design (or system). The designer

Figure 5-1 This landscape requires significant maintenance inputs to keep the hedge sheared, trees limbed up, and herbaceous plants lined up in rows without touching each other.

hopes to predict an outcome of the entire design, having considered the impact that each component will have on the end result. Landscape designers using this approach will possess an increased awareness of what impact the design will have on the environment as the plantings develop and mature into a functional ecosystem.

HOW LANDSCAPES FUNCTION AS ECOSYSTEMS

Landscapes should be multifunctional, fulfilling utilitarian, recreational, and aesthetic needs as well as contributing to ecological cycles and environmental enhancements (Dunnett and Clayden 2000). An ecological approach to design and management will help the landscape become a multifaceted ecosystem.

John Tillman Lyle's work (1985) has been particularly important in shaping this new approach to design and to viewing landscapes as ecosystems. There are two aspects of his work with direct relevance to designing and managing landscapes as ecosystems:

There needs to be a critical investigation of the landscape design process in the context of an ecosystem—its function, structure, and ecology—rather than just economic rationality.

Management issues need to be addressed as an integral part of ecosystem design because ecosystems have a variable future and it is difficult to predict what changes will take place over time.

The general implication of his work is that design is an ongoing process; it should not be the objective. His work was forward thinking because it acknowledged the need for management strategies to develop over time while accounting for how the landscape has matured. In some cases, the management strategy may include redesigning a portion of the landscape to make it more functional.

Along with Lyle's approach to design is an understanding of the impact plant selection can have on how the landscape functions as an ecosystem. Proper plant selection can influence the designed landscape in two ways: an increase in habitat and biodiversity and an increase in the genus loci (local distinctiveness or sense of place) of the landscape. Plantings with a local distinctiveness help maintain the ecological diversity of an area and make aesthetic sense (Color Plate 5-1). These types of plantings are usually based on local native plant communities and can also reflect local cultural uses of plants in gardens and the wider landscape (Kendle, Rose, and Oikawa 2000).

As stated earlier, biodiversity is essential to a sustainable ecosystem. Traditional landscape plantings more closely represent a monoculture with a smattering of trees and shrubs and a few annuals thrown in for color (Figure 5-2). This is partly a result of limited plant availability, an unimaginative design approach, and the planned management of the site aimed at preserving a desired species mix and size (Dunnett and Clayden 2000). Combining a mix of species with varied mature sizes, branching habits, and growth rates with a dynamic and adaptive management strategy can result in a functional and

Figure 5-2 Yews (*Taxus* spp.) are a staple in many commercial landscapes because of their low maintenance and general adaptability. This landscape includes a limited number of species and no annual color.

aesthetic planting that also increases habitat value. This planting approach can be an important part of naturalistic areas in a landscape as well as more managed spaces.

Historically, many landscape design concepts focused on the short-term goals of a project. Yet the overall design of the landscape will have both short- and long-term impacts on how it functions. Similar to Lyle, Wann (1996) introduced a different approach to design. He highlighted the need for a more enduring view of the landscape. Much of his work addressed the importance of designing sustainable landscapes that allow the integrity of the original landscape design to be maintained indefinitely.

> Designing for a sustainable landscape necessitates a holistic and integrative outlook that is based on ecological understanding and awareness of the potentialities and limitations of a given landscape. Such understanding ensures that in accommodating future uses their impact on existing ecosystems and essential ecological processes and biological and landscape diversity is anticipated. This will allow for healthy ecosystems and long-term ecological stability (Wann 1996).

Lyle (1985) and Wann (1996) both acknowledged the role of humans in the design, installation, and management of landscape ecosystems. In their work, they successfully incorporate the human species in ecological theory rather than suggest that humans are separate from nature and that our impact on an ecosystem is always negative. Both suggested that landscape professionals can initiate positive environmental changes within a landscape ecosystem. One example of the positive role humans can have on developing and managing an ecosystem can be seen in many gardens and parks. Numerous ecology studies, including Gaublomme et al. (2008) and Loram et al. (2008), demonstrate that gardens and parks typically have greater biodiversity than natural systems because they include a select number of nonnative species. In comparison, landscapes devoted wholly to native plant species have a much more limited level of diversity.

Building on the work of Lyle (1985) and Wann (1996), today's landscape designers, installers, and managers have an operational framework on which to base their effort. Using this paradigm, the landscape ecosystem can be viewed as a set of complex relationships among the growing environment (soil, moisture, light patterns, and temperature), plants (trees, shrubs, annuals and perennials, ground covers, and turfgrass), animals (wildlife, birds, and insects), and people. These multiple relationships and the interactions among them result in a landscape ecosystem.

CONSIDERATIONS IN DESIGNING A NEW LANDSCAPE ECOSYSTEM

Careful design and plant selection can produce beautiful and functional plant communities that are ecologically sophisticated. This section will address both the designer's intent and the plant materials in regard to creating a landscape ecosystem. Chapters 2 and 3 describe plant materials—existing vegetation and selecting new species—in the broad context of sustainable design. This chapter will focus on plant materials in the context of creating landscape ecosystems.

Designer's Intent in Creating a Landscape Ecosystem

Chapter 2 outlined the concept of design intent as part of the landscape design process. This concept is also relevant when creating a landscape ecosystem. In addition to focusing on the aesthetic and functional goals of the landscape, however, the designer must also address ecosystem services. The design focus may be on creating new ecosystem services or on enhancing existing services such as erosion and sediment control or habitat function. Whatever the intent, in order for the goals to be achieved, the designer, landscape contractor, and maintenance professionals must communicate throughout the project.

Much of current conventional landscape planting design is characterized by the use of a limited number of species and cultivars with relatively simple compositions (Figure 5-3). These compositions include shrub masses with or without ground covers, street trees with or without turf below, and mown amenity turf (Thoday, Kendle, and Hitchmough 1995). A result of this design approach is that most of these plantings fill aesthetic and functional roles but provide limited ecosystem services. Often the plantings are maintained to produce a static effect. To achieve this effect, considerable resource inputs in site preparation, plant establishment, and long-term maintenance are required (Benson and Roe 2000).

Amenity turf is turf used for aesthetic purposes.

Figure 5-3 Upright evergreens are combined with deciduous flowering shrubs to create a simple composition that provides year-round aesthetic appeal.

In broad terms, the designer's intent for a landscape ecosystem should meet these minimum criteria:

- Require limited inputs, albeit more during the plant establishment phase and less during the long-term management phase.
- Reflect local character.
- Include native or site-adapted species.
- Contribute to the local biodiversity.
- Have a dynamic growth and development progression that allows for self-regeneration and nutrient cycling.

A final consideration is the social implications of the design. In order for a landscape ecosystem to be truly sustainable, it must also be publicly acceptable and aesthetically pleasing. In some cases to gain larger acceptability, it may be necessary to include landscape elements, such as annual plantings for color, that do not meet the objectives listed previously. One approach is to have a multidimensional design with showy and highly manicured areas near building entrances. As you move away from this public space, the landscape becomes more natural and less maintained. This approach helps a designer satisfy

Figure 5-4 In this housing development, a large portion of the site was developed to re-create the native habitat and function as a wetland ecosystem.

multiple objectives. Provided the overall move is toward sustainability, sometimes both pragmatic and flexible approaches are necessary when meeting social or cultural needs (Dunnett and Hitchmough 1996).

When all of the objectives that constitute the designer's intent are achieved, a sustainable landscape ecosystem is created (Figure 5-4). This ecosystem will meet the aesthetic needs of the project, serve in a functional capacity, and provide multiple ecosystem services.

Plant Materials for Creating a Landscape Ecosystem

A logical first step in landscape ecosystem development is to start with existing materials on the site. This includes the existing vegetation, soil conditions, drainage patterns, and light exposure. Retaining existing vegetation of value provides both a cost savings and an initial framework for additional species selection and design. It also influences whether all or just part of the site must be designed and planted. Preserving and integrating existing vegetation where possible has aesthetic, functional, and ecological value (Dunnett and Clayden 2000).

Natural Regeneration of Site-Adapted Species to Create a Landscape Ecosystem

An alternative to retaining existing vegetation or incorporating new plant species is to encourage natural regeneration of vegetation on the site. Natural regeneration requires little management input and allows species already adapted to the growing environment to colonize the area. The natural competition that develops as a result of the colonization will result in a diverse mix of species, each well suited to the unique microclimates on the site. However, this type of natural regeneration is also unpredictable. There is no guarantee that the preferred species will regenerate and that the desired plant community will develop (Dunnett and Clayden 2000). The natural progression may result in a landscape ecosystem that lacks biodiversity and is not aesthetically acceptable during early successional phases. Often plant species introduced by birds and animals can have a major influence on the plant community that develops (see Table 10-1). In these instances, some form of landscape management, including the removal of unwanted species and the addition of desirable species, may be required to achieve a fully functional landscape ecosystem.

Sometimes soil management may be necessary to ensure the desired species mix establishes on the site. A minimal amount of soil modification, such as adding organic matter to improve drainage and nutrient content, may be necessary to allow these desirable, though less well adapted, species to thrive. When possible, soil modifications should be done early in the site regeneration process to minimize damage to roots.

Selecting New Species to Create a Landscape Ecosystem

When natural regeneration does not result in the desired landscape ecosystem, or when little to no

Successional phase refers to the succession, or change, in the vegetation found in a plant community over time.

existing vegetation has been left on a landscape site, it will be necessary to select species to create the landscape ecosystem. Although many plant species grow best in a narrow range of environmental conditions, most can still grow adequately across a broader range. This is important in a landscape ecosystem because of the desire for a diverse species mix, which is often linked to the need for diverse growing requirements. Further, as successional growth in the landscape occurs, some of the environmental conditions on the site will change, and plants must adapt to these changes in order to survive.

Selecting regionally adapted species or those from similar native habitats gives the landscape the best chance of survival and increases the likelihood it will reach its full potential and the designer's intent. One example of using regionally adapted species is incorporating species native to the Mediterranean area in plantings located in the western United States. Mediterranean species are adapted to growing in mild climates with extended dry periods. Because of this, many of these species (Table 5-2) are well suited to growing in western Washington and Oregon and parts of California, where the climate, including seasonal precipitation patterns, is similar (Figure 5-5).

The ultimate goal of a functional landscape ecosystem is twofold. First, it should serve the needs of those who use the landscape, mainly humans and animals. Second, the resulting plant community should require minimal inputs (water, fertilizer, pesticides, maintenance labor) as it matures and reaches a level of natural equilibrium. Incorporating existing vegetation, allowing natural regeneration to occur, and adding site-adapted plant species all contribute to successfully creating a functional landscape ecosystem.

TABLE 5-2 Abbreviated List of Mediterranean Native Species Well Adapted to the Growing Climates of Western Oregon and Washington

Common Name	Scientific Name
Herbaceous Perennials	
Artemisias	*Artemisia* spp.
Bear's breeches	*Acanthus mollis*
Cupid's dart	*Catananche caerulea*
Mulleins	*Verbascum* spp.
Rockrose	*Cistus* spp.
Spurge	*Euphorbia* spp.
Ground Covers	
Candytuft	*Iberis sempervirens*
Saint-John's-wort	*Hypericum calycinum*
Thyme	*Thymus* spp.
Vinca, common periwinkle	*Vinca minor; Vinca* spp.
Evergreen Shrubs	
Heath	*Erica* spp.
Laurustinus	*Viburnum tinus*
Lavender	*Lavandula* spp.
Rosemary	*Rosmarinus officinalis*
Trees	
Atlas cedar	*Cedrus atlantica*
Italian cypress	*Cupressus sempervirens*
Portugal laurel	*Prunus lusitanica* (can be invasive)
Savin juniper	*Juniperus sabina*
Strawberry tree	*Arbutus unedo*

Source: Table compiled from Bell, VanDerZanden, and McMahan (2001); Mesogeo Gardens and Greenhouse (http://mesogeogarden.com/wpblog/); and the Mediterranean Garden Society (http://www.mediterraneangardensociety.org/).

ESTABLISHMENT STRATEGIES FOR A NEW LANDSCAPE ECOSYSTEM

The twin forces of succession and disturbance are constantly at work in a newly planted landscape. The

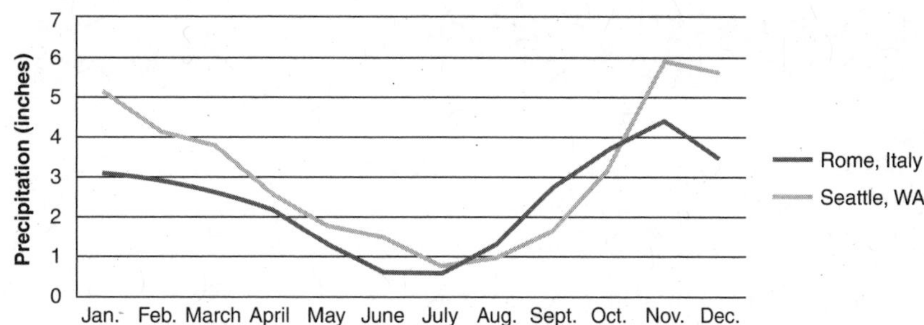

Figure 5-5 Seasonal rainfall distribution for Seattle, Washington, and Rome, Italy, both of which have a Mediterranean growing climate.

disturbance created by installing a new landscape creates the opportunity for seeds existing on the site to germinate and sets in motion the forces of succession. The new plant community that has been installed will change over time and, without some form of human intervention (landscape management), will develop into an ecosystem that may or may not meet the designer's intent. (Refer to Chapter 8 for specific strategies on the planting and establishment of landscape plants.)

As the serial progression of a landscape ecosystem occurs and the planting moves from the establishment phase into the growth and maturation phase, there will be a change in management needs (Figure 5-6). The establishment phase requires intensive management, including limiting competition from weeds for water and nutrients and mulching to conserve soil moisture and limit weed germination. This input-intensive phase enables the planting to become well established and grow rapidly into a functional ecosystem. The level of inputs should decrease as the landscape progresses toward a climax phase. During this phase, plantings will still require some level of management if they are to develop into a functional landscape ecosystem. Allowing a planting to revert to its natural pattern and processes, with no management input, is seldom a desirable approach to short- and long-term management of the site.

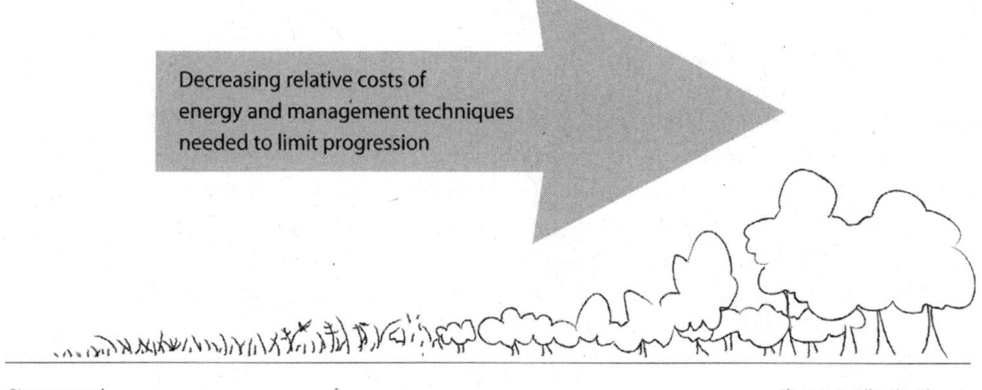

Figure 5-6 Illustration showing the serial progression of a landscape ecosystem and the accompanying change in management requirements.

MANAGEMENT STRATEGIES FOR A LANDSCAPE ECOSYSTEM

Postplanting Succession, Plant Attrition due to Changing Microclimates, and Encroachment of Nonplanted Species

A landscape manager's involvement with a site normally encompasses a much longer time frame than that of the designer or installation contractor. Because of this long-term interaction with the site, landscape managers should be involved in discussions and decisions about the project from the very beginning. To help landscape managers approach landscape maintenance in a sustainable way, the Sustainable Sites Initiative (2009a) has developed a comprehensive guide to developing and implementing a landscape maintenance plan (Table 5-3). The guide can be used by the integrated team (designer, installation contractor, and landscape manager) to develop a landscape maintenance plan that identifies the long-term desired outcomes for the site and the short-term plans to achieve these goals. This tool provides an excellent framework for communication between all parties involved in the project.

Management of a landscape ecosystem requires an understanding of natural plant cycles and a flexible and dynamic approach to plant care. Purposeful management throughout the life span of the planting is necessary. When possible, the focus of this type of management should be on the natural evolutionary change of the landscape over time. Research has shown that ecosystems near their climax successional state, or natural equilibrium, need less management than landscapes that are in an early successional state (Brooker and Corder 1986; Handley and Bulmer 1987). However, the ecosystem that results from a designed and managed landscape is far from natural and will always require some management.

In fact, these ecosystems are often in a slowly progressing state of flux over the lifetime of the planting. Sometimes this fluctuation is small, progressive, and easy to integrate. An example of this type of change is the attrition of full-sun species due to the increasing shade density from maturing tree canopies (Figure 5-7). In other cases, larger, more extreme influences will impact the ecosystem's growth and development. An example of this type of change is the loss of overstory trees as a result of extreme weather events such as flooding or ice storm damage (Figure 5-8). In these extreme cases, significant management intervention will be necessary to preserve the overall functionality of the landscape.

A major component of long-term landscape ecosystem management is postplanting succession. The species mix of the planting often changes over time due to microclimate changes and plant attrition. Occurring parallel with this serial progression is the encroachment of nondesirable species into the landscape ecosystem. Although these species may not be desirable, not all of these new arrivals are invasive. Invasive species, on the other hand, do need to be managed intensively to preserve the ecosystem and to limit their impact on surrounding natural and artificial landscapes.

Postplanting Succession

Plant succession accounts for the change in species mix of a plant community over time. Landscape succession can be seen on many scales. Examples of large-scale succession include the thousands of acres (hectares) burned in Yellowstone National Park in the United States in 1988, the extreme flooding that remade the landscape in Northern Italy in 2000, and the decimation of the native pine population in the first decade of this century in the Rocky Mountains of the United States due to the mountain pine beetle (*Dendroctonus ponderosae*). Small-scale succession may occur when a new building site is cleared or a gap in the existing tree canopy is created when a mature shade tree is removed in an urban landscape. The multiple types of succession are often due in part to changes in microclimates within the plant community. The serial progression, or succession, of a new landscape ecosystem is unavoidable, and landscape managers are responsible for directing succession in a desirable way (Figure 5-9).

TABLE 5-3 Sustainable Sites Initiative Sample Landscape Maintenance Plan Matrix

WORKSHEET: SITE MANAGEMENT PLAN						
Maintenance plan topics to be addressed by the integrated design team (including the maintenance contractor or manager)	Required or optional?	10-year desired outcome from maintenance practice	Required actions to achieve 10-year desired outcome (include specific details below)			
			Specific activities	Skill level required	Timeline/ schedule	Other details
Plant Stewardship						
Plant maintenance: Describe the process for maintaining vegetation according to long-term plans for the site and adhering to recognized standards for professional horticultural practice.	Required for all sites					
Plant health: Describe the process for monitoring plant health to prevent problems. Identify the proper techniques for addressing dead, diseased, or pest-infested vegetation.	Required for all sites					
Site safety: Describe the process for maintaining vegetation to ensure site safety and meet the needs of the intended users of the site.	Required for all sites					
Plant replacement: Provide a list (include the common and scientific names) of potential appropriate, noninvasive plants that can be used for replacing plants. When replacing plants, consider maintenance needs of plants and design approach.	Required for all sites					
Pest management: Control pests, diseases, and any unwanted species of plants and animals using integrated pest management (IPM) techniques.	Required for all sites					
Invasive Species Management						
Provide a list (include common and scientific names) of plant species identified in the area that are currently on any of the following lists as invasive: regional lists, state noxious weed laws, or federal noxious weed laws.	Required for all sites					

Figure 5-7 The sun-loving perennials originally planted in this landscape have died out over time as the tree canopies above have matured. Those that remain are weak and should be replaced with shade-tolerant species.

Figure 5-8 These mature trees are being pruned significantly or removed entirely as a result of a major ice storm. The resulting landscape will look much different as new plants are installed based on the changed site conditions.

Plant Attrition Due to Changing Microclimates

Landscapes transform over time as a result of environmental changes (including changes in site microclimates), variations in plant growth rates, and plant death (attrition). A body of research describes the important role population dynamics play in plant attrition in an ecosystem (Breshears et al. 2008; Stilma, Keesman, and Van der Werf 2009). The continual and dynamic biological and environmental processes that impact a landscape

DOES MAINTENANCE OF NATURALISTIC LANDSCAPES ALWAYS REQUIRE FEWER INPUTS?

A common assumption is that maintenance of naturalistic landscapes requires fewer inputs compared to other types of landscapes (Dunnett and Clayden 2000). This type of blanket statement doesn't always hold true. One example is the maintenance of amenity turf. A naturalistic approach might include fewer mowings over the course of the growing season so the turf has a taller, more natural appearance. Clearly, this would require fewer inputs (i.e., labor and fuel) than mowing the turf more frequently to maintain it at a shorter mowing height. However, it isn't quite that simple. Although the taller turf requires fewer mowings, each mowing requires more time and energy compared to more frequent mowings that remove less leaf tissue each time. Another issue with this maintenance approach is that the taller grass will generate significant green waste with each mowing, which must be disposed of off-site. This results in an additional cost compared to mowing more frequently with a mulching mower and leaving the clippings on-site, because less leaf tissue is being removed. A better approach is to analyze the desired outcome of the maintenance practice and then balance the maintenance inputs with outputs.

DISCUSSION POINTS

At this 10-acre (4 ha) commercial landscape site, the landscape manager has recently noticed a significant increase in the number of broadleaf weeds in the planting beds and turf area. What are some probable causes for this change to the landscape? Describe potential management strategies for this scenario.

ecosystem result in an ever-changing mix of species. As some species lose their ability to grow in the new environment, they are replaced by better-adapted species.

Examples of species changes due to microclimate changes include the following:

- Full-sun species being replaced by those that can handle an increasing shade level due to maturing tree canopies (Color Plate 5-2)
- Loss of some herbaceous species because they are unable to compete for the reduced soil moisture as trees and shrubs mature and require more water
- Loss of some species because of an increase in foliar diseases due to decreased air circulation caused by increased foliage density from the maturing plants

Figure 5-9 This commercial landscape is carefully managed to maintain the native species that were planted and to create the appropriate genus loci.
Courtesy Rick Martinson, WinterCreek Restoration, Bend, Oregon.

NATURAL SUCCESSION

The natural process of succession generally includes a sequential series of events. Included here is a succession scenario for an eastern deciduous forest in the United States described by the Brooklyn Botanic Garden (2009). It describes vegetation change, acknowledging some regional differences, on abandoned farmland left undisturbed for many years.

> Millions of seeds that lay dormant in the exposed soil germinate, causing an explosion of physiologically tough, aggressive annuals like horseweed (*Conyza canadensis*) and common ragweed (*Ambrosia artemisiifolia*). These plants, called pioneer species, dominate the first season. In a few years, biennials like mullein (*Verbascum* spp.) and Queen Anne's lace (*Daucus carota*) become common, along with a few perennial wildflowers like asters (*Aster* spp.) and goldenrods (*Solidago* spp.). After five years or so, grasses and wildflowers turn the area into a meadow. Within a few years young maples (*Acer* spp.), ashes (*Fraxinus* spp.), dogwoods (*Cornus* spp.), cherries (*Prunus* spp.), pines (*Pinus* spp.), and cedars (*Cedrus* spp.), many present as seedlings in the earliest stages, rapidly transform the meadow into "old field." This habitat is an extremely rich, floriferous blend of pioneer trees, shrubs, and herbaceous species particularly favored by wildlife. Given enough time without major disturbance, perhaps several centuries, a mature or old-growth forest will once again be found on the site.

As this natural attrition takes place, it is often necessary for a landscape manager to add new species to ensure the ecosystem continues to have adequate biodiversity. One strategy landscape managers can use to limit the amount of replacement species needed is to incorporate plants that grow in a range of light conditions (Table 5-4). These species can adapt over time to the changing light levels and still perform their ecosystem function. Landscape managers must monitor these progressive changes and make the necessary adjustments to direct the changing species mix in order to preserve the aesthetic, functional, and ecosystem services of the landscape.

TABLE 5-4 Ornamental Trees, Shrubs, Perennials, and Ground Covers That Are Adaptable to Growing in a Range of Light Conditions from Full Sun to Full Shade

Scientific Name	Common Name
Evergreen Trees	
Picea glauca	White spruce
Picea glauca var. *densata*	Black Hills spruce
Pinus cembra	Swiss stone pine
Pinus flexilis	Limber pine
Pinus mugo	Mugo pine
Pinus strobus	White pine
Taxus cuspidata 'Capitata'	Japanese yew
Thuja occidentalis 'Techny'	Techny arborvitae
Deciduous Trees	
Acer saccharinum	Silver maple
Nyssa sylvatica	Black gum
Sassafras albidum	Common sassafras
Evergreen Shrubs	
Large (5–10 feet) (1.5 to 3 meters)	
Juniperus chinensis 'Maney'	Chinese juniper
Picea glauca 'Conica'	Dwarf Alberta spruce
Rhododendron ×	Numerous hybrids, including 'Helsinki University', 'Mikkeli', 'Northern Starburst', 'Olga Mezitt'
Taxus × *media*	Anglojap yew
Tsuga canadensis 'Lewis'	Lewis hemlock

Scientific Name	Common Name
Small (under 5 feet) (under 1.5 meters)	
Buxus microphylla var. *koreana* 'Wintergreen'	Wintergreen boxwood
Euonymus fortunei 'Emerald 'n' Gold'	Emerald 'n' Gold wintercreeper
Euonymus fortunei 'Moonshadow'	Moonshadow wintercreeper
Juniperus horizontalis 'Mother Lode'	Mother Lode creeping juniper
Juniperus horizontalis 'Wiltonii'	Blue rug creeping juniper
Juniperus sabina 'Blue Forest'	Blue Forest savin juniper
Picea abies 'Nidiformis'	Bird's nest spruce
Picea pungens 'Montgomery'	Montgomery Colorado blue spruce
Rhododendron ×	Numerous hybrids, including: 'Pink Beauty' and 'Snowbird'
Deciduous Shrubs	
Large (8–12 feet) (2.5 to 3.5 meters)	
Exochorda racemosa	Common pearlbush
Exochorda serratifolia 'Northern Pearls'	Northern Pearls pearlbush
Hamamelis vernalis 'Autumn Embers'	Autumn Embers vernal witch hazel
Philadelphus coronarius	Sweet mock orange
Rhamnus frangula 'Columnaris'	Columnar glossy buckthorn
Viburnum × *burkwoodii*	Burkwood viburnum
Viburnum dentatum 'Morton'	Northern Burgundy viburnum
Viburnum dentatum 'Ralph Senior'	Autumn Jazz viburnum
Viburnum dentatum 'Synnestvedt'	Chicago Lustre viburnum
Viburnum farreri	Fragrant viburnum
Viburnum lantana	Wayfaringtree viburnum
Viburnum × *rhytidophylloides*	Lantanaphyllum viburnum
Viburnum × *rhytidophylloides* 'Alleghany'	Alleghany lantanaphyllum viburnum
Medium (4–8 feet) (1 to 2.5 meters)	
Aronia arbutifolia	Red chokeberry
Calycanthus floridus	Common sweetshrub
Clethra alnifolia	Summersweet clethra

(*Continued*)

TABLE 5-4 (Continued)

Scientific Name	Common Name
Clethra alnifolia 'Ruby Spice'	Ruby Spice clethra
Exochorda serratifolia	Korean pearlbush
Fothergilla major	Large fothergilla
Hydrangea arborescens 'Annabelle'	Annabelle hydrangea
Ilex glabra	Inkberry
Kerria japonica	Japanese kerria
Myrica pensylvanica	Northern bayberry
Rhodotypos scandens	Black jetbead
Spiraea × *vanhouttei*	Vanhoutte spirea
Symphoricarpos albus	White snowberry
Small (under 4 feet) (under 1.5 meters)	
Daphne × *burkwoodii*	Burkwood daphne
Daphne × *burkwoodii* 'Carol Mackie'	Carol Mackie daphne
Daphne × *burkwoodii* 'Somerset'	Somerset burkwood daphne
Forsythia × 'Arnold Dwarf'	Arnold Dwarf forsythia
Itea virginica	Virginia sweetspire
Itea virginica 'Henry's Garnet'	Henry's Garnet sweetspire
Itea virginica 'Sprich'	Little Henry sweetspire
Rhus aromatica 'Gro-Low'	Gro-Low sumac
Salix purpurea 'Nana'	Dwarf purple oiser willow
Stephanandra incisa 'Crispa'	Cutleaf stephanandra
Symphoricarpos × *chenaultii* 'Hancock'	Chenault coralberry
Ground Covers	
Ajuga reptans	Bugleweed
Euonymus fortunei	Wintercreeper euonymus
Euonymus fortunei 'Coloratus'	Purple wintercreeper
Vinca minor	Common periwinkle

Scientific Name	Common Name
Perennials	
Achillea spp.	Yarrow
Aquilegia hybrids	Columbine
Campanula carpatica	Carpathian bellflower
Centaurea montana	Mountain bluet
Chelone lyonii	Turtlehead
Heuchera hybrids	Coralbells

Encroachment of Nonplanted Species

Part of the constantly changing landscape ecosystem is the encroachment of nonplanted species on the site. Many forces lead to this distribution, including humans, animals, and environmental factors such as wind and water. Recently, some landscape ecology research has evaluated how and what changes to both natural and managed landscapes may be attributed to climate change (Breshears et al. 2008; Kelly and Goulden 2008; Kendle, Rose, and Oikawa 2000). In particular, they are focusing on what impact climate change has on plant distribution and encroachment into landscape ecosystems.

Even a subtle change in plant distribution can have a significant impact on the landscape. It is important for landscape managers to be able to distinguish between the arrival of species that will have a clear and undesirable impact on ecosystem function (invasive species) from those that simply represent ecosystem flux due to serial progression. The arrival of invasive species in natural and managed landscapes leads to a number of problems, including displacement of native species, which must be addressed through sound landscape management strategies (California State Parks 2009) (Figure 5-10). In contrast, the species representing flux can be essential to maintaining a level of ecosystem stability. These new species are able to grow where previously established species have become less viable (Williams 1997) and can ensure the landscape will still fill its aesthetic, functional, and ecosystem service roles.

Population dynamics is the branch of life sciences that studies short- and long-term changes in the size and age composition of populations, and the biological and environmental processes influencing those changes (Wikipedia 2010a).

Identifying Invasive Species

In contrast to native species that are indigenous to a particular area or region, invasive species are plants that are not native to a given ecosystem and that cause, or are likely to cause, economic, ecological, or environmental harm (Wikipedia 2010b). It is often because of this economic and environmental impact that some of the "introduced," "exotic," or "alien" species used in landscapes today get a bad name. Clearly, not all introduced species are invasive. In many cases, they are well-behaved, functional, and aesthetic parts of a landscape.

In general, invasive species are more often associated with a species of plant rather than a plant cultivar. Because the majority of cultivars are reproduced through budding or grafting, which requires human intervention, there is little likelihood they will spread extensively unless planted by humans. Further, many

(a)

(b)

Figure 5-10 (a) Butterfly bush (*Buddleia* spp.) has invaded the edge of this stream and has choked out native vegetation. (b) English ivy (*Hedera helix*), seen here climbing up tree trunks, has become a significant problem in some parts of the United States.
Images courtesy of Linda R. McMahan and Brad Withrow-Robinson, Oregon State University Extension Service.

of the newer tree cultivars readily available through the nursery industry do not produce viable seed via pollination so seed dispersal and subsequent spread of the plant does not occur (Ramstad and Orlando 2009).

However, there are exceptions. Recent data suggests that cultivars of two common urban trees, Norway maple (*Acer platanoides*) and Bradford pear (*Pyrus calleryana*), have exhibited invasive tendencies in native woodland areas (Ramstad and Orlando 2009). There is similar evidence that some native species, western juniper (*Juniperus occidentalis*) for example, are spreading beyond their native habitats and significantly changing otherwise intact ecosystems. Table 5-5 lists a number of native species that have become invasive in certain parts of the world. While native plants are an important part of a sustainable landscape, the species in the overall context of the design and growing environment must be considered when determining if it is the best choice. Although a particular species is native, in some instances it may become a landscape liability. It is important to check local resources to determine if these species are a problem in your area.

COMMON INVASIVE SPECIES TRAITS INCLUDE THE FOLLOWING:

- Ability to reproduce both asexually and sexually
- Fast growth rate
- Rapid reproduction
- High dispersal ability
- Phenotypic plasticity (the ability of a plant to alter its growth form to suit current environmental conditions)
- Tolerance of a wide range of environmental conditions
- History or evidence of successful invasions

Source: Wikipedia (2001b).

TABLE 5-5 Plant Species Native to the United States That Have Been Classified as Invasive

Scientific Name	Common Name
Shrubs and Subshrubs	
Bocconia frutescens	Plume poppy
Caragana arborescens	Siberian peashrub
Citharexylum caudatum	Juniper berry
Clidemia hirta	Soapbush
Hypericum canariense	Canary Island Saint-John's-wort
Lantana camara	Large-leaf lantana
Maclura pomifera	Osage orange
Mahonia nervosa	Oregon grape
Rubus argutus	Highbush blackberry
Trees	
Calocedrus decurrens	Incense cedar
Catalpa bignonioides	Southern catalpa
Catalpa speciosa	Northern catalpa
Juniperus virginiana	Eastern red cedar
Pinus ponderosa	Ponderosa pine
Pinus strobus	Eastern white pine
Populus balsamifera	Balsam poplar
Pseudotsuga menziesii	Douglas fir
Robinia pseudoacacia	Black locust
Thuja occidentalis	Eastern arborvitae

Source: Adapted from the Invasive Plant Atlas of the United States (http://www.invasiveplantatlas.org/index.html).

SUMMARY

Landscape ecosystems are multifunctional and fulfill aesthetic and functional needs while providing ecosystem services. Ecosystem services contribute to ecological cycles and environmental enhancements. Ongoing collaboration among the landscape designer, installation contractor, and landscape manager is essential to creating landscape ecosystems that function in both the short term and the long term. A well-designed and well-managed landscape ecosystem will require more inputs (labor, resources such as water, fertilizer, pesticides) during the early phases of succession but will ultimately require fewer inputs as the entire system evolves into a functional ecosystem at a semi–steady state of equilibrium. To accomplish this, the landscape management plan must account for planting succession due to plant attrition and the encroachment of nonplanted species.

STUDY QUESTIONS

1. Describe the climax stage of an ecosystem.
2. Define "ecosystem services." List 10 examples.
3. Describe the concept of "ecological design" from the 1960s through the late 1980s. How has this influenced current landscape design approaches?
4. Define "amenity turf."
5. Describe what is meant by design intent with regard to creating landscape ecosystems.
6. Define "succession phase."
7. Describe natural regeneration in a landscape context. Give an example in a natural landscape and in a built landscape.
8. What is postplanting succession? What can landscape managers do to address this situation?
9. Describe the relationship between plant attrition and microclimates.
10. List five factors that contribute to plant attrition.
11. Define an "invasive species." What happens when they invade a landscape? Why should they be managed?
12. If a species is invasive in one part of the world, is it necessarily invasive in another part of the world? Explain.
13. Should only plants native to an area be used to create a landscape ecosystem? Explain.

chapter 6

Environmental Issues

INTRODUCTION

Environmental concerns about landscape management practices have been raised by environmental groups, governmental organizations, health care professionals, writers, parents, and private citizens. A common viewpoint of critics is that fertilizers and pesticides are overused in the urban environment; are largely unnecessary; and pose unreasonable threats to humans (especially children), pets, and wildlife (particularly fish and birds) (Robbins and Sharp 2003). Traditional approaches to landscaping are criticized for producing ecologically sterile plant monocultures devoid of normal micro- and macroorganisms associated with natural environments (Robbins and Sharp 2003). Finally, use of outdoor power equipment is thought to increase noise pollution and degrade air quality, negating the positive impacts landscapes have on oxygen production and carbon sequestration.

Not surprisingly, the majority of those working in the landscape industry have a different perspective. This group comprises landscape contractors; maintenance contractors; sports field managers; golf course superintendents; and manufacturers of fertilizers, pesticides, irrigation equipment, mowers, and other power equipment. Typically, these stakeholders defend the use of fertilizers and other chemicals as necessary, power equipment as indispensible, and landscape plantings as diverse and overwhelmingly positive environmental enhancers. Many fear that concerns about the environmental impacts of maintenance practices may lead to regulations that will make it impossible for them to provide cost-effective and profitable services to customers.

Because one of the reasons for managing landscapes sustainably is to reduce the environmental concerns associated with management practices, it is important to consider some of the more important landscape management issues and options that exist.

This chapter will discuss the following:

- Nutrient leaching and runoff
- Pesticide leaching and runoff
- Health concerns associated with pesticides
- Fish and wildlife issues associated with pesticides
- Air pollution due to power equipment emissions
- Depletion of water resources
- Sustainability and environmental rhetoric
- Perspectives on environmental issues regarding pesticide use

NUTRIENT LEACHING AND RUNOFF

Nitrogen and phosphorus are important nutrients for healthy landscape plants. Both are potential pollutants of surface water and groundwater. While both nutrients can cause eutrophication of streams, rivers, and lakes (i.e., uncontrolled algae growth due to nutrient enrichment), much recent research has focused on the role phosphorus plays in eutrophication of urban bodies of water (Petrovic and Easton 2005; Soldat and Petrovic 2008). In urban and suburban areas, potential sources of nitrogen and phosphorus include the following:

- Leaching and runoff from lawns, shrub beds, and flower beds
- Runoff from direct misapplication of chemicals to sidewalks, driveways, and streets
- Leaching from septic systems
- Leaching from lawn clippings and tree leaves that accumulate in or are purposely placed in streets (Figure 6-1)
- Leaching from flower petals, fruits, and nuts of trees (Figure 6-2)
- Deposition of airborne particulate matter, including tree pollen and dust
- Runoff of eroded soil and organic mulch (Figure 6-3)
- Animal urine/feces, roadkill, and food waste
- Soaps and other chemicals

Historically, phosphorus was considered relatively immobile in soils and most likely to move off landscapes only in eroding soil or organic residues. Though quantities are small, it is now clear that phosphorus can also move in dissolved form (Hart, Quin, and Nguyen 2004; Soldat and Petrovic 2008). Nitrate nitrogen from fertilizers leaches readily and is also common in runoff. Research consistently shows that, as fertilizer application rates increase, runoff and leaching increase for both nitrogen and phosphorus.

Phosphorus

Phosphorus is important in all energy reactions occurring in plants. As one of the macronutrients, it is needed in modest quantities by all plants. It is

(a)

(b)

Figure 6-1 (a) Tree leaves and (b) lawn clippings can both contribute to nitrogen and phosphorus pollution if placed in the street.

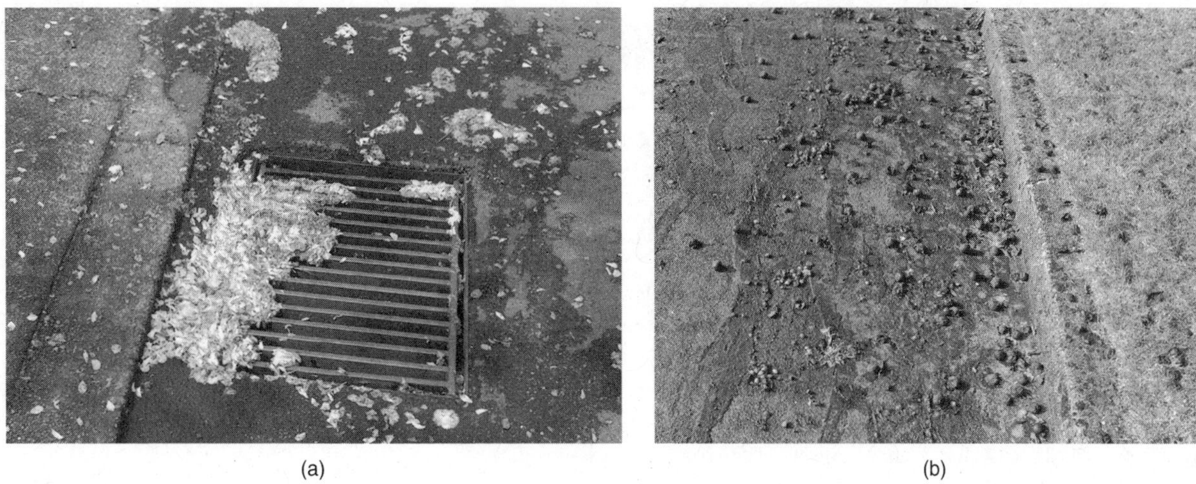

(a) (b)

Figure 6-2 (a) Petals from flowering trees often accumulate in storm sewers during spring rains and can contribute to nutrient pollution. (b) Later in the season, fruits from street-side trees can also contribute to nutrient pollution.

included in all complete fertilizers (those containing nitrogen, phosphorus, and potassium). Because plants need much less phosphorus than nitrogen or potassium, it is easy to overapply, resulting in a gradual buildup of phosphorus in soil.

Several states have enacted laws restricting the use of fertilizers containing phosphorus. Extensive soil testing in those states has demonstrated that many lawn soils have accumulated phosphorus far beyond the amount needed for healthy plant growth.

(a) (b)

Figure 6-3 Soil from erosion or careless handling during building and landscape construction can be an important source of phosphorus pollution. (a) Properly protected site and (b) improperly protected site.

Figure 6-4 Once nitrogen and phosphorus reach streams or lakes, they stimulate algae growth.

By restricting phosphorus application to lawns, they hope to reduce pollution of lakes and streams (Figure 6-4).

In 2002, Minnesota became the first state to restrict phosphorus and require lawn fertilizers to have 0 percent phosphorus. By law, phosphorus can only be applied to lawns during establishment or if soil tests indicate a deficiency (www.mda.state.mn.us/phoslaw). By 2007, a progress report on the impact of the law restricting phosphorus in Minnesota noted numerous changes, including increased availability of phosphorus-free fertilizers, a 38 percent reduction in the use of fertilizers containing phosphorus, and general acceptance of the regulations by the public. An unintended consequence was a reduction in the number of organic fertilizers available because many organic materials naturally contain relatively high levels of phosphorus (Rosen and Horgan 2005). As of 2007, officials in Minnesota were unable to document the impact of phosphorus-restricted fertilizers on phosphorus levels in water bodies.

Michigan researchers using a statistical modeling program claimed a 25 percent reduction in phosphorus loading (phosphorus accumulating in bodies of water) in lakes and rivers after only one year due to a local ordinance similar to the Minnesota law (Lehman, Bell, and McDonald 2009).

Because other research has shown that increases in phosphorus concentrations in bodies of water are directly related to application rates, it is likely that phosphorus restrictions will reduce the amount of phosphorus loading in lakes and streams due to fertilizer applications. Because there are many other sources of phosphorus in surface waters, including sediments in lake bottoms, it remains unclear just how big an impact laws restricting phosphorus will have on phosphorus pollution (Figures 6-1, 6-2, and 6-3b).

As a result of research, best management practices regarding phosphorus pollution include the following:

- Use soil test data to guide phosphorus applications so as to keep phosphorus levels at the low end of adequate.
- Apply phosphorus at low rates [0.5 lb P_2O_5/1000 sq ft/application (2.5 g P_2O_5/m^2/application)] only as needed and only during the main growing season.
- Time applications to avoid heavy postapplication rainfall events.
- Irrigate enough after application to remove fertilizer from foliage and wash it into the soil.
- Avoid fall applications of phosphorus in climates where frozen soil and snow cover occur in winter.
- Maintain nitrogen fertility high enough to produce dense turf, which reduces dissolved phosphorus runoff and nearly eliminates sediment loss.
- Return clippings when feasible because clippings do not increase phosphorus runoff under turf conditions (Bierman et al. 2009).
- Avoid applying soluble phosphorus sources. Organic sources of phosphorus may result in less runoff loss (Hart, Quin, and Nguyen 2004).

Nitrogen

Nitrogen is the primary nutrient needed to stimulate grass color and growth. Lawns are darker green and denser when nitrogen is applied as fertilizer. Removing clippings from lawns during mowing rapidly removes available nitrogen from the system and increases the need for supplemental nitrogen.

Grasses are very efficient in absorbing nitrogen so the likelihood of large increases of nitrogen in surface water or groundwater due to lawn fertilization is small. In most reports, nitrate losses from watersheds are two to five times higher from agriculture than from suburban/urban landscapes, which, in turn, are higher than nitrate losses from forested areas (Groffman et al. 2004). In the study by Groffman et al. (2004), nitrogen inputs in suburban areas included [10 lb N/acre/y (11.2 kg N/ha/y)] from atmospheric deposition (nitrogen in rainfall and dust) and [13 lb N/acre/y (14.4 kg N/ha/y)] from fertilizer. In a similar study in Arizona (Baker et al. 2001), input from pet waste totaled [15 lb N/acre/y (17 kg N/ha/y)]. This indicates that nitrogen fertilizer inputs over entire urban ecosystems make up about one-third of the total nitrogen entering the ecosystem (Baker et al. 2001). Landscape areas in which lawns were a major component retained 75 percent of added nitrogen in plant and soil material, thus reducing the amount of nitrogen available for leaching or runoff (Groffman et al. 2004).

The ability of lawns to absorb and retain nitrogen changes with age as do lawn nitrogen requirements. As lawns age, more nitrogen is stored in the root zone area, and lawns require less nitrogen for adequate growth. Research indicates that older lawns need less nitrogen and are prone to increased leaching losses if nitrogen application rates remain at establishment levels (Frank et al. 2006). For example, on mature Kentucky bluegrass (*Poa pratensis*), continued high-nitrogen applications of [5 lb N/1000 sq ft/y (24.5 g N/m^2/y)] resulted in a loss of 11 percent of applied nitrogen. Low nitrogen rates of [2 lb N/1000 sq ft/y (9.8g N/m^2/y)] resulted in only 1 percent nitrogen loss.

Pollution potential from nitrogen fertilization of shrub beds has not been extensively researched. One published account compares runoff and leaching between newly established Saint Augustinegrass (*Stenotaphrum secundatum* (Walt.) Kuntze) and a newly planted mixed tree, shrub, and ground cover bed in a tropical environment (Erickson et al. 2001). Runoff was insignificant from both areas, but the landscape bed lost 30 percent of applied nitrogen to leaching while the lawn lost less than 2 percent of applied nitrogen. These results are predictable, because the landscape planting had not achieved 100 percent ground coverage while the sodded lawn covered the entire ground surface immediately. To better understand the dynamics of this situation, additional testing needs to be done over a period of years to see what long-term trends develop.

Best management practices established from research regarding nitrogen pollution include the following:

- Apply nitrogen at times when lawns and other landscape plants are actively growing.
- Avoid late-fall or dormant nitrogen applications.
- Use lowest effective rates of nitrogen, avoiding soluble sources when possible.
- Avoid nitrogen applications prior to expected heavy rainfall events.
- Design lawn and landscape beds so that runoff is retained on-site.
- Reduce applied nitrogen rates when clippings are returned.

For additional details on nutrient management in landscapes, see Chapters 8 and 9.

PESTICIDE LEACHING AND RUNOFF

Pesticides encompass a wide array of chemicals, including herbicides, fungicides, insecticides, miticides, nematicides, moluscicides, rodenticides, and fumigants. Among these chemicals, some are registered for use in landscapes, some for agriculture, and some for structural pests (termites). In general, more chemicals are registered for use on warm-season grasses than on cool-season grasses (see Chapter 10). Because pest species vary from region to region, pesticides commonly used in one area may not be used in another area. Regulations vary by country, so not all pesticides are available in all countries. Understanding the environmental impact of pesticides requires specific knowledge of the site and the chemicals involved.

Most research on pesticide fate in landscapes (whether it accumulates, leaches, runs off, or breaks down) has been directed at lawns and golf course turf. Research aimed at leaching and runoff behavior is generally carried out using a worst-case scenario approach. For example, in many small-plot studies, irrigation is applied at a rate of [2 to 6 inches/h (5 to 15 cm/h)], sometimes within 24 hours after application, to purposely cause runoff or leaching (Baird et al. 2000). In some trials, a preapplication irrigation event is followed by postapplication irrigation (Harrison et al. 1993).

For a short and concise analysis of the fate of pesticides used on turf, see Hull (1995). An in-depth discussion of the fate of pesticides is presented by Balogh and Walker (1992), Racke and Leslie (1993), and Clark and Kenna (2000).

Some general research findings on pesticide fate include the following:

- For commonly used landscape pesticides, runoff is more of a problem than leaching and is more likely to occur if precipitation occurs shortly after application.
- Once chemicals dry on foliage or become bound up in thatch or soil, leaching and runoff potential decrease.
- Leaching potential increases as the solubility and persistence of individual chemicals increases.
- Dense turf or ground cover reduces runoff significantly.
- Most chemicals break down fast in dense vigorous lawns, reducing the potential for leaching and runoff.
- Chemicals purposely or inadvertently applied to concrete or asphalt are extremely prone to runoff and are slow to degrade (Mumley and Katznelson 1999).

Best management practices gleaned from leaching and runoff studies with pesticides include the following:

- Reduce the potential for runoff by designing landscapes that direct runoff to on-site bioswales rather than to storm sewers, streams, or lakes.
- Establish vegetative no-spray buffer zones between treated areas and waterways.
- Avoid application of pesticides when soil moisture levels are high or when heavy precipitation is likely within 24 hours.
- Use pesticide formulations with low runoff or leaching potential. Runoff is generally greater with granular than wettable powder formulations. Water-soluble formulations are more likely to run off than low-water-soluble formulations. Pesticides with high adsorption affinity are less likely to run off or leach than materials that are not adsorbed (Baird et al. 2000).
- Avoid application of pesticides to impervious surfaces such as sidewalks, driveways, and roads.
- Use pesticides only in the context of a well-formulated integrated pest management (IPM) plan (see Chapter 10).

HEALTH CONCERNS ASSOCIATED WITH PESTICIDES

Health concerns associated with pesticide use in commercially maintained landscapes include direct toxic exposure to applicators, human bystanders, and pets; exposure via dislodgeable residues; long-term exposure; and exposure to multiple chemicals. Beyond direct toxic effects, the greatest concern is potential carcinogenicity associated with short- and long-term exposure to pesticides.

The greatest risk to applicators using common pesticides applied in turf and landscape situations comes from insecticides. Fungicides pose less risk and herbicides the least. The actual risk depends on the specific chemical, the dosage, and the extent of exposure (Ottoboni 1997). Licensed applicators who follow all label-recommended safety precautions are unlikely to be exposed to toxic levels of pesticides during mixing and handling (Leonard and Yeary 1990).

Research has generally concluded that bystander exposure to the widely used broadleaf herbicide 2,4-D is unlikely under normal homeowner or professional applicator procedures. According to studies on bystander exposure to herbicides and insecticides, dislodgeable residues drop rapidly in the first 24 hours after application (Sears et al. 1987). In the case of diazinon, a 24-hour re-entry waiting period dramatically reduces potential exposure due to contact with plant foliage. Similar results were obtained in studies using 2,4-D (Thompson, Stephenson, and Sears 1984). Excretion of absorbed 2,4-D by applicators applying product daily as part of their job was well below the established daily dietary intake of 0.3 mg/kg, indicating minimal absorption. In a test of absorption and excretion of 2,4-D in bystanders, Harris et al. (1990) were unable to detect 2,4-D in urine samples from bystanders in the first four days after application.

Although the health impacts from exposure to individual or multiple chemicals are difficult to study, many trials have been conducted on such issues as exposure of children to lead in paint, insecticides applied to foundations for termite control, landscape pesticides, pest strips, and flea collars. Others deal with agricultural pesticide use and potential effects on applicators or the public.

Case-control studies are the most common way to study the health effects (such as cancer) associated with pesticides. Typical studies compare one group of people with cancer to another group of people from the same population who don't have cancer. Participants are asked a series of questions about their use of chemicals and other lifestyle behaviors. The questions may ask participants to recall events that occurred several years to decades ago. Using this data, researchers look for correlations between the history of pesticide use or exposure and the incidence of cancer.

Odds ratios are developed that associate the disease with exposure to one or more chemicals or lifestyle characteristics. Odds ratios above 1.0 indicate that there may be an association of an activity or exposure with the incidence of disease. Case-control studies are not very precise because they don't account for details such as chemical application rates, formulations, actual dates of exposure, and duration of exposure. The odds ratios do not offer any absolute risk factors, only that there may be an association (Ottoboni 1997).

Numerous case-control studies have indicated that 2,4-D appears to be associated with an increased incidence of non-Hodgkin's lymphoma (Blair and Zahm 1995; Buckley et al. 2000; Hoar et al. 1986). Buckley et al. (2000) found a high association of cancer in children of families with a history of high pesticide use but were not able to identify specific chemicals or exposure parameters and suggested more research.

In Canada, Ritter et al. (1997) conducted an in-depth analysis of the relationship between public exposure to pesticides and incidence of cancer. They concluded that phenoxy herbicides (2,4-D and related compounds) may pose a risk to applicators who handle the chemicals regularly but that there was no indication that the general public was at risk from exposure to these herbicides. They also concluded that there was no evidence that lawn and garden pesticides in general are likely to be a major cause of cancer. They called for more sophisticated research studies to better determine the risks associated with pesticide use. It should be noted that, in their opinion, case-control studies have limited value.

There is no consensus among scientists or the public on the relative risks of exposure to pesticides. Groups opposed to pesticides are strong advocates of the precautionary principle in dealing with the potential side effects of pesticide use on human health. The Rio Declaration on Environment and Development (the Rio Declaration) defines the precautionary principle as follows:

> In order to protect the environment, the precautionary approach shall be widely applied by States according to their capabilities. Where there are threats of serious or irreversible damage, lack of full scientific certainty shall not be used as a reason for postponing cost-effective measures to prevent environmental degradation. (Wikipedia 2010)

Simpler interpretations include "better safe than sorry" and "look before you leap." In the context of landscape pesticide exposure, the precautionary principle makes it the responsibility of users to demonstrate that no harm will come from the use of pesticides in landscapes. This has become the crux of an ongoing debate concerning pesticide use because obviously there is no way to demonstrate that no harm will ever come from their use.

The following best management practices reflect concerns raised by the precautionary principle:

- Avoid the use of pesticides as much as possible through a well-conceived IPM plan.
- In all cases, select low-risk pesticides first.
- Take advantage of all available precautions to reduce the exposure to pesticides by applicators and bystanders.
- Use signs to inform bystanders that pesticide applications have been made.
- Alert neighbors of treatments as required by law.
- Avoid re-entry on sprayed properties for 24 to 48 hours or as prescribed by the pesticide label.
- Do not use pesticides in situations where young children or pets are likely to be exposed.

FISH AND WILDLIFE ISSUES ASSOCIATED WITH PESTICIDES

Fish, birds, and other wildlife are potential casualties in areas treated with pesticides (Figure 6-5). In high enough concentrations, insecticides can kill fish or disrupt their reproduction (Mumley and Katznelson 1999). For instance, salmon are susceptible to direct kills at high dosages and suffer from reduced growth when subjected to sublethal doses of organophosphate or carbamate insecticides for exposure periods as short as four days (Baldwin et al. 2009). Bird kills due to direct poisoning have resulted in restrictions on the use of organophosphate insecticides (Stone and Gradoni 1985). Carbaryl (an insecticide) and benomyl (a fungicide) are both toxic to earthworms and can reduce populations in lawns by 60 percent or more for up to 20 weeks after a single application (Potter et al. 1990). In the same study, chlorpyrifos (an insecticide) reduced spider, rove beetle, and

Figure 6-5 Birds are particularly sensitive to insecticide treatments.

predatory mite populations for up to six weeks after a single treatment. Potter (1994) noted that regular pesticide applications to lawns may destabilize the lawn ecosystem and increase the number and severity of pest outbreaks.

To avoid the negative consequences of indiscriminate pesticide use, consider the following best management practices for landscape pesticide use:

- Use pesticides only in the context of a well-conceived IPM plan.
- Determine if the proposed treatment area provides habitat for birds and fish as well as other wildlife and alter plans as needed to avoid their exposure.
- Analyze potential pesticides from a nontarget perspective to avoid inadvertently selecting pesticides posing a high risk to wildlife.
- Create no-spray buffer zones near streams and lakes as defined by local, state, or federal law.
- Avoid regular use of insecticides so arthropod, spider, and mite populations can remain healthy and function properly as beneficial organisms.

See Chapter 10 for additional information on IPM and pest control options.

AIR POLLUTION DUE TO POWER EQUIPMENT EMISSIONS

Landscapes are potential environmental moderators and offer many functional benefits. For instance, Beard and Green (1994) discussed the benefits associated with lawns, including:

- Excellent soil erosion control and dust abatement
- Improved recharge and protection of groundwater quality
- Entrapment and biodegradation of synthetic organic compounds
- Soil improvement and restoration
- Urban heat dissipation–temperature moderation
- Reduced noise, glare, and visual pollution problems
- Decreased noxious pests and allergy-related pollen

In spite of the positive impacts landscapes have on the urban environment, there are drawbacks. Commercial maintenance of landscapes requires the use of noise- and exhaust-producing power equipment. Mowers, edgers, trimmers, chain saws, blowers, chippers, tractors, and trucks are all used regularly or occasionally on commercial landscapes. The internal-combustion engines used to power this equipment create unwanted noise and air pollution.

Until recently, emissions from engines less than 25 hp were not regulated in the United States (U.S. Environmental Protection Agency 1998). The U.S. Environmental Protection Agency (EPA; 1998) estimates indicated that small engines contributed about 5 percent of the total hydrocarbon emissions from internal-combustion engines in the country. In Australia, tests on two- and four-stroke engines indicated that lawn mowers produced 5.2 percent of the carbon monoxide and 11.6 percent of the nonmethane hydrocarbons toward the total emissions in the study region (Priest, Williams, and Bridgman 2000). While both engine types produce significant pollution, studies have demonstrated that two-stroke engines produce from 7 to 20 times more hydrocarbons than four-stroke engines (Priest, Williams, and Bridgman 2000; White et al. 1991).

Small-engine emissions are significant because they are primarily concentrated in residential and commercial areas. In the United States, Phase 1 emission controls were initiated in 1997 by the EPA and involved changes in fuel–air mixing ratios and enhanced exhaust controls. Phase 2 sets stricter exhaust emission levels, beginning in 2011. The new regulations require improvements in fuel systems, engine combustion, and, in some cases, the addition of catalysts (U.S. Environmental Protection

Agency 2008). These changes are predicted to reduce new hydrocarbon and nitrogen oxide emissions by 35 percent and reduce evaporative emissions by 45 percent. Phase 3 standards are in the proposal stage and will bring small-engine emissions in line with those of automobiles.

Other sustainable strategies for engine-powered cars, trucks, and small equipment are being explored by numerous landscape maintenance companies. Some companies have shifted to biodiesel or propane fuel for mowing equipment. Others have replaced fleet vehicles with gas/electric hybrids or more fuel-efficient conventional vehicles. Currently, the most effective way to reduce emissions is to buy new equipment. As technology allows, expect to see more electric mowers and, ultimately, different power sources such as methanol, natural gas, fuel cells, and even hydrogen (Konrad 2009).

Noise issues concern both operators and bystanders. Noise regulations vary by city and country. Noise limits are based on decibel levels at the operator's ear and for specific distances from the source. While there are no universal standards, maximum acceptable decibel levels of 90 at the operator and 60 at 50 ft (15 m) are typical. Larger engines may have higher limits than smaller engines. The nature of small-engine operation makes noise reduction challenging.

DEPLETION OF WATER RESOURCES

Water shortages have long been a concern in arid climates, but humid climates also are increasingly experiencing water shortages as the population increases. In many countries, aging water capture and conveyance systems are inadequate and environmental issues preclude new major water capture projects. With future water supplies uncertain, city utilities will concentrate on protecting existing sources, increasing water reuse, and, in some areas, increasing desalinization (Richardson 2008). Additionally, the use of potable water for irrigation will decrease worldwide as higher-priority uses prevail (Duncan, Carrow, and Huck 2009). Nonpotable water from sewage treatment facilities is likely to become more important for landscape uses because it is available in quantity and is close to end users. Golf courses have effectively used treated wastewater for many years (Figure 6-6). Use of nonpotable water for irrigation is discussed in Chapters 2 to 4. Guidelines and details regarding optimal irrigation strategies and options for reducing irrigation are presented in Chapters 8 and 9.

Figure 6-6 Where available, treated sewage water can be an important source of irrigation water as on this golf course.

SUSTAINABILITY AND ENVIRONMENTAL RHETORIC

When contemplating life in urban and suburban areas, landscapes seem like the perfect counterbalance to concrete, steel, and asphalt. Imagine life in Manhattan without Central Park. Manicured city parks make life in large metropolitan areas more enjoyable, and attractively landscaped commercial developments make appealing workplaces. If you consider the perspective of the environmental movement, however, it often seems like there is more wrong than right with this landscaped world. Since Rachel

Carson fired the first shots decrying the mindless use of insecticides in forests, the war of words attacking and defending the use of fertilizers and pesticides has been constant. Amid this battle, the truth is hard to find.

Because lawn care is a major focal point for those questioning the use of fertilizers and chemicals in landscapes and because lawns also account for a significant area of commercial landscapes, much of the following discussion will focus on them. Lawns as a symbol of misguided social priorities have been discussed by several authors (Bormann, Balmori, and Geballe 2001; Jenkins 1994; Robbins 2007; Steinberg 2006). Referring to the lawn care reform movement in Canada, Sandberg and Foster (2005) noted that "entrenched battles have inspired civic debate about land stewardship, human health, economic governance, property rights, civic responsibility and aesthetics." They also noted that the "... politics of lawn care reform stand for larger social and cultural dynamics." This theme was carried further by Robbins (2007), who suggested that lawns are something other than "passive products of aggregated consumer choices ... to which an industry responds ... ." In his view, people are subjugated by lawns because of what lawns demand of them.

Given the level of rhetoric, it is enlightening to examine the claims and counterclaims about lawns and lawn care and their effect on the environment. Following are three examples of rhetoric along with discussion of their veracity, which will demonstrate the types of questions that should be raised when claims are made by either side in the ongoing debate about landscapes and the environment.

Claim:
Lawns are the single largest crop grown in the United States.

Source:
http://www.epa.gov/greenacres/nativeplants/factsht.html#Replacing%20Your%20Lawn.

To determine if this claim is true, the first step is to determine how many acres (square kilometers) of lawns there are in the 48 contiguous states (i.e., the lower 48 states). This is not an easy task because of the complexity of landscape configurations. The most commonly quoted study based on satellite imagery estimates the total area in the lower 48 states covered in some form of lawn at approximately 40,458,600 acres (163,800 km^2) (Milesi et al. 2005). This estimate includes residential, commercial, institutional, and park lawns plus all golf courses and athletic fields and amounts to 1.9 percent of the 48 contiguous states. The study doesn't discriminate between lawn area and shrub beds so it probably more accurately reflects total landscaped area.

The next step is to determine the size of croplands. According to the 2007 U.S. census of agriculture, the total area of farmland is 922,095,840 acres (3,734,488 km^2). Table 6-1 shows how landscapes, which are not part of the U.S. census of agriculture, compare with total cropland, total irrigated cropland, and the five largest crops.

Conclusions:
Landscapes cover a significant land area but are nowhere near the largest crop and are equal to only 4.4 percent of the total farmland in the 48 contiguous states.

Claim:
Lethal lawns: diazinon use threatens salmon survival.

Source:
Oregon Pesticide Education Network (http://www.pesticide.org/diazsalmon.pdf).

An article from the Oregon Pesticide Education Network, titled "Lethal Lawns: Diazinon Use Threatens Salmon Survival," discusses the effects of diazinon on salmon and connects the use of diazinon on lawns directly to salmon health issues. While the general information in this document appears to be accurate and truthful with regard to the effect of diazinon on salmon, the author's attempt to connect diazinon use on lawns with observed levels of diazinon in San Francisco Bay is completely wrong.

TABLE 6-1 Crop Areas in the 48 Contiguous United States

Crop	Total Acres	Total Square Kilometers	Percentage of Total
All crops*	922,095,840	3,734,488	100
All corn*	92,228,203	373,524	10
Soybeans*	63,915,821	258,859	6.9
Forage*	61,455,483	248,895	6.7
Hay*	58,121,003	235,390	6.3
Wheat*	50,932,969	206,279	5.5
Landscapes†	40,458,600	163,800	4.4

*2007 U.S. census of agriculture data.
†From Milesi et al. (2005).

To create the connection, the author refers to a study carried out in Alameda County, California, that determined that diazinon in the bay came from a small number of homes in the surrounding area. According to the lethal lawns report: "The researchers followed up this monitoring study by hiring commercial applicators to apply diazinon to two home lawns in the watershed. This research verified that applications of diazinon at recommended rates and in accordance with directions on the product label caused contamination at the levels that had been measured in the block by block monitoring study." This passage seems to make a direct connection between diazinon use on lawns and diazinon concentration in San Francisco Bay.

The author's statement does not make sense based on research regarding diazinon behavior when applied to lawns. Research has consistently demonstrated that diazinon does not run off lawns because it is bound up in thatch (Niemczyck, Krueger, and Lawrence 1977). Diazinon also has a short residual life (less than a month) in lawns due to rapid breakdown in the lawn canopy (Branham and Wehner 1985).

A review of the original research by Mumley and Katznelson (1999) gives a different version of the final trial. According to Mumley and Katznelson: "The final stage of monitoring evaluated diazinon runoff from individual homes. Two homes were selected for intensive source area sampling. Diazinon was applied to each home at recommended rates and in accordance with label instructions. Source area samples were collected from roof drains, patios and driveways following rainfall events for fifty days after application." They concluded with the following: "The largest source areas were patios and driveways, followed by roof drains." Lawns were never mentioned in this report. The authors applied diazinon to driveways, patios, and roof drains, which explains why runoff could be measured for 50 days after application.

Conclusions:
In this case, there was no relationship at all between diazinon use on lawns and diazinon runoff into San Francisco Bay. The product was applied by the researchers and not professional applicators, and applications were made directly to the driveways, patios, and roof drains to control ants. Lawns were never treated. A better title for the report would have been "Lethal Driveways and Patios: Diazinon Application to Impervious Surfaces Threatens Salmon Survival."

Claim:

All of our pesticide products are legal and registered by the EPA as practically nontoxic.

Source:

Promotional material used by some pesticide applicators, distributors, and manufacturers (U.S. General Accounting Office 1990).

In 1990, the U.S. General Accounting Office (GAO) submitted a report to the U.S. Senate concerning the ongoing use of prohibited safety claims by manufacturers, distributors, and users of landscape pesticides. It pointed out that, despite clearly stated rules on what can and cannot be said about pesticides, prohibited claims were continuing. EPA regulations prohibit statements that are "false or misleading" and claims "as to the safety of the pesticide or its ingredients, including statements such as 'safe,' 'nonpoisonous,' 'noninjurious,' 'harmless' or 'nontoxic to humans and pets' with or without such a qualifying phrase as 'when used as directed.'"

In the 1990 report, the GAO criticized the EPA for not taking enforcement action against manufacturers and distributors for making prohibited claims. The GAO also criticized the Federal Trade Commission (FTC) for failing to protect consumers against false advertising and failing to take enforcement action against applicators, manufacturers, and distributors.

In 2003, the state of New York levied a $2 million fine against Dow AgroSciences for making prohibited safety claims about its pesticide products from 1995 to 2003. In addition to the financial penalty, Dow AgroSciences was required to stop making safety claims about its products and to implement a compliance program (http://www.ag.ny.gov/media_center/2003/dec/dec15a_03.html).

Conclusions:

By law, prohibited safety claims about pesticides cannot be made. Because the EPA is not an enforcement organization, violations of these regulations have seldom been prosecuted.

PERSPECTIVES ON ENVIRONMENTAL ISSUES REGARDING PESTICIDE USE

In the ongoing debate between environmental advocates and the landscape industry, environmental groups have become proactive while the landscape industry has been more reactive. Environmental groups force the action by challenging the industry in the courts of law and public opinion. The industry groups react with counterclaims, lobbying, and lawsuits via manufacturers and industry groups. Meanwhile, the EPA and its counterparts in other countries are charged with trying to satisfy both sides. This awkward arrangement has resulted in ongoing changes in testing requirements, increasing restrictions on pesticide use, and loss of registration for products demonstrated to cause unacceptable health or environmental damage (Table 6-2).

TABLE 6-2 Partial List of Pesticides Banned or Severely Restricted from Use in Landscapes*

United States†	Canada‡	European Union§
Herbicides	**Herbicides**	**Herbicides**
2,4,5-T	2,4-D all forms	2,4,5-T and its salts and esters
2,4,5-TP	Amitrole	Simazine
2,4-D isooctyl ester	Dicamba	
4,6-Dinitro-o-cresol	Dichlobenil	
Bromoxynil butyrate	MCPP	
Calcium arsenate	Simazine	
Dinitrobutyl phenol		
Dinitro-o-cresol		
Insecticides	**Insecticides**	**Insecticides**
Aldrin	Carbaryl	Acephate
Chlordane	Endosulfan	Alachlor

(*Continued*)

TABLE 6-2 (Continued)

United States[†]	Canada[‡]	European Union[§]
DDT	Malathion	Aldicarb
Diazinon	Phosalone	Aldrin
Endrin	Pyrethrins	Arsenic compounds
Gamma-lindane	Rotenone	Carbaryl
Heptachlor		Chlordane
Lead arsenate		DDT
Sodium arsenate		Diazinon
Sodium arsenite		Dieldrin
		Endrin
		Heptachlor
		Lindane (gamma-HCH)
		Malathion
		Permethrin
Fungicides	**Fungicides**	**Fungicides**
Cadmium compounds	Captan	Mercury compounds
Mercury compounds	Copper sulfate	Zineb
	Ferbam	
	Folpet	
	Thiophanate-methyl	
	Zineb	

*This list is intended only as an example and is not intended to be exhaustive.

†http://scorecard.org/chemical-groups/one-list.tcl?short_list_name=brpest.

‡http://www.ene.gov.on.ca/en/land/pesticides/class-pesticides.php.

§http://www.pan-uk.org/PDFs/Banned%20In%20The%20EU_April%20 Update.pdf.

In Canada, the debate has heated up in recent years as indicated by attempts to ban or restrict cosmetic pesticide use in landscapes. Compare the following comments from Health Canada's Pest Management Regulatory Agency (PMRA) with the campaign by environmental groups.

"After undertaking a detailed review of 2,4-D, the PMRA (2008) determined that 2,4-D meets Canada's strict health and safety standards and can be sold and used in Canada." The PMRA noted that its findings were consistent with regulations in the United States, New Zealand, and countries of the European Union, as well as the World Health Organization.

In closing its report, the PMRA noted that "Health Canada understands that the public may have concerns over use of pesticides and would like to convey that all registered pesticides undergo a thorough science-based risk assessment and must meet strict health and environmental standards before being approved for use in Canada." PMRA's reasoned and scientific assessment did little to assuage the fears of the public.

Environmental and health groups throughout Canada campaigned vigorously against cosmetic pesticides in Quebec and Ontario and, most recently, New Brunswick. Each of these provinces passed legislation to ban pesticides on home lawns and restrict their use on golf and sports turf. In announcing the New Brunswick ban, the Canadian Association of Physicians for the Environment (CAPE) singled out 2,4-D along with other products and noted that over 700,000 citizens were now protected from unnecessary spraying and that the province's ecosystems were safer (Khan 2010). To garner support for the ban of pesticides, a CAPE fund-raising letter noted that people exposed to pesticides are at increased risk for brain, prostate, kidney, and pancreatic cancer, and children are at increased risk for leukemia. The letter also noted that polls showed 8 out of 10 New Brunswick residents were in favor of a ban on nonessential pesticides and that they believed they posed potential health risks to humans. Finally, the CAPE fund-raising letter stated the following: "With overwhelming support from the public, health groups and the environmental community, it makes perfect sense for governments to do away with lawn poisons." The PMRA findings were not even mentioned. CAPE's goal is to ban lawn pesticides throughout Canada.

Campaigns to ban or restrict pesticides generally focus on the public's fear of cancer and the overuse of unnecessary pesticides. It is challenging to prove these claims but easy to invoke the precautionary principle to encourage people to err on the side of caution.

There is also the question of overuse. Just as fast-food restaurants make money by selling fast food, spray companies make money by spraying chemicals. Because they are in the business of spraying pesticides, they are responsive to the desires of owners and site managers who have their own standards for aesthetic quality. It is easy to assume that every lawn at every site is being deluged with chemicals, but a detailed and systematic study of pesticide use in commercial landscapes that would confirm or deny this assumption has yet to be conducted.

The question of pesticide use in landscapes for cosmetic purposes is more complicated than just safety or overuse claims. For example, attitudes about the appropriateness of lawns as the main element in landscapes appear to be changing (Bourdieu 1984; Hirsch and Baxter 2009). No longer does the entire public subscribe to the standard of a pure grass lawn, free of weeds. Those who do strive for perfect lawns often simply want to fit in and avoid conflict with their neighbors. This contributes to the use of pesticides in landscapes (Robbins and Sharp 2003). This idea is supported by Hirsch and Baxter (2009), who found three key implications based on their study:

1. "Environmental health risk policy should consider the notion that social and contextual influences can more powerfully affect the way laypeople think than risk perceptions alone."
2. "Residents may desire change, such as reductions in neighbourhood pesticide use, but are unwilling to engage in antagonistic relations with neighbours."
3. Mandatory bans versus voluntary ones "... deflect much of the responsibility for alternative yard aesthetics away from the individual homeowner."

The constantly increasing pressure to ban or further restrict pesticides has definitely put the landscape industry on alert. In some cases, it has split commercial lawn care providers into two factions: one side is adamant that there is no scientific reason to ban the use of pesticides deemed necessary by applicators (Gathercole 2009); the other side maintains that it is fruitless to oppose the changes taking place nationwide and it is time to move away from business as usual and embrace IPM and alternative strategies for lawn and landscape care (Lanthier 2009). At this time, there does not appear to be a consensus of opinion within the industry.

If the changes in Canada reflect a change in global attitudes about pesticide use, then they also present an opportunity for innovative sustainable landscape management practices. The following excerpt from a paper by an agronomic and arboricultural consultant in British Columbia regarding pesticide safety sums up the attitudes and concerns about pesticide spraying among commercial applicators in Canada at the present time:

> The horticulture industry is under scrutiny over the use of pesticides in urban areas. The public opinion is that pesticides are dangerous and that we (the users) are not careful enough. Part of that criticism is valid. It will remain valid as long as some people spray without protective clothing, in contravention of common sense and in contravention of the label itself.
>
> We need to tell our story. We need to tell the public we require these products to manage serious problems, and we use these products only when justified and following recognized safety practices. But we also need to answer the public concern of unnecessary pesticide use. Our industry associations must encourage on-going training on non-pesticide methods that are effective in commercial programs.
>
> I say "let's move on." Let's respect the pesticide labels, which say to wear protective clothing.... Let's respect provincial legislation,

which says we must use IPM and seek non-pesticide methods of control. Let's respect the public opinion, which says we must use less pesticides and more natural methods. It may not be easy, but it can be done. (Lanthier 2009)

SUMMARY

Environmental issues in landscape management are real and need to be dealt with in a professional manner. Leaching of nitrogen and phosphorus from landscapes can be managed by design and through best management practices. Likewise, leaching and runoff of applied pesticides can be controlled using integrated pest management strategies and best management practices during and after application. Health concerns associated with pesticide use primarily affect applicators but are equally important for bystanders, pets, and wildlife. To minimize potential hazards, pest control activities need to be carefully thought out and executed with safety utmost in mind. The industry needs to develop alternative methods for effective pest control. Air pollution associated with power equipment is decreasing due to new emission control regulations and will continue to decrease as new technology and regulations evolve.

Water resources are in a state of flux, and landscape access to potable sources of water will continue to decline as higher-priority uses emerge. In addition, alternate sources of water need to be developed for use in landscapes.

Agenda-driven rhetoric makes it very difficult to know what is true in the debate over the environmental impact of landscaping practices. Careful analysis is needed to arrive at the truth. The examples presented in this chapter demonstrate how important it is to look behind claims. With perspectives on environmental issues diverse and often extreme, moderate voices are often not heard. The final guidelines presented here offer a blueprint for maximizing environmental health while achieving acceptable landscape quality.

STUDY QUESTIONS

1. How do the views of environmental groups differ from those of many landscapers with regard to environmental issues?
2. What are the basic goals of sustainable landscape management as far as environmental issues are concerned?
3. Nitrogen and phosphorus fertilizers have been targeted as potential sources of water pollution. What can managers do to reduce the possibility that these nutrients will end up in streams, rivers, and lakes?
4. To date, how effective have phosphorus fertilizer bans been in reducing phosphorus levels in water?
5. What are the potential problems associated with the use of pesticides in landscapes? How can you manage applications to minimize these problems?
6. Who faces the greater risk from pesticides used in landscapes, the applicators or the bystanders? What can managers do to limit bystander exposure to pesticides?
7. What is the significance of case-control studies regarding the risk of cancer in humans? What are some of the drawbacks to case-control studies?
8. What is the precautionary principle and how does it relate to the discussion about health risks associated with the use of pesticides?
9. What problems do landscape pesticides (insecticides mainly) pose for wildlife? Is it possible to use pesticides without endangering fish and birds? Explain.
10. As long as we use power equipment for maintenance, there will be air pollution. Based on current technology, what is the most effective way to minimize that pollution?
11. Where do landscapes fall on the priority list for using potable water? How does that impact our approach to design and maintenance of future landscapes?

12. As the saying goes, "Don't believe everything you read." How does that apply to the ongoing environmental rhetoric? Why don't both sides simply strive to find the truth? In your opinion, does the end goal justify the means?
13. Find three examples of environmental rhetoric and analyze each one to determine just how truthful the claims are. See if you can find the truth behind the claims.
14. Based on the discussion about pesticide bans in Canada, what do you think the likelihood is that the same thing will happen in the United States?
15. How will lawn and shrub bed care be impacted if pesticide use is banned in those areas in commercially maintained landscapes in your climate zone?
16. Which of the following regions would have the toughest time producing attractive landscapes at existing sites if pesticides were banned for cosmetic purposes?
    a. Northern Europe
    b. Southern Italy
    c. Northwestern Australia
    d. Virginia and North Carolina
17. Is there a place for pesticides in sustainable landscapes? In your opinion, how should the pesticide issue be addressed in your region?

chapter 7

Sustainable Soils for Landscapes

INTRODUCTION

Healthy soil is central to the development of sustainable landscapes. Healthy soils are biologically active and texturally and structurally suited to healthy root growth of trees, shrubs, and lawns. In the context of landscapes, soils serve many functions, including that of plant growth medium, substrate/habitat for soil fauna/flora, nutrient recycling, sink for pollutants, and source of pollutants (Bullock and Gregory 1991). Unfortunately, soils are often damaged during building and landscape construction, resulting in an altered growing environment that may suffer from compaction, poor drainage, and altered soil fertility.

This chapter will discuss the following:

- Healthy soils
- Sustainable options in developing soils for landscapes
- Managing soils sustainably

HEALTHY SOILS

An excerpt from the National Cooperative Soil Survey describes soil as "natural bodies, made up of mineral and organic materials that cover much of the earth's surface, contain living matter and can support vegetation outdoors, and have in places been changed by human activity.... Soil consists of the horizons near the earth's surface which, in contrast to the underlying rock material, have been altered by the interactions, over time, between climate, relief, parent materials, and living organisms" (Fenton and Collins 2000).

The principal components of the mineral fraction of soils are sand, silt, and clay. Under natural conditions, these minerals plus organic matter develop over long periods of time into defined layers called "soil horizons." The conditions under which soils develop determine their properties and morphology. In the U.S. system, there are 12 orders that characterize soil (Table 7-1). Each order of soil can be further subdivided into as many as six additional taxonomic categories, with the lowest level called a "soil series." A soil series is a group of soils that have horizons similar in arrangement and characteristics (Fenton and Collins 2000). This hierarchical system demonstrates that in nature soils are highly ordered with predictable properties.

Urban soils don't fit well into the categories used to describe natural soils. Urban soils may consist of material having a nonagricultural, artificial surface layer more than 20 inches (50 cm) thick that has been produced by mixing, by filling, or

TABLE 7-1 Natural Soil Orders Based on the U.S. System of Classification

Order	Percentage of World's Ice-Free Land Surface	Characteristics
Alfisols	10	Soils with clay minerals leached out of the surface layer and into the subsoil layer. Form under forest or mixed vegetation and are productive crop soils. Located in semiarid to moist areas.
Andisols	1	Minerals lack orderly crystalline structure, and soil has high nutrient- and water-holding capacity. Highly productive crop soils. Common in cool areas with high precipitation.
Aridisols	12	Minimally weathered soils that often accumulate gypsum, salt, and calcium carbonate. Common desert soils.
Entisols	16	Occur in areas with recently deposited parent materials. Found in many environments, including floodplains, dunes, and steep slopes.
Gelisols	9	Soils with permafrost near the soil surface. May be affected by frost churning and ice segregation. Found at higher latitudes and higher elevations.
Histosols	1	Soils with high organic matter and no permafrost. Can be saturated or free-draining. Commonly called bogs, moors, peats, or mucks.
Inceptisols	17	Moderately weathered soils common to semiarid and humid environments. These soils have a wide range of characteristics and are found in many different climates.
Mollisols	7	Soils with a dark surface horizon relatively high in organic matter. Tend to be quite fertile. These form under grass in climates with pronounced seasonal dry periods.
Oxisols	7	Highly weathered soils common in tropical and subtropical regions. Found on land surfaces that have been stable for a long time. Tend to be infertile and have low cation exchange capacity.
Spodosols	4	Weathered soils with organic matter and aluminum deposited in the subsoil. Common where soils are formed from coarse-textured deposits. Common in coniferous forest regions and tend to be acidic and infertile.
Ultisols	8	Humid-area soils formed from intense weathering and leaching. Typically acidic with nutrients concentrated near the surface.
Vertisols	2	Soils containing high levels of expanding clay minerals. Expand when wet and shrink when dry. Fertile soils but retain water when wet.

Source: Adapted from http://soils.usda.gov/technical/soil_orders/.

by contamination of the land surface (Maechling, Cooke, and Bockheim 1974). Taxonomists struggle to categorize urban soils because of their extreme diversity (Evans, Fanning, and Short 2000).

In spite of the taxonomic difficulties, healthy urban soils are achievable. Healthy soils are characterized by the composite of their physical, chemical, and biological properties. Physical properties such as structure and water-holding capacity; chemical properties such as pH, nutrient-supplying ability, and salt content; and biological properties such as mineralization capacity and microbial associations are specific examples of factors affecting soil health (Pankhurst, Doube, and Gupta 1997).

Soil health has been defined by Doran and Safley (1997) as "the continued capacity of soil to function as a vital living system, within ecosystem and land use boundaries, to sustain biological productivity, promote the quality of air and water environments, and maintain plant, animal and human health." While soil quality focuses primarily on the physical and chemical properties of a soil, soil health factors soil biota into the equation. Soil biota include living roots, microflora (e.g., bacteria and fungi), microfauna (e.g., nematodes, protozoa, and rotifers), mesofauna (e.g., mites, collembolans, and enchytraeids), and macrofauna (e.g., spiders, larger insects, earthworms, ants, and termites) (Coleman and Wall 2007). The living biological components of soil make up less than 10 percent of the total organic matter in the soil but are involved in a wide range of soil processes, including nutrient cycling, organic matter decomposition, soil structure development, and the fate of agrochemicals and soil pollutants. Of the soil organisms, microflora (e.g., fungi and bacteria) make up 75 to 90 percent of the total while microfauna and macrofauna (nematodes, earthworms, microarthropods, and protozoa) make up 5 to 10 percent (Coleman and Wall 2007).

Soil health indicators collectively tell whether the soil is functioning normally (Pankhurst, Doube, and Gupta 1997). Physical indicators of soil health include bulk densities low enough to allow normal root development, water-holding capacity high enough to support plant growth between irrigation or precipitation events, and adequate pore space to maintain aerobic conditions suitable for root growth. Chemical indicators include pH in the range of 5 to 7.5, low to moderate electrical conductivity, cation exchange capacity adequate to retain nutrients, organic matter levels high enough to support high microbial activity, presence of major nutrient elements, and absence of heavy metals. The physical and chemical indicators are fairly constant and do not change much over time unless humans intervene.

Biological Factors

Biological indicators of soil health are harder to interpret (Pankhurst 1994). Scientists are still learning how soil micro-, meso-, and macroorganisms interact to produce healthy soils. Some of the attributes that have been considered include microbial biomass, abundance of microorganisms, soil respiration rates, microbial biodiversity, and soil microfauna and macrofauna biodiversity. Soil enzymes mediate and catalyze most soil processes and have the potential to provide an assessment of soil health (Dick 1997). At present, we lack simple meaningful measures of biological activity as indicators of soil health.

Soil Ecological Food Web

In contrast to simple measures, studies of soil ecological food webs prove useful in characterizing communities of micro- and macroorganisms normally associated with different plant communities. For example, ecologists have used nematode population and community structure to determine the characteristics of the detritus food web (the community of organisms that decompose organic material). Because nematodes feed on bacteria and fungi, the assemblage of microbial populations will be reflected in the makeup of the nematode population (Ferris and Matute 2003). Lawn soil food webs are categorized as highly enriched (high fertility) but poorly to moderately structured (less microbial diversity) compared to undisturbed natural grasslands that are usually highly structured (high microbial diversity) but poorly enriched (low soil fertility) (Cheng et al. 2008). Fertilizer inputs increased the enrichment index in this study, but had no impact on the nematode community. Disturbance such as tillage or application of organic materials with high nitrogen content (low carbon-to-nitrogen ratio) increased the enrichment-opportunistic nematodes due to stimulation of bacterial growth by the organic source material (Ferris and Matute 2003).

WHAT IS THE SIGNIFICANCE OF THE CARBON-TO-NITROGEN RATIO?

The C/N ratio refers to the relative amount of carbon in organic material compared to the amount of nitrogen. Organic material that is high in carbon but low in nitrogen is slow to decompose, because microorganisms cannot get enough nitrogen to grow and assimilate the carbon in the organic matter. To initiate decomposition, the microbes scavenge for soil nitrogen, which depletes the amount available for plants to use. When organic debris is composted properly by adding nitrogen fertilizer or green waste that is high in nitrogen, microbes rapidly break down the organic matter and produce the finished compost, which has a much lower C/N ratio. The relatively higher amount of nitrogen in the finished compost is released from dead microbes and is available to plants as a fertilizer.

Mycorrhizae

Mycorrhizal fungi are essential components of native plant communities, including forests and grasslands. Mycorrhizae form symbiotic associations with the vast majority of vascular plants. Plant benefits include increased uptake of water and phosphorus and protection against root pathogens (Bardgett 2005). Because mycorrhizae benefit some plants more than others, they can affect the structure of plant communities by preferentially increasing the competitiveness of certain plants (Grime et al. 1987). Soils with strong mycorrhizal associations are generally healthy soils, but many plants can perform well without mycorrhizae. Management inputs of fertilizers or fungicides may or may not decrease mycorrhizal activity.

Earthworms

Earthworms are important contributors to healthy soils in constructed landscapes. They facilitate aggregate and crumb formation in soil and increase pore formation. They also facilitate the breakdown of organic matter via fragmentation, burial, and mixing of residues (Coleman and Wall 2007) (Figure 7-1). Earthworms are generally abundant in natural forests and grasslands in temperate and tropical climates. In constructed landscapes, earthworms may be present or absent, depending on the source of soil. Soils can be improved by introducing earthworms. Several insecticides and fungicides are toxic to earthworms and can reduce or eliminate populations when used regularly. Lawn thatch levels increase when earthworms are killed by pesticides because the fragmentation and mixing function is gone (Potter, Powell, and Smith 1990).

The dominant earthworms in many constructed landscapes in cool temperate climates include *Lumbricus terrestris* L., *L. rubellus* Hoff., *Apporectodea longa* Ude., and *A. trapezoides* Duges. High soil organic matter, periodic fertilizer applications, and soils kept moist via regular irrigation foster higher species diversity and density.

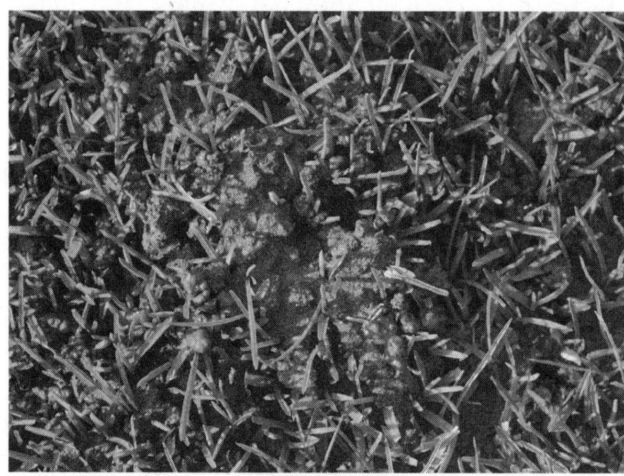

Figure 7-1 Healthy earthworm population in a lawn as indicated by worm casts.

The picture emerging from the limited research on lawn community ecosystems indicates a system with a range of flora and fauna, grazing and detritus food webs that are well developed but skewed toward high enrichment (high fertility) and low structure (less microbial diversity), and a key role for earthworms in system development. Tree and shrub plantings in landscapes have been less well researched than lawns so it is difficult to describe the structure of soil food webs associated with them. In healthy plantings, strong mycorrhizal associations may or may not be present, detritus food webs in typical acidic soils will be dominated by fungi rather than by bacteria (Cheng et al. 2008), and strong earthworm populations are likely. These factors will result in good soil structure and healthy vigorous plants.

Figure 7-2 Layering quality topsoil over compacted subsoil and gravel is a poor way to produce a good growing medium.

SUSTAINABLE OPTIONS IN DEVELOPING SOILS FOR LANDSCAPES

A landscape soil conservation plan should be developed before building construction occurs. This plan designates protected areas, creates soil stockpiling areas, and orchestrates the entry and exit areas for machinery. The goal is to do no harm to on-site soils when possible and to maintain the integrity of existing topsoil. Unfortunately, given the nature of building construction, soil planning is often neglected early in the process and may only involve bringing in topsoil to assist in achieving final grades. The following sections introduce options for addressing soil issues. For soil specifications and engineering standards, see Craul (1999) and Urban (2008).

Fill Soils

Fill soils may include sand and gravel, subsoil construction spoils, or construction debris such as concrete rubble and asphalt chunks. In a given fill area, there is rarely continuity so physical characteristics may vary significantly from one section to another. Fill material is often heavily compacted after placement to avoid settling prior to landscape installation. Soil scientists refer to fill material as "having great spatial variability."

Fill soils are generally not intended for use as planting soils but, in effect, become the subsoil to whatever topsoil is placed over them. Because of the poor water movement properties of compacted fill soils, drainage system installation has to be considered prior to or after adding topsoil. If drainage is not accounted for, the finished landscape will suffer from poor drainage, because water moving through the topsoil cannot move into and through the fill material below (Figure 7-2).

On-Site Soils

Because much urban and suburban development occurs in areas of former farmland, it is possible that on-site soils are of good quality and generally suitable for a wide range of landscape plantings. The strategy in these situations is to remove the topsoil from the building footprint area and parking lot areas and place it in stockpiles for later use. Areas that will be undisturbed during building construction should be fenced and otherwise protected to prevent unplanned heavy-equipment traffic, dumping, and contamination during construction. Once elevations have been established, the stockpiled soil can be incorporated with existing topsoil to achieve final grades.

The advantages of using on-site soils include:

Soil uniformity across the site

Unimpeded natural drainage through the profile

Minimal need for amendments

Known fertility status

Minimal need to import soil

The disadvantages of using on-site soils include:

Soil type may not be suitable for planting.

Quantity may not be adequate to meet grades.

Soil seed bank may contain noxious weeds.

The 2009 version of the Sustainable Sites Initiative offers soil restoration criteria, including a root zone depth of 12 inches (30 cm), maximum dry bulk density or cone penetrometer readings appropriate for a range of soil textures from sand to clay, appropriate soil organic matter levels, and restoration of soil organism activity and diversity based on on-site reference soils. For details, see: http://www.sustainablesites.org/report/.

Amending On-Site Soils

Even when on-site soils are generally suitable, they may have been compacted during construction or require pH adjustment prior to use. Soils slated for flower or shrub beds may be too fine textured (excess clay) and require amendments to decrease the bulk density and raise the porosity to acceptable levels.

Amending on-site bed soils is commonly done by adding composted organic matter at rates ranging from 10 to 50 percent by volume (Figure 7-3). Adding 33 percent food waste compost by volume to a sandy loam soil reduced the bulk density from 1.5 g/cm^3 to 1.2 g/cm^3 in uncompacted soil and from 1.8 g/cm^3 to 1.5 g/cm^3 in compacted soil. In both cases, the bulk density of the amended soil was below the threshold for potential root restriction (Rivenshield and Bassuk 2007). Root restriction in sands occurs at bulk densities above 1.6 g/cm^3 (Aubertin and Kardos 1965). When compost was added to clay loam soils, the bulk density actually increased at the 33 percent volume and didn't decrease until the compost volume increased to 50 percent (Rivenshield and Bassuk 2007). This may be an anomaly because this particular compost contained sand, but it appears that using compost to reduce the bulk density of clay soils may require too much amendment to be practical.

Figure 7-3 Adding and then tilling compost into surface soils can improve fertility, aeration, and water retention.

Because commercial composts are only partially composted, decomposition continues once they are incorporated into soil. The ultimate volume reduction of the incorporated compost due to decomposition may run 50 to 75 percent (Urban 2008). When large amounts of compost are mixed with soil, significant settling will occur. Incorporating compost into the top 8 inches (20 cm) of soil will alleviate compaction to that depth, will decrease the bulk density initially by physical dilution, and may provide long-term structure enhancement as the compost decomposes. Settling and decomposition loss of added

Figure 7-4 Prior to planting, the soil on the right side of this photo was amended with 6 inches (15 cm) of compost, while the soil on the left received nothing. Note the increased growth in the amended soil.

organic matter of an 80 percent/20 percent compost mix may reduce final soil volume by 10 to 15 percent to the depth of incorporation (Urban 2008).

Compost may also affect numerous soil characteristics. These include pH and nutrient status, and if the original soil is sandy, compost will increase the water-holding capacity. Composts vary in their state of decomposition, pH, and nutrient status, and, without testing, there is no way of knowing what impact individual materials might have. Except in annual flower beds, compost can only be incorporated into soil once. In planting beds with herbaceous perennials and woody plants, additional applications can only be made from the surface. The impact of a one-time compost incorporation in a silty clay soil on the growth of rhododendrons (*Rhododendron* spp.) is illustrated in Figure 7-4.

There are several potential problems with adding compost, including:

Uniform on-site mixing is difficult to achieve.

Amended soil volume may settle significantly as compost decomposes.

Excessive tilling during mixing may destroy the original soil structure.

Effective incorporation depth is limited so there is no impact on soil deeper than the tillage depth.

Soil may become loaded with phosphorus from compost.

Compost may be cost prohibitive on large areas.

From a practical point of view, bed areas are often amended with organic matter, whereas lawn areas are not. Where existing soils are used for lawns, general preparation requires only enough tillage to facilitate grading.

Adding sand to heavy-textured on-site soils to improve porosity and drainage is a risky endeavor. Research has shown that small quantities of sand, even when mixed uniformly, decrease the porosity (micropores and macropores) of amended soils (Spomer 1983). As sand proportions increase, the porosity decreases until the quantity of sand is large enough that remaining soil particles cannot fill all the voids between sand grains. Practically speaking, sand must make up in excess of 80 percent of the final amended soil by volume before it increases macropore space. This in itself makes adding and tilling sand into on-site soils impractical.

Importing, Manufacturing, or Augmenting Landscape Soils

Often existing soils have not been protected, and construction activities have ruined the soil via compaction, layering, gravel incorporation, or contamination with paint or other chemicals. In such situations, a common practical option is to remove the existing surface soil to a depth of 10 to 18 inches (25 to 45 cm) and replace it with imported soil. Though effective, this is the least sustainable approach for improving soil because the original soil is now suited only for fill and the imported soil has to be mined from another location. This is probably the most common strategy in use currently, and it will be a difficult practice to abandon for most contractors.

Figure 7-5 In this case, a loamy sand soil was placed over the original silty clay loam soil, resulting in nutritional and drainage issues.

It was once possible to obtain true topsoil harvested from farmlands or stripped from other construction sites. Today, it is more common to get whatever soil is being harvested as gravel operations open up new pits. These soils are variable, often ranging from sandy loams to loamy sands. By nature, they are easy to work, relatively free-draining, nutrient poor, and may contain undesirable weeds such as horsetail (*Equisetum* spp.) or nutsedge (*Cyperus* spp.). Sometimes imported soils are not topsoil but instead are clean fill soil harvested from deep pits (Figure 7-5).

Imported soils are often placed over subsoils to fill up the excavated area. Where excavation has exposed subsoils and created a pit surrounded by foundations and sidewalks, drainage problems may result. Because the imported soils are often porous, the subsoils are impervious, and the pit is surrounded on all sides, water tends to accumulate, leading to perpetually wet soils. To avoid this, drainage needs to be installed at the interface between subsoil and topsoil. Details on drainage design can be found in Craul (1999).

When soil is imported to augment existing soil and establish final grades, it is most often layered over the original soil. When possible, use soil that is similar in texture to the original soil and till on-site soil lightly before placement to break up the interface between the original soil and the imported soil. If sandy soil is placed as a shallow layer over an existing finer-textured soil, it should be uniformly incorporated to eliminate layering.

Manufactured soils are typically mixtures of soil, sand, and organic matter or just sandy soil plus organic matter. These are mixed off-site and delivered as a homogeneous product. Premixed soils may be proprietary and may be inoculated with mycorrhizae or other microorganisms. Where project value is high enough, custom mixes may be specified by landscape architects or consulting engineers.

Sustainable soils are manufactured soils that use sustainable components such as sand from river dredging, composted garden waste, mine tailings, or other waste materials suitable for use in manufactured soil mixes (Craul 1999). The goal is to assemble a mix that will support plant growth, drain well but hold adequate water, and retain nutrients. Organic sources such as peat moss are not considered sustainable because of current fears that peat bogs are being destroyed by overharvesting. Thorough testing of prospective mixes is necessary to determine their suitability for use (Craul 1999).

Structural soils have been developed to improve the survival potential of urban street trees planted in paved areas (Grabosky, Bassuk, and Trowbridge 2002). The planting mix consists of a stone matrix mixed with a small portion of clay loam soil. The stone provides a stable medium to support the trees, and the soil provides nutrient-holding capacity and enhances water retention. Roots grow in the voids between rocks. The system is compatible with engineering compaction needs and allows root growth to develop in an aerated environment that is not prone to plugging or further compaction (Grabosky, Bassuk, and Trowbridge 2002).

This approach has shown promise in difficult planting situations during establishment and early development, but because it is new, the long-term function of the system is unknown. In North Carolina, tree growth in structural soil was equal to growth of the same trees in compacted soil and produced greater total root length than other treatments. Tree growth in uncompacted soil was notably better than that in structural soil (Smiley et al. 2006). This reinforces the notion of using structural soils only in situations where uncompacted soils are not feasible to maintain.

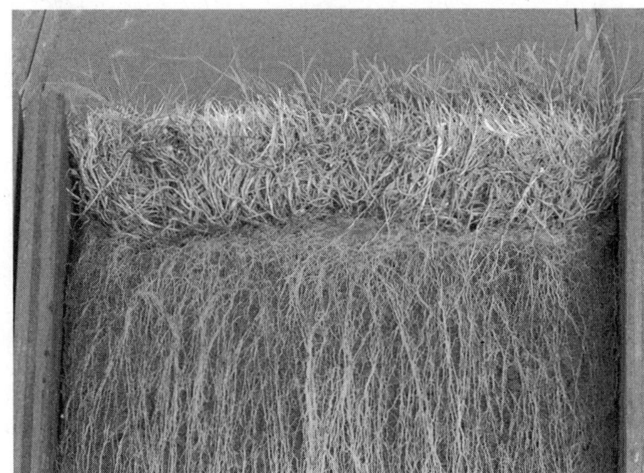

Figure 7-6 The fibrous nature of grass roots helps to improve soil structure.

MANAGING SOILS SUSTAINABLY

Once bed soils are in place, regardless of how they were selected or amended, the goals become the same. In order for soil to function over time, it needs to support healthy soil fauna and flora communities, absorb and move water, maintain soil oxygen levels high enough to sustain healthy root growth, and replenish organic matter to fuel growth of soil organisms. The natural process in tree and shrub bed soils is for added organic matter to decompose down to an end point organic matter percentage. The structure resulting from decomposition by-products is transient without continued inputs of organic matter. As a result, infiltration and percolation rates decline along with soil aeration. Without continued inputs, bed soils become harder, less receptive to water, and less hospitable for root growth.

Lawns, by nature, tend to build soil organic matter, and the fibrous nature of the root systems builds structure (Figure 7-6). Returning clippings to the lawn encourages general vigor and can stimulate earthworm activity, which incorporates clipping debris, reduces thatch accumulation, enhances aeration, and may increase infiltration rates (Potter, Powell, and Smith 1990). The main threat to this process is compaction resulting from foot and machinery traffic. If compaction is severe, the natural system breaks down, and soil becomes denser, more impermeable, and less suitable for root growth.

Mulch

In bed areas, mulching is an important means for maintaining surface permeability, enhancing soil biological activity, conserving water, and preventing a general decline in soil health. Mulches may also help with weed suppression, as discussed in Chapter 10. The impact of organic mulch depends somewhat on its composition.

Mulches with high carbon-to-nitrogen (C/N) ratios include the following:

- Most bark materials (large and small nuggets, fine grades, hardwood, and softwood; most have high lignin content)
- Wood chips (cellulose)
- Sawdust (cellulose)
- Pine needles (lignin, cellulose)
- Coconut husks (lignin, cellulose)
- Ground recycled pallets (cellulose)
- Arborist mulch (mix of wood chips, bark, and leaves)

Materials with high C/N ratios are slow to decompose. It is not clear what impact these mulches might have on soil properties, and there is only a limited amount of research from which to draw. In a study comparing ground recycled pallets with composted garden refuse and unmulched bare soil, Tiquia et al. (2002) measured several soil and microbial properties over a three-year period. The ground wood pallets had a C/N ratio of 114:1 at the time of application. After three years, this mulch had no effect on soil nutrient status, pH, or soil microbial biomass compared to the unmulched bare soil area.

Low C/N mulches include:

Composts

Hemlock bark

Mulches that have been thoroughly hot composted have low C/N ratios. In theory, they should provide nutrients, improve soil structure, and enhance soil microbial activity. In the trial by Tiquia et al. (2002) discussed earlier, composted garden refuse with a C/N ratio of 17:1 increased soil organic matter, soil potassium, soil pH, soil respiration, extractable nitrogen, and microbial biomass compared to bare soil. Compared to ground recycled pallets, it increased soil organic matter, weak Bray extractable soil phosphorus, soil potassium, total extractable soil nitrogen, and dissolved organic nitrogen. In this case, compost really did have significant impacts on the soil. Other research has demonstrated that low C/N composted garden refuse not only stimulates soil microorganism growth but also increases the available soil nitrogen and stimulates both growth and flowering of rhododendron (*Rhododendron* spp.) and growth of river birch (*Betula nigra*) (Lloyd et al. 2002).

There are many reasons for applying mulch to planting beds, but if the goal is to enhance physical, chemical, and biological soil properties, the best choice is compost. For weed control, mulches with high C/N ratios are the ideal choice. Bark products are among the slowest mulches to decompose so they last longer than other organic materials. After many years' use of high C/N mulches, it is probable that impact on soil properties will be similar to compost effects measured in short-term trials.

One of the problems associated with conventional landscape management is that virtually all plant debris is removed from the landscape. In a natural setting, plant debris falls to the ground and becomes part of the detritus food web. In typical constructed landscapes, natural debris is collected and hauled to recycling facilities and then returned to the landscape as compost. Finding ways to keep plant debris in beds will not only reduce waste but will also contribute to the development of healthy soils in a sustainable way.

WHAT IS HOT COMPOSTING?

Hot composting describes aerobic decomposition of organic material in which a series of microorganisms attack the organic matter using carbon in the organic material as an energy source. As mesophilic organisms (which tolerate moderate temperatures) attack raw organic matter, respiration rates increase and heat is produced. At about 110°F (45°C), thermophilic microorganisms (which are heat tolerant) take over and raise temperatures as high as 150°F (65°C) as they consume the remaining organic matter. At these high temperatures, pathogenic organisms and most weed seeds are killed, and decomposition proceeds rapidly, causing a reduction in the volume of organic material. Turning the pile maintains aerobic conditions, and decomposition occurs rapidly before temperatures drop, mesophilic organisms recolonize, and the compost cures. Hot composting is a controlled process that yields a predictable product with a low C/N ratio that is stable and rich in nutrients.

Moisture, Compaction, and Aeration

Soil moisture, compaction, and aeration are all interrelated. Compaction reduces macropores in soil and hampers aeration. Infiltration and percolation rates

Figure 7-7 In compacted soils, trees often develop very shallow root systems with many surface roots.

Figure 7-8 Mulch is useful for retaining soil moisture, but when coupled with regular irrigation or lots of rain, soils under mulch can become saturated and anaerobic. This image shows saturated soil with excess water at the mulch-soil interface.

of water decline under compacted conditions. Compaction also reduces root depth and may result in surface rooting (Figure 7-7). Compacted soils are difficult to wet when dry and, once wet, are slow to dry out. Wet soils are more prone to further compaction and further reductions in soil aeration. The goal in managing soils is to minimize compaction and optimize aeration. It is then possible to manage moisture with careful irrigation.

Moist aerated soil with a ready source of organic matter stimulates strong soil fauna and flora communities. Mulching combined with periodic irrigation during extended dry periods helps maintain soil moisture at optimal levels. This combination will maintain vigorous microflora, microfauna, and macrofauna growth throughout the growing season. Excessive irrigation, common in many mulch beds, may result in wet surface soils and can cause anaerobic conditions to develop (Figure 7-8). Anaerobic soils will kill aerobic microorganisms. Sustainable irrigation strategies for beds are discussed in Chapter 8.

Mechanical options for compaction relief and aeration for lawns include coring machines and solid-tine aerators. Unfortunately, these machines are not suited for use in landscape beds, and there are limited practical options available for improving aeration in landscape beds. Traditional methods include soil augering with or without backfills, vertical slotted pipes placed in auger holes with or without gravel, and water jets used to bore into soils around plants. Using these techniques, researchers found no differences in tree growth over a two-year period (Pittenger and Stamen 1990). They also concluded that where soil moisture is consistently maintained in the readily available range, tree growth in compacted sandy loam soils does not appear to be affected.

Other approaches have been developed to relieve soil compaction in tree root zones. The Grow Gun and Terralift both use high-pressure air discharge to blow holes in the soil and then fill the holes with some type of porous material. In sandy clay and clay loam soils, neither machine decreased the bulk density. Oxygen diffusion was increased at soil fracture layers but not beyond, and the long-term impact was not measured (Smiley et al. 1990). Other research has demonstrated decreased bulk density, increased macroporosity, and increased saturated hydraulic conductivity when the Terralift was used in sandy loam soil but not in a loam soil (Rolf 1992). Soil injection with high-pressure nitrogen gas using the Terrravent machine was not effective in decreasing the soil bulk density or improving tree growth in compacted soils (Hascher and Wells 2007; Smiley 2001).

A detailed review of compaction and amelioration treatments failed to find any postplanting treatments that could be recommended with confidence (Day and Bassuk 1994). The authors commented that multiple site-specific variables make it difficult to predict results. The difficulties in relieving compaction in planted landscape beds attest to the importance of proper bed preparation prior to planting and the need to maintain mulch cover after planting to minimize compaction.

SUMMARY

Long-term sustainability of landscapes is dependent on a healthy growing environment for plants. Healthy growing conditions start with quality soil that is biologically healthy. Sustainable site preparation uses on-site soils when possible. Soils high in sand tend to be well aerated but prone to drought, whereas soils high in clay tend to be fertile but prone to compaction and poor water movement. Both extremes of soil types can be amended with organic matter prior to planting to enhance performance after planting and meet sustainability goals. In situations where on-site soil is not suitable for use, manufactured soils are a viable option. Once soils are in place and plants are growing, ongoing efforts are needed to minimize the negative impacts of compaction on soil aeration and soil moisture status. Mulch plays a major role in maintaining soil health and preventing compaction after landscape installation while relatively few options are available for alleviating compaction in existing landscapes.

STUDY QUESTIONS

1. Define "soil." What are soil orders? Where do urban soils fit into the traditional soil classification system?
2. Define "soil health." How does soil health differ from soil quality?
3. What are the important types of soil biota? What makes them so important in determining soil health?
4. What are the key physical and chemical components contributing to soil health?
5. How do soil ecological food webs relate to soil health? What are examples of soil food webs?
6. What does it mean to say that lawn soil food webs are highly enriched but poorly structured? Is that a value judgment or just a way of categorizing lawn soils? Explain.
7. What is the difference between mycorrhizae and endophytic fungi (see Chapter 10)? What functions does each serve?
8. Do earthworms serve any beneficial purpose in landscape soils? Explain.
9. Compare the properties of fill soils, undisturbed on-site topsoils, and imported soils.
10. Why is it desirable to save on-site soils? Are there any notable problems with keeping on-site soils?
11. What are the goals of amending on-site topsoils? What is bulk density and why is it important? How do amendments affect bulk density?
12. What soil properties are affected by added compost? Is there a difference in soil response to compost and noncomposted amendments?
13. How effective is sand in improving soil physical properties? How much sand is needed to improve soil porosity?
14. Importing soils to landscape sites is almost standard practice. From a sustainable perspective, what is wrong with imported soils? Are imported soils generally more or less fertile than undisturbed on-site soils?
15. What kind of weed problems are associated with imported soils? Is there any way to avoid these problems?

16. What is the difference between manufactured soils and sustainable soils?
17. What are structural soils and where in the landscape are they best used? Are they intended to replace topsoils in all bed and lawn areas?
18. What happens to compost after it is incorporated into on-site soils? Once in place, is there any way to further enhance soil organic matter content?
19. Explain the concept of the carbon-to-nitrogen ratio in organic mulches. Why is the carbon-to-nitrogen ratio important? What is the optimum carbon-to-nitrogen ratio to enhance soil properties? What if the mulch is intended for weed control?
20. What happens to soil aeration, drainage, and rooting when soils become compacted? What choices do you have to effectively decrease compaction in bed soils?

chapter 8

Managing Trees, Shrubs, and Beds Sustainably

INTRODUCTION

Sustainable management of trees and shrubs requires proper planting, thoughtful care during establishment, and regular follow-up. Maintenance contractors often spend a great deal of time rescuing plants that suffer from poor planting, lack of follow-up fertilization, misguided pruning, and inadequate irrigation. Attentive pruning, intelligent irrigation, and periodic tasks such as edging, mulching, and weed control will develop sound trees, shrubs, and ground covers.

This chapter will discuss sustainable strategies for:

- Planting
- Fertilization
- Irrigation
- Pruning
- Managing the waste stream

PLANTING

This section will discuss preparation of the planting hole and the planting process. Opportunities for handling and placing soils during construction were discussed in Chapter 7.

One of the basic goals in planting is to place plant roots in contact with the soil in which they will be growing. While this seems simple and intuitive, failure to achieve good root-to-soil contact is one of the most common reasons for planting failures. Techniques used to grow plants in nurseries may contribute to planting problems due to extreme root loss or root system distortion. Characteristics of the most common production systems are discussed next.

Field-Grown Bare-Root Stock

Field-grown bare-root stock is a technique for producing deciduous trees and some deciduous shrubs. It involves growing plants in soil until they reach market size and then harvesting them with mechanical diggers that undercut the plants and sever the roots. Plants are harvested in late fall or early winter once the plants are fully dormant. After digging, plants are graded and stored in sawdust or other mulch prior to shipping to nurseries where they are sold locally in early spring prior to leaf-out. Bare-root plants are typically small with stems around 0.75 to 1.5 inches (2 to 4 cm) in diameter, and they have up to 95 percent of their roots removed during digging (Figure 8-1). Planting can only be done for a short time in spring while they are still dormant so the window of opportunity for bare-root stock is small.

Figure 8-1 Most of the roots on this bare-root tree have been removed during digging.

(a)

(b)

Figure 8-2 (a) This balled-and-burlapped Oregon grape (*Mahonia aquifolium*) (plant on right) has about 5 percent of the root system remaining after digging. Root-balls should be handled carefully to avoid breaking up the soil mass. (b) This much larger spade-dug tree is placed in burlap lining the wire basket. The basket ensures the root-ball will not fall apart during handling.

Bare-root plants are easily planted because they are free of soil and roots are immediately placed in contact with soil, thus avoiding interface problems common to other plant production systems. Because the planting season for bare-root stock is short, leftover plants are often transferred to pots filled with organic planting media. If held in the nursery for most of the season, they essentially become container-grown plants and face the same challenges associated with that method of plant production.

Balled-and-Burlapped and Spade-Dug Stock

Field-grown stock not suited to bare-root transplanting was historically hand dug with the intact and undisturbed root-ball placed in burlap, which was then bound with twine (Figure 8-2). With the development of mechanical spades, trees today are commonly dug and placed in wire baskets lined with burlap. The burlap and basket are then secured with twine. This system is widely used for conifers, larger deciduous trees, and many shrubs. Even though as much as 95 percent of the root system is removed during digging, the remaining roots are undisturbed and the fine roots are intact, resulting in generally high transplant survival rates. In many cases, stock can be stored and then planted at any time during the growing season. Balled-and-burlapped and spade-dug plants are heavy and must be handled with care to avoid fracturing the root-ball. Plants placed in pots after digging often develop distorted root systems with proliferation of roots at the surface, which increases the potential for girdling roots once the plants are planted out. Postplanting irrigation problems arise when the soil in the ball differs significantly from the backfill soil. Problems also result from failure to remove the twine from around the plant stem at the time of planting. This is particularly important if nonbiodegradable twine is used to secure the root-ball.

Tree spades are frequently used to transplant large trees with trunk diameters 2 to 10 inches (5 to 25 cm) or larger. In these situations, trees are generally dug and placed in wire baskets or boxes for transport (Figure 8-2b). In cases where trees are already growing on-site, tree spades can be used to move them directly to their new location. This involves digging the planting hole with the spade, discarding the soil on-site, and then digging the tree and placing it in the new planting hole. Large spade-dug trees have generally high survival rates but often grow slowly after planting for several years until the root system regenerates.

Container-Grown Stock

Container-grown nursery plants are the most common plants available today. The system employed by most growers uses lightweight organic growing media designed to drain rapidly once placed in plastic containers. Media may be entirely composed of ground bark or a mixture of bark with small portions of sand, soil, or other material. Container-grown plants are easily transported and can be planted at any time of the year. Root systems tend to be vigorous and often become distorted as roots quickly fill the container and either circle around the base of the container or grow upward to the surface (Figure 8-3a). Roots may develop on the surface of the container and develop into girdling roots as they enlarge over time (Figure 8-3b). Container stock planted in spring establishes well in most cases. Stock held over through the growing season, however, often becomes pot bound and is more likely to struggle after planting. Container plants tend to have high transplant survival rates but often grow poorly once planted in the landscape. Because most landscaping is done during the main growing season and into the fall, containers are the system of choice for planting shrubs.

The Planting Hole

People have been planting plants for a long time, so it is not surprising that there are many different recommendations on how to plant properly. Many time-honored practices work just fine but often involve more effort than is necessary. As research has caught up to folklore, planting guidelines have changed significantly. Current recommendations stress the following.

Planting holes should be wider than they are deep. Typical recommendations call for the planting hole to be two to three times the diameter of the root-ball. Therefore, a plant with a 12-inch (30-cm) root-ball should be placed in a hole 24 to 36 inches (60 to 90 cm) across. The outer edges of the hole can be tapered down from the edge of the hole to the bottom, creating a bowl-like cross section (Figure 8-4). This recommendation is based on studies demonstrating that roots tend to develop laterally from the ends of cut roots or from within the center of the root-ball and that relatively few roots initially develop downward (Watson and Himelick 1997).

(a)

(b)

Figure 8-4 Planting holes that are wide and tapered from the edges to the center provide optimum conditions for rapid establishment and root system recovery.

Planting holes should be just deep enough to accommodate the plant. Digging a giant pit is a lot of work that accomplishes very little and may cause plants to sink below grade when settling occurs. This is particularly true when planting balled-and-burlapped or spade-dug trees. The holes should be just deep enough so that when the root mass is placed on the compacted bottom of the hole, the root-stem juncture is at or slightly above grade level (Watson and Himelick 1997).

Figure 8-3 (a) Plants that grow too long in containers often have distorted root systems. (b) This maple was held too long in a small container and then moved to the field, with its distorted root system intact. Now several potential girdling roots are apparent.

In normal soils with average structure, there is no need to amend the soil prior to backfilling (Gilman 2004; Smalley and Wood 1995; Whitcomb 1975, 1987). Because amending soils with organic matter is one of the time-honored practices in horticulture, this may seem counterintuitive. Most research shows that plant growth in sites with amended soils is about the same as plant growth in unamended soils. Under normal conditions, amending the backfill soil in a planting hole does not affect the rate of transplant survival.

In highly compacted soils (or disturbed soils with poor structure), soil replacement or large-scale amendment of the entire area may be needed (see Chapter 7). Amending the soil in the planting hole may provide a better environment for initial establishment but only if drainage is included to prevent accumulation of water in the amended planting hole. For detailed information on working with these soils, consult Craul (1999) or Urban (2008).

Plants grown in containers are prone to becoming root bound, and the root system structure is often tangled and circular. Breaking up this container mass immediately before planting will improve root contact with the soil. When plants are removed from containers and planted with this compacted root mass intact, an interface is created between the soil and the porous, free-draining container medium. In these instances, water entering the container plant root zone tends to drain freely into the surrounding soil. Because water is held more tightly in the soil than in the container medium, it does not move back into the container plant root zone and drought stress occurs (Costello and Paul 1975; Spomer 1980). Further, because plant roots often stay in the container medium, which does not retain nutrients, deficiencies often occur. The result is a plant that is under drought and nutritional stress and therefore slow to establish roots into the surrounding soil (Figure 8-5).

Figure 8-5 This container plant was planted undisturbed in gray clay. After five years, the plant had not grown and showed several nutrient deficiencies. After it was dug up, it was apparent that the roots had never grown into the surrounding soil.

There are two common options available to avoid the container interface problem. In young container plants that are not yet root bound, shake out some of the medium or bare-root the plant completely (Color Plate 8-1). Feather out the roots and spread them into the surrounding soil prior to backfilling. If planting in the spring or fall under moist conditions, some root pruning can be done to reduce tangling roots and to improve the lateral spread of the root system. A faster and simpler strategy involves laying the plant on its side and using a spade to slice through the root mass from the base toward the root-stem interface. This technique, commonly

Figure 8-6 One year after planting in soil, note the greater root development in the butterflied plant on the right versus the undisturbed container plant on the left.

called "butterflying," opens up the root system, thus facilitating better root-to-soil contact without severely damaging the root system (Figure 8-6).

Firmly pack the soil into the hole after plant placement but do not compact. The goal is to pack the soil returned to the hole enough to securely hold the plant in place and prevent tipping. Additional packing causes loss of soil structure and increases compaction. It is okay for the soil to have clods and small air pockets when planting is completed.

Other Amendments

There are many proponents of adding microbial preparations such as mycorrhizae, compost tea, and biostimulants such as cytokinins and humic substances to the backfill soil or after planting as surface applications. These materials are successfully marketed because they promise a healthy soil teeming with microbes and the ability to withstand the rigors of environmental stress (Lowenfels and Lewis 2006). Anecdotal testimonies often predict dramatic effects and claim these additives are the most important part of the planting process.

There is limited research to support claims about compost tea, cytokinins, and humic substances, and it remains to be seen whether research bears out the initial claims. Results from extensive research conducted over decades supports the general role mycorrhizae play in plant growth and survival in natural habitats such as forests. In natural environments, mycorrhizal effects on increased phosphorus uptake are well documented (as are increased survival rates in stressful environments particularly where drought is severe) (Steinfeld, Amaranthus, and Cazares 2003). Growth responses in landscape environments where plants have been inoculated with commercial preparations of mycorrhizae have been difficult to demonstrate (Appleton et al. 2003; Gilman 2001). Following is a summary of plant responses to mycorrhizal associations under natural and landscape conditions:

A high level of mycorrhizal infection of roots is normal in any soil formerly supporting forests (Iyer, Corey, and Wilde 1980). In constructed landscapes planted with nursery-grown plants, the mycorrhizal infection rate is variable and ranges from no infection to levels typically found in natural settings.

The principal impact of mycorrhizae is increased absorption of nutrients by host plants. This is particularly valuable in nutrient-poor soils. Phosphorus is the best-documented nutrient.

Mycorrhizal associations often decrease when plants are grown in fertile, irrigated soil.

Fertilization and irrigation in landscapes can largely substitute for mycorrhizal functions in many cases.

Because of the trend toward more sustainable landscapes that receive fewer inputs such as fertilizer and irrigation, it is likely mycorrhizae will become increasingly important for healthy plant growth. Since most landscape plants have some level of natural mycorrhizal infection, it is important to determine the degree of natural infection to avoid needlessly applying commercial mycorrhizal products (Iyer, Corey, and Wilde 1980).

Postplanting Care

The goal of postplanting care is to encourage rapid establishment of roots and to enhance plant vigor. In commercial settings, postplanting care for trees may include minimizing competition by removing grass or ground covers around the base, staking, mulching, fertilizing, and irrigating. Pruning at the time of planting may also occur.

Minimizing Competition

Creating a free space around the base of newly planted trees reduces the chances that trees will get struck by mowers and reduces competition between grass roots and developing tree roots for nitrogen and moisture. Numerous studies have demonstrated that grass roots can significantly reduce tree root growth, root extension rates, and shoot extension (Messenger 1976; Green and Watson 1989; Harris, Clark, and Matheny 2003). A circular free space 4 to 5 feet (1 to 1.5 m) in diameter will generally minimize competition during the establishment period and reduce the chance that trees will be damaged by landscape maintenance equipment.

Staking

Researchers generally conclude that, in most cases, staking is not necessary and may even delay establishment by reducing root development and slowing trunk diameter growth (Harris, Leiser, and Davis 1978). The value of staking is holding trees straight and protecting them from damage. Problems with staking often result from staking rigidly, which prevents normal root and trunk development, and from using wire or plastic ties that girdle trunks as the tree diameter increases over time (Figure 8-7).

Figure 8-7 Staking causes damage in the landscape when stakes and ties are left on too long. Wire ties eventually will cut into and girdle stems if not removed in a timely fashion.

Staking should meet the following criteria:

Avoid staking when trees are able to stand straight without assistance and there is no need for protection from wind or machinery.

Place stakes away from the trunk and below the lowest branches. When planting balled-and-burlapped or spade-dug trees, avoid driving stakes into the intact root-ball.

Attach ties to the trunk loosely and as low as possible. The idea is to support the tree while allowing some movement of the trunk. Movement is what stimulates both increased root growth and trunk diameter growth.

Remove stakes and ties as soon as possible. In many cases, the stakes can be removed by the end of the first growing season after planting (Figure 8-8).

(a)

(b)

Figure 8-8 This example of staking shows (a) the optimum placement of stakes originally and (b) how removing stakes one year after planting avoided damage to the trunk.

Mulching after Planting

Mulching after planting gives the installation a finished look and provides sustainable benefits by reducing weed encroachment and preventing the soil surface from rapidly drying (thereby assisting in quicker establishment and increased shoot growth) (Ferrini et al. 2008; Montague et al. 2007).

In general, mulches derived from composted organic debris with a carbon-to-nitrogen ratio (C/N) of 20:1 or lower positively affect establishment in new plantings as compared with noncomposted wood waste with a C/N ratio above 50:1, which tends to tie up soil nitrogen during subsequent decomposition. Due to the volume of compost mulches applied around the base of newly planted trees or shrubs, much of the increased growth observed may be due to nitrogen release by the mulch. Mulch should be 2 to 4 inches (5 to 10 cm) deep and applied so as not to cover the base of the tree trunk.

FERTILIZATION

Fertilization of landscape plants is a surprisingly controversial topic among researchers and landscape professionals (Siewart et al. 2000). In its simplest form, fertilization involves determining optimum rates of fertilizer, application timing, and the combination of nutrients needed to produce vigorous healthy landscape plants in much the same manner as for other crop plants. While in many cases it is that simple, some experts question the very idea of fertilizing because trees and shrubs growing in the wild seem to do just fine without fertilizer (Miller 2000). Others argue that conditions at landscape sites are vastly different from natural environments; soils are more likely to be impoverished, and fertilizer is absolutely necessary. Research trials often add to the confusion: some demonstrate strong growth responses to fertilizer while others show no response at all.

Goals in developing a fertilization program include the following:

Enhancing establishment and early growth after transplanting

Stimulating growth to more rapidly achieve functional landscape size

Maintaining plant health over time

Overcoming known nutrient deficiencies that affect plant health

There are other situations where fertilization is likely to be necessary, including trees growing in confined root zones caused by construction activities or plants growing in containers. This section will address fertilizing new transplants, stimulating growth in young trees, and maintaining plant health over time.

Fertilizing Transplants during Establishment

Young trees in new landscapes may take several years before they become big enough to impact the landscape. During the establishment period, which can last from one to four years, trees may grow weakly or not at all (Color Plate 8-2). Several studies have demonstrated significant growth from annual applications of nitrogen fertilizer to trees, particularly those with continuous (indeterminate) growth habits such as tulip poplar (*Liriodendron tulipifera*) (Figure 8-9), sweet gum (*Liquidambar styraciflua*), and elm (*Ulmus* spp.). Typical response patterns show modest increases in growth and color in the first year, followed by increased growth in height, caliper, and canopy spread in succeeding years (van de Werken 1981). Trees in temperate climates receiving annual fertilizer applications generally develop denser branching and retain leaves longer during fall as noted in Color Plate 8-3.

Other research has found that some newly transplanted trees do not respond to added fertilizer for the first one to three years after planting (Day and Harris 2007). This may be due to local environmental conditions or because determinate species were used that are less responsive to nitrogen fertilizer than the indeterminate species discussed earlier. Determinate trees generally don't show much response in year 1 other than darker foliage color in nitrogen-deficient soils as shown in Color Plate 8-4.

Maintaining Long-Term Plant Health

In generally healthy growing environments with mature trees or shrubs, it is hard to recommend continuous annual fertilization. Mature trees growing in lawns typically have extensive root development extending out into the lawn area (Figure 8-10). Because tree and lawn roots largely occupy the same area, trees compete freely for fertilizer applied to the lawn area. Likewise, trees near or in planting beds will compete for nutrients with shrubs. Maintaining an aerated root zone, which encourages strong microbial activity, and alleviating compaction in tree root zones are probably more important than regular fertilization in mature landscapes.

Alleviating Nutrient Deficiencies

Iron deficiency occurs in soils with a pH above 7.5, because iron tends to form insoluble compounds at high pH and is unavailable for plant root absorption. Research has shown that soil injections of iron solutions can alleviate symptoms for one or more years. Iron trunk implants can have a similar effect. A better solution is to avoid planting trees like pin oak (*Quercus palustris*) and maples (*Acer* spp.), which are prone to iron deficiency, in areas with high-pH soils. Sustainable practice dictates that the best approach is to avoid these types of landscape problems rather than to create problems and then search for solutions.

(a) (b)

Figure 8-9 Trees like tulip poplar (*Liriodendron tulipifera*) with indeterminate growth are very responsive to nitrogen fertilizers even when young. (a) In this trial, unfertilized trees were tall and spindly with small canopies. (b) Fertilized trees were taller with nearly double the trunk diameter and much larger canopies.

DETERMINATE VERSUS INDETERMINATE GROWTH

In temperate climates, all trees start growth in spring by elongation of preformed shoots contained in terminal buds. With determinate trees, the preformed leaves and shoots elongate and may produce a few more leaves before setting a new bud. Under normal conditions, once the bud is set, growth is finished for the rest of the year. The actual period of shoot elongation may last only a few weeks. With indeterminate trees, growth starts out by elongation of the preformed leaves and stems, but the apical meristem (growing point) continues to produce new leaves as long as conditions are conducive to growth. Indeterminate trees may continue to grow throughout the entire growing season sometimes for as long as 150 days.

HOW IS TREE RESPONSE TO FERTILIZER MEASURED?

There are a number of different parameters that can be used to evaluate the effect of fertilizer on plant growth. These include increase in vertical height, increase in lateral shoot extension, increase in canopy area, and increase in trunk caliper at a specified height above the ground. Because it is easy to measure increases in trunk caliper, this measure is often the choice of researchers.

COMMON TREE RESPONSES TO SPECIFIC NUTRIENTS AND APPLICATION METHODS

- Nitrogen is the most important nutrient and is most likely to stimulate growth.
- All types of nitrogen fertilizers are effective in stimulating color and growth.
- Growth responses to phosphorus are likely only when a deficiency is demonstrated.
- Potassium does not appear to affect growth in a measurable way.
- Tree responses are similar for all methods of application.
- Broadcasted tree fertilizer tends to stimulate weed growth in mulch beds and overstimulate lawn grasses.
- Tree responses to nitrogen applied by the broadcast method have been reported at rates ranging from 1 to 6 pounds N/1000 square feet (5 to 30 g N/m^2).
- Maximum plant growth occurs from early-spring applications, followed closely by fall and summer applications.
- Fertilizer growth responses continue to show for one or more years after applications are stopped.
- Fertilizer responses are less apparent in mature trees with larger root spreads.

Figure 8-10 Tree roots generally spread a long way from the base of the trunk as shown in this photo of elm tree roots uncovered over 50 feet (15 m) from the tree.

Assessing Fertilizer Needs

Accurate techniques for assessing landscape fertilizer needs could help landscapers use fertilizers more efficiently. Soil testing and plant tissue analysis are the most common methods used to estimate fertilizer needs, but both have limitations. For example, there are no simple and effective soil tests to help guide nitrogen applications (Scharenbroch and Lloyd 2004). In general, more research is needed to develop the potential of soil and plant analyses for guiding landscape fertilizer applications.

IRRIGATION

Irrigation is an important practice for landscapes in many different climate zones. While criticism of landscape water use is often directed at lawns, it is fair to say that a significant amount of total water use occurs in bed areas. Because landscape watering is so visible and water is such a precious commodity, it is important that it be used efficiently. The following sections will address options for improving irrigation efficiency and reducing water use in general.

Irrigating New Plantings

In many climates, irrigation is critical for successful establishment of transplanted plants (Anella, Hennessey, and Lorenzi 2008). Bare-root, balled-and-burlapped, and spade-dug trees all suffer in excess of 95 percent root loss during digging. Container plants retain their root systems, but due to excessive drainage from porous container media, they often suffer from rapid drought stress (Costello and Paul 1975). As a result, all types of plants benefit from regular irrigation for at least the first year after transplanting. Research has demonstrated that regular irrigation during the establishment year benefits root system development as much as five years later, even if no additional irrigation occurs after the first year (Gilman et al. 2003; Gilman 2004). In situations in which automated irrigation is not feasible for street trees, soaker bags provide an effective way to maintain consistent moisture during establishment (Figure 8-11).

Irrigating Mature Plantings

Pop-up sprays are the most common heads for beds. With precipitation rates of 1.5 to 2 inches/ h (4 to 5 cm/h), water application rates far exceed the infiltration rates of even the most porous soils. A general strategy has evolved toward daily irrigation or every-other-day irrigation, often in conjunction with lawn irrigation systems. This is the case in spite of

Figure 8-11 Tree survival in areas without irrigation systems has been improved by using soaker bags like the one shown here.

a general consensus that shrubs and trees are more tolerant of drought than lawns and require less irrigation. Until recently, irrigators have had limited methods to reduce irrigation in bed areas other than using judgment based on personal experience. New head technology such as stream rotor nozzles for pop-up spray head bodies offers a chance to reduce precipitation rates significantly and help reduce runoff potential in shrub bed areas.

With the advent of weather-based controllers, it is now possible to irrigate based on evapotranspiration (ET). Evapotranspiration is the water lost from surface evaporation added to that lost from transpiration from plants. Using weather station data, computers calculate the daily ET and adjust the run times of controllers to match the total ET since the last irrigation event. Properly analyzed, ET is a fairly accurate measure of water use by plants. (For more information on ET measurements, see Chapter 9.) The use of calculated ET values to guide irrigation is an improvement, but there are still many obstacles that make efficient irrigation difficult. Some of these difficulties include excessive precipitation rates, poor system uniformity or unknown system uniformity, and unknown water requirements for most commonly used landscape plants.

Researchers have determined regionally accurate ET values for lawn grasses, but it has been difficult to measure water needs for landscape plants, although some research in this area has been conducted. Costello et al. (2000) used two methods to estimate water requirements for landscape plants in California.

One approach involves landscape coefficients and potential ET measurements, which are useful for estimating actual irrigation needs in landscapes. The other approach is Water Use Classification of Landscape Species (WUCOLS), which relies heavily on expert opinions based on field observations to categorize plant water requirements for 1900 plant species. Water needs are listed as low, medium, and high, and are used to delineate five regional climates. The WUCOLS ratings provide a useful guide for designers who want to create plant groupings with similar water needs.

While determining landscape plant water requirements depends on both art and science, accurately applying water in landscape beds may be an even greater challenge. Poorly designed landscapes that create awkward, difficult-to-irrigate areas (see Chapter 2) are among the problems landscape maintenance contractors must confront to meet this challenge. Poor system maintenance and poor decision making by irrigators add to the problems. Considering these factors, efficient irrigation is more than just knowing about plant water requirements.

In some cases, the most efficient way to irrigate landscape bed areas is drip irrigation. Improved water filtration and pressure-compensating in-line emitters have increased the practical value of drip irrigation in commercial landscapes. Water can be applied directly to the root zones of individual plants and is not wasted on bare areas, sidewalks, and roadways.

Reducing Irrigation in Landscape Beds

As simple as it sounds, the best way to reduce the amount of water used for irrigation is to apply less water. Tremendous strides have been made in determining plant water requirements through estimates of ET, and the irrigation industry has improved controllers and created a number of devices to prevent overwatering. Unfortunately, the industry's fascination with ET has inadvertently led to the assumption that irrigated woody landscape plants need regular systematic applications during the entire growing season simply because they use water. This assumption ignores the physiological ability of plants to tolerate drought, and that inevitably has led to overirrigation. This is even apparent in arid regions, where it is common to see mature landscapes planted with native drought-adapted plants being irrigated regularly. In many climates, landscapes will perform just fine with far less irrigation than they currently receive.

Improving Irrigation System Performance

Improving system performance starts with analyzing the irrigation system and studying the plants and the site conditions. Because pop-up spray irrigation systems are designed in the studio and installed when landscape plants are small (and not likely to interfere with water spray patterns), the first thing to investigate is how plant growth has affected water distribution. When mature plants obscure sprinkler throw (Figure 8-12), raise the sprinkler heads or move the heads to allow proper throw. Also straighten the heads and check and clean the nozzles and filters. On older systems, it may be best to systematically replace the nozzles.

Once the system has been adjusted, head pressures can be measured with pitot gauges, and in some situations, uniformity can be tested and precipitation rates can be measured. Where uniformity tests cannot be conducted, manufacturers' tables can be used to estimate precipitation based on nozzle and measured head pressures. If the landscape professional does not know how much water the system is applying, there is no way to apply the right amount of water.

Figure 8-12 Shrub bed irrigation is complicated by growth of plants in the bed. In this case, shrub foliage has distorted the spray pattern, rendering this head ineffective.

While adjusting landscape irrigation systems, it is useful to run adjacent lawn sprinkler systems to see how they are impacting the beds. Lawn sprinklers may have to be adjusted to prevent excessive overthrow into shrub beds. In shrub beds where precipitation rates are above 1.5 inches/h (4 cm/h), it may be worthwhile to change heads to stream rotors with similar throw but much lower precipitation rates. This is an all-or-none option because spray heads and rotor heads cannot be mixed due to different precipitation rates. Finally, study past irrigation programming and calculate how much water has been applied seasonally based on past run times and known precipitation rates. Consider cutting back on days irrigated or run times per irrigation.

For drip systems, check the entire system for line breaks or plugged emitters. With a little digging, it is possible to place containers under emitters to determine if actual drip rates match manufacturer's specifications. On new plantings, make sure emitters are close enough to the base of the plant to actually water the roots. This becomes irrelevant on most mature plants because they get water from shared emitters from adjacent plants or from adjacent lawn areas. Review run times from previous seasons and explore options for reducing days or run times for the upcoming season.

Adjust zone run times according to the type of plants, the bed microclimate, and the maturity of the plants. At some point, determine whether irrigation is even needed for the beds in question. Trees in beds often get all the water they need from surrounding lawn irrigation systems, and no direct irrigation is needed.

As the next irrigation season approaches, wait as long as possible before initiating irrigation. After the peak irrigation season is over, turn off shrub zones as early as possible. In cool temperate marine climates where irrigation is needed from June to early September, it is common to see irrigation systems running as early as March and as late as December. This wastes water and gives the industry a bad reputation.

PRUNING

Most pruning references focus on plant-centered pruning techniques. Plant-centered pruning is based on maintaining a plant's natural form and timing pruning to maximize flowering. Many books include pruning encyclopedias with specific tips on most of the important species (Brickell and Joyce 1996; Brown and Kirkham 2004).

Pruning Shrubs and Ground Covers in Commercial Landscapes

Pruning in commercial settings is always a challenge and reflects a host of limitations such as poorly articulated goals, lack of horticultural knowledge, inadequately trained workers, and constant pressure to reduce time spent on-site.

Commercial pruning of shrubs and ground covers is anything but plant centered. Normally, it focuses on size control and on creating a neat and tidy look at all times. Shrubs are often sheared into cubes, spheres, cylinders, spires, mounds, pom-poms, and any other three-dimensional objects the pruner can dream up (Figure 8-13). The appeal of shearing should be obvious: it is fast; involves little training; and requires virtually no knowledge of plant materials, growth habits, or flower habits. Unfortunately, many plants lose their charm when sheared, and many beautiful plant compositions fail to achieve the desired effect because differences in texture, size, and form do not develop. This situation is another disconnect among designers, owners, and maintenance companies that results in uninteresting and sometimes bizarre-looking landscapes. A more sustainable approach would have designers, owners, and maintenance personnel work together to articulate the design intent and determine an aesthetic and economical way to achieve it.

Figure 8-13 In many cases, mindless shearing makes it impossible to determine what the designer was trying to achieve with the plant composition.

Pruning Trees in Commercial Landscapes

Tree maintenance in commercial landscapes runs the gamut from untouched, to sheared, to selectively pruned. Large boulevard trees or those in parklike settings are generally pruned selectively by arborists once the trees move beyond the establishment period. These trees are likely to be pruned in natural form except in countries where convention dictates pollarding or other nonnatural styles. Small trees below 15 feet (5 m) are likely to be pruned by landscape maintenance firms in styles ranging from sheared to natural form (Figure 8-14).

Pruning Strategies for Young Trees

Young trees may need regular pruning for 5 to 10 years after planting to develop desirable structure and form in the context of their surroundings. For example, boulevard trees need straight trunks and crowns high enough to provide clearance on adjacent roads and sidewalks. Trees in open areas may need high crowns on a straight trunk or may be allowed to retain lower branches and develop a dense canopy right down to ground level.

The general goal is to produce trees with strong branch attachments without included bark, good branch spacing, and crowns raised slowly to a height appropriate for the location in the landscape.

(a)

(b)

Figure 8-14 (a) Shearing small trees creates an almost surreal, cartoonish look. (b) Selective pruning produces a more natural look.

Excurrent Trees

Excurrent trees naturally develop a central leader, and many, such as tulip poplar (*Liriodendron tulipifera*) and sweet gum (*Liquidambar styraciflua*), have indeterminate growth. Training involves removing lower branches annually as needed to raise the crown gradually to its desired height (Figure 8-15). Additional annual pruning may be needed to remove competing leaders that may develop or to retrain leaders lost to injury or dieback. This is easy to do because the natural tendency of these trees is to grow with a single leader.

Decurrent Trees

Decurrent trees such as some oaks (*Quercus* spp.) and many maples (*Acer* spp.) naturally lose the terminal leader and develop into multileader trees. If a straight trunk is needed for any period of time, attention has to be paid during the training process. Vigorous trees may maintain a dominant leader for several years, but often competing leaders develop very quickly, making it impossible to develop the desired form. The goal is to maintain a single trunk up to the point where permanent scaffold branches will develop. At that point, emphasis shifts to selecting main branches that are strongly attached to the crown and allowing the natural growth habit to take over. The process is illustrated in Figure 8-16. In field situations, trees can be allowed to develop low crowns with major branches at or near ground level if that suits the desired appearance in the landscape.

Pruning Strategies for Shrubs and Ground Covers

There are several techniques commonly used in pruning shrubs.

Selective Pruning

Selective pruning involves removing a modest number of shoots annually to maintain an overall natural look, maintain a balance between old and new shoots, and manage size (Figure 8-17). Branches are pruned using point-of-origin, drop-crotch, and heading cuts (Figure 8-18).

(a) (b)

Figure 8-15 Excurrent trees naturally tend to maintain central leaders. (a) Training involves raising the crown by removing low branches and (b) removing competing leaders when they develop in maturing trees.

Shearing

Shearing, as described earlier, involves trimming plants into geometric shapes using only heading cuts. Once started, shearing has to be done regularly in order to maintain rigid form. Shearing is appropriate for hedges but generally diminishes the beauty of most freestanding shrubs. It also results in a thin dense shell of foliage at the outer edge and a dead zone in the interior of the plant (Color Plate 8-5). Given the prominence of shearing in commercial landscapes, designers may want to rethink their planting schemes by choosing plants that are suited to shearing and have naturally slow growth rates.

Periodic Rejuvenation

Periodic rejuvenation involves cutting plants back near ground level in spring with heading cuts generally just as new growth begins or just after spring flowering shrubs have bloomed. Rejuvenation pruning can be used to create special effects, such as red stems in red twig dogwood (*Cornus sericea*), or to restructure a shrub whose form has been destroyed by shearing (Figure 8-19).

(a) (b) (c)

Figure 8-16 Decurrent trees tend to rapidly lose the central leader so regular pruning is needed. (a) Before pruning, numerous branches need to be removed. (b) After pruning, form is re-established. (c) The final goal is to make sure branches are strongly attached and spaced to avoid future structural problems.

(a) (b)

Figure 8-17 Flowering shrubs like the bigleaf hydrangea (*Hydrangea macrophylla*) perform best when selectively pruned. (a) Good balance of young and older shoots after pruning leads to (b) attractive form and strong flowering.

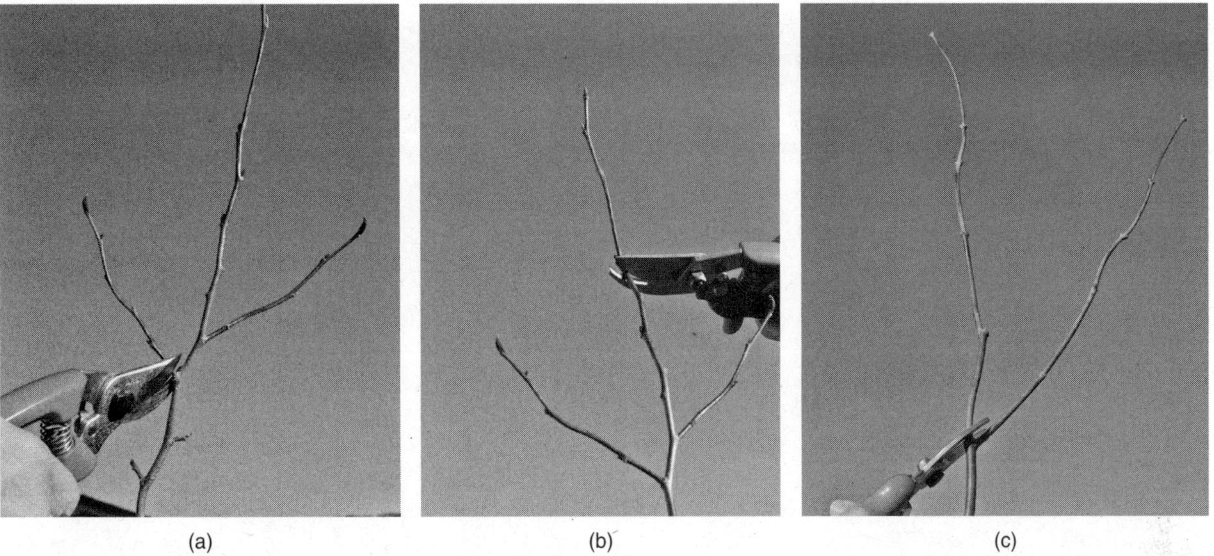

(a) (b) (c)

Figure 8-18 (a) Thinning cuts remove branches at their point of origin, resulting in normal growth and form. (b) Heading cuts remove branches arbitrarily without regard to their point of attachment and always leave a stub. Regrowth is vigorous from buds located below the cut. Shearing is just frequent heading of all shoots. (c) Drop-crotch cuts remove the main shoot just above a lateral shoot of similar size oriented in the same direction as the parent shoot. Regrowth is intermediate between thinning and heading.

Annual Rejuvenation

Annual rejuvenation involves cutting shrubs back with heading cuts each spring and then allowing them to grow without additional pruning during the course of the growing season. In this case, plants can be pruned to the ground or to a permanent framework of branches chosen by the pruner. This is a useful technique for plants that flower in summer from newly developed shoots such as Bumald spirea (*Spiraea* × *bumalda*) (Color Plates 8-6a and b).

Periodic Mowing of Ground Covers

Periodic mowing of ground covers to keep the height down is a practice that should be used more often. Even low-growing ground covers will eventually begin to mound up on themselves and develop a vertical wall of sheared foliage around the edges topped by interior areas that look wild and unmanageable. The appearance is a little like a haircut, in which the sides are shaved off and the top is long.

Problems Associated with Questionable Pruning Decisions

Maintaining a balance between lower, middle, and upper branches is the key to a natural-looking shrub. Removing too many of the lower branches destroys the natural form and turns shrubs into small, ungainly trees that look top-heavy. Often the only solution is either to rejuvenate the plant or to replace it (Figure 8-20). When plants start to get too big, it is better to reduce the size by starting at the top and working down, leaving as many lower branches as possible. Once the lower branches have been removed, it is hard to get them back except by rejuvenation.

Figure 8-19 Red twig dogwood (*Cornus sericea*) responds to periodic rejuvenation. (a) This plant illustrates appearance after several years' growth without pruning. (b) The plant is cut down to the ground in spring. (c) After a season of regrowth, the new shoots show good winter color.

Waiting too long to prune conifers leads to the awkward quasi-bonsai shrubs seen so often in landscapes. Many conifers are essentially one-way plants because they are not able to produce new shoots when cut back to bare wood. Sheared conifers turn into blobs and lose the qualities that make them distinctive (Figure 8-21a). The key with most conifers is to prune regularly using point-of-origin and drop-crotch cuts throughout the entire canopy (Figure 8-21b). Once conifers get too big, they need to be removed and replaced.

The Impact of Construction and Design Decisions on Pruning

A common landscape construction problem involves laying out plants without consideration of the ultimate size of the plants placed near the perimeter (edge) of a planting area. While plantings may look good initially, it doesn't take long for those near edges to grow into walkways or over roadside curbs. When this happens, offending plants often get sheared off on the outfacing side (Figure 8-22). If the design

Figure 8-20 (a) This viburnum (*Viburnum* spp.) was disfigured by regular shearing. (b) A nearby plant that was cut to the ground in early spring grew back from crown buds to its natural form.

Figure 8-21 (a) Shearing conifers results in round blobs and destroys the character of the plants. (b) With practice, junipers and other conifers can be quickly pruned selectively and retain their natural attributes.

intent was to create a naturally growing cluster of one type of plant, the effect is lost. Parking strips that are narrow should have plants placed in the middle so once they grow they will naturally fit the space. If plants are staggered or planted on a grid, inevitably the edge plants will create pruning problems.

Why this is such a common problem is not clear. It could be an error on the part of the designer, who didn't think about the consequences of the layout scheme. Perhaps too many plants were specified for the area, and installers simply made sure all the plants were used. Possibly construction laborers

Figure 8-22 Plants located too close to the edge of the bed quickly encroach on sidewalks and are sheared to keep them out of people's way. The solution is to plant them farther from the edge of the bed.

were instructed to spread the plants evenly and fill the bed, which indicates poor training and lack of supervision. Figure 8-23 illustrates the impact of this problem.

Failure to articulate the design intent forces pruners to guess what the designer had in mind (Figure 8-24). After studying hundreds of commercial landscapes, we find it is often impossible to determine what (if anything) the designers were trying to accomplish. Difficulty in identifying the design intent is exacerbated when plants die en masse, further obscuring the composition. This leads to ever-expanding mulch beds and complete loss of the overall design (Color Plate 8-7).

Long-term pruning and general maintenance will improve when designers work together with maintenance and construction contractors during and after the planning and construction phases. Designers need to incorporate input from maintenance specialists regarding plant selection, placement, and long-term maintenance. Timely inspections during construction and follow-up annual reviews of maintenance will guide project development and will also improve the final product.

General Pruning Strategies

Mass plantings are created with the assumption that plants will grow into each other (Figure 8-25). One of the advantages of massing plants is less exposed ground and fewer niches for weeds to invade. The

(a)

(b)

Figure 8-23 (a) Junipers (*Juniperus* spp.) planted too close to the edge of the bed will quickly be sheared in order to keep them off the sidewalk. (b) The solution is to remove the entire row of plants next to the edge of the sidewalk and then selectively prune elongating shoots.

(a)

(b)

Figure 8-24 (a) The natural look as the designer envisioned. (b) As interpreted by the pruning crew. Where was the breakdown in communication?

Figure 8-25 Densely planted beds help reduce inputs of mulch and herbicides and help reduce erosion and compaction.

goals are to keep the dense mass of plants while maintaining proportion to each other and controlling size as needed. Pruning is largely selective and involves thinning cuts (branches removed at points of origin) as needed to keep the planting in bounds. It may also involve periodic rejuvenation of overgrown plants or removal and replacement as needed. Avoid shearing at the perimeter of the planting unless it is part of the design intent. Periodic mowing of ground covers to keep height down may be warranted.

Some plantings may be intended to mimic desert vegetation and contain a mix of small trees and shrubs (Figure 8-26). The goal of this design concept is to allow specimen shrubs to grow naturally with minimal pruning. Pruning is largely selective or uses light shearing prior to major growth to control size but maintain a natural appearance. Specimen plants generally look best when they remain foliated from top to bottom. Avoid shearing individual plants into formal-looking geometric shapes because it ruins the natural desert look.

Defining the edge where ground covers meet sidewalks, curbs, or beds requires regular mechanical edging. If conventional vertical-blade edgers are used, the edge becomes hedged and looks unnatural (Figure 8-23a). Soft edges are created by using string trimmers, but it is easy to obliterate plants at the edges, resulting in a 6 to 8 inch (15 to 20 cm) wide area of exposed soil that looks odd and facilitates weed encroachment (Figure 8-27). Meanwhile, the ground covers themselves begin to build up higher and higher until they look more like shrubs. Ultimately, these become a pruning nightmare as it

(a) (b)

Figure 8-26 (a) Desert plants have been randomly sheared with no thought to the overall appearance. (b) Plants have been allowed to grow more naturally, resulting in an attractive planting requiring less effort to maintain.

(a) (b)

Figure 8-27 (a) Soft edging with string trimmers where beds meet lawns or curbs potentially looks more natural than hard edges, but often produces a ring of bare ground that looks ugly. (b) A combination of soft and hard edging with periodic mowing produces a more attractive edge.

is difficult to wade into the area to cut back stray shoots. This is a common problem with low-growing junipers (*Juniperus* spp.) and many cultivars of cotoneaster (*Cotoneaster* spp.).

One design strategy to reduce maintenance is to select ground covers that can be mowed periodically to control height buildup (Figure 8-27a). The key is to mow at least annually. This quasi-rejuvenation approach works best during the growing season rather than at the end of the season when regrowth is unlikely. Periodic selective pruning at edges will further reduce the buildup problem. Ground covers other than lawns look best when they appear to just reach the edge of the bed.

MANAGING THE WASTE STREAM

Debris generated from pruning, deciduous tree leaves, lawn clippings, and other organic waste materials, by convention, have been removed from maintenance sites. Decades ago, this material was routinely sent to landfills, where it contributed to excess volume, methane gas production, and leaching into soil. A current and somewhat more sustainable approach involves hauling green waste to local composting facilities for a fee and then repurchasing the finished compost for use in the landscape. Although this approach is a type of recycling, it consumes a great deal of time and energy loading and hauling debris and, ultimately, eats into profits. The advantage is that it allows contractors to leave each site looking neat and tidy at all times. As sustainable options for landscape maintenance are explored, it will be necessary to find better ways to handle the waste stream created from landscape management practices.

A better sustainable goal is to find ways to reduce the amount of waste removed from the site but not necessarily to eliminate it all at once. A 50 percent reduction in waste removal would be significant for most contractors. For example, as pointed out in Chapter 9, clippings can easily be returned to many lawn areas, eliminating a large component of green waste. Clipping removal can still be practiced in high-profile areas, which require higher aesthetic standards. Likewise, pruning debris can be chipped on-site and stored for aging at a discreet on-site location or can be immediately applied to beds that are in less prominent locations than the main entrance. Contractors complain that currently available chippers do not create a product attractive enough to spread on high-visibility beds. This poses an opportunity for chipper manufacturers to find ways to get a more acceptable chip with one pass through the chipper.

Managing Leaf Drop

Currently, deciduous tree leaves are collected and removed from all beds and lawns. While this results in well-groomed landscapes, it is time consuming and costly. It also interferes with the natural organic matter decomposition cycles in bed areas and lawns. In many landscapes, there are beds where leaves can be concentrated without detracting from the site appearance (Color Plate 8-8). Likewise, mulch mowing leaves on lawns where feasible will help recycle leaf organic matter into the soil (Color Plate 8-9). At peak leaf drop, leaves can be collected and used for deep mulching beds or waste areas around parking lots where invasive plants such as blackberries (*Rubus* spp.) are often a problem (Figure 8-28). Designers can facilitate on-site recycling of leaves by including staging areas in discreet locations on corporate campus facilities that accommodate storage and handling of debris. With this practical approach, organic waste can be viewed as an asset rather than as a liability.

Figure 8-28 When the main leaf drop occurs, use on-site disposal when possible. This area was infested with blackberries (*Rubus* spp.). After removal of vines, the deep mulch of leaves will help slow reinvasion.

SUMMARY

Sustainable maintenance of commercial landscapes involves all parts of the landscape. Proper plant selection and thoughtful plant placement lead to better growth and reduced pruning needs as plants mature. Best planting techniques ensure long-term survival of plants and eliminate problems caused by distorted root systems, stake ties, or maintenance equipment. Intelligent use of fertilizer can speed the growth and vigor of young plants and increase plant survival. Irrigation may be necessary in most landscapes but is often used inefficiently. Sustainable irrigation requires careful system design, constant maintenance and upgrading, and a commitment to avoid overirrigation. Pruning is challenging in commercial landscapes due to lack of time, inadequate staff training, poorly articulated goals, and poor designs. Improved interaction among designers, owners, and maintenance contractors is needed to move away from indiscriminate shearing and toward site-appropriate pruning techniques. Improved waste management solutions should aim to leave waste on-site and incorporate it into the landscape rather than hauling it away to composting facilities or landfills. While challenges are many, so are opportunities for improvement in all aspects of commercial landscape care.

STUDY QUESTIONS

1. Explain the advantages and disadvantages of each of the following in terms of transplanting:
   a. Bare-root stock
   b. Balled-and-burlapped stock
   c. Container stock
2. Why might container plants suffer more from drought stress after planting than bare-root plants? How can this problem be avoided?
3. What is the logic for digging planting holes wide and bowl shaped?
4. Does it make sense to add organic matter to planting backfill soil in all cases? Are there exceptions? Is there anything wrong with adding organic matter?
5. In situations where soil is compacted or otherwise not suitable for planting, what are your options for improving the site?
6. What role do mycorrhizae play in the survival and growth of plants? Does it make sense to add mycorrhizae to planting soils? Explain.
7. If you plant a tree in a lawn and let the grass grow right up to the base of the tree trunk, what impact will the grass have on the growth and vigor of the tree? What is the obvious solution to this problem?
8. Staking is good because it ensures trees will stay straight until they are established. What can go wrong when trees are staked? What is the best way to approach staking?
9. Which is better for plant nutrition, mulch with a high carbon-to-nitrogen ratio or mulch with a low carbon-to nitrogen-ratio? Why?
10. Make a case for fertilizing young transplanted plants. Make a case for not fertilizing young transplants.
11. What is the best time of the year to fertilize? For how many years should plants be fertilized on a regular basis? Which element is most important for growth and color?
12. What is the difference between determinate and indeterminate growth in trees? How does growth style affect response to applied fertilizers?
13. What impact does irrigation of young transplants have on establishment and long-term plant vigor? Do all trees and shrubs require regular irrigation once they have matured? Will the answer to that question change in different regions?
14. What is WUCOLS? How can this system guide irrigation? What are its limitations?
15. What is the major obstacle to accurately irrigating bed areas? What can you do to remedy this problem?

16. What is plant-centered pruning? How does it differ from typical commercial site landscape pruning?
17. Why is indiscriminate shearing so prevalent in commercial landscape work? How can this be changed? Or can it?
18. What is the difference between excurrent and decurrent tree growth habits? How does growth habit affect the initial training and pruning of young trees? Is it important that all trees have a single central trunk? Explain.
19. Explain the basic approach to each of the following shrub pruning styles:
    a. Selective pruning
    b. Shearing
    c. Periodic rejuvenation
    d. Annual rejuvenation
20. How does shearing affect the impact of mass plantings and characteristics of individual plants?
21. A common pruning problem with many evergreens and conifers is the tendency to cut out all the lower shoots, which turns every plant into a small treelike structure. Why is this bad practice? How does it affect bed maintenance?
22. When conifers become overgrown or ugly from years of bad pruning, what is the best option? How can you go about rejuvenating most conifers? Explain.
23. How should ground cover plants be arranged in a planting bed to avoid future pruning problems?
24. How should ground cover beds be handled to avoid the tendency to hedge up the sides while leaving the top to grow wild and tangled? In planning a ground cover planting, what should you look for in selecting the plant material?
25. How can tree leaves be managed in fall to avoid removing them from the site?

chapter 9

Lawns in Sustainable Landscapes

INTRODUCTION

Modern lawn care began to evolve after World War II with major growth in the 1960s. The postwar era was defined by the baby boom; large-scale development of the suburbs (e.g., Levittown); unprecedented economic growth; increased personal wealth; technological changes in equipment, fertilizers, and pest control chemicals; and an increase in campus-style corporate headquarters with extensive landscape plantings. Along with these changes, the lawn care industry developed rapidly to serve the needs of the burgeoning commercial property maintenance and residential care market.

Mowing, fertilization, pest control, irrigation, and grass selection have largely become standardized throughout much of the world where lawns are planted. Typical maintenance programs offer weekly mowing often with clippings removed, targeted applications of fertilizer three to six times per year as appropriate for the climate zone, and, in some areas, set applications of herbicides and insecticides. Professional lawn care serves both a segment of the residential market and much of the commercial market, including everything from fast-food restaurants to corporate headquarters. Many full-service landscape maintenance companies complete all work in-house, while others contract out fertilizer and pesticide applications.

Professional lawn care has been broken into a discrete set of practices conducted on a calendar basis. In much of the industry, all lawns receive the same level of care regardless of their location in the landscape or their function in the design. In order to fit lawns into a sustainable model, they need to be properly sited, their components need to be carefully selected, and they need to be appropriately maintained. The key to maximizing sustainability of lawns will be a willingness on the part of designers, owners, and maintenance professionals to change the way lawns are used in landscapes and the way they are managed.

LAWN OR TURF?

Turf typically denotes mowed turfgrasses kept pure by regular use of herbicides and is appropriate when talking about golf courses and sports fields. *Lawn* is a broader term that describes mowed vegetation often containing significant broadleaf plants as well as grass. Lawns are generally maintained at a lower standard than turf.

This chapter will discuss the following:

- Matching grass types to climate in theory and practice
- Impact of grass breeding programs
- Species for sustainable lawns
- Sustainable maintenance strategies

MATCHING GRASS TYPES TO CLIMATE IN THEORY AND PRACTICE

Lawn grasses are categorized as either cool season or warm season. Cool-season grasses are predominantly grown in cool temperate and cool marine climates typical of much of Europe, parts of northern

TABLE 9-1 Zones of Adaptation for Common Lawn Plants*

Zone 1—Cool Temperate Continental Climates

Temperate climates suited primarily for cool-season grasses. Warm but rarely hot summers, with winters cold enough and long enough to limit survival of all but the hardiest warm-season grasses. Precipitation is variable, ranging generally from 8 to 40 inches per year (20 to 100 cm per year), often as snow in winter periods. Irrigation is required in drier areas for survival of lawns.

Zone 2—Cool Temperate Marine Climates

Temperate climates suited to cool-season grasses and favoring bentgrasses (*Agrostis* spp.). Summers are variable but generally mild though occasionally as warm as zone 1. Winters are mild and wet with precipitation ranging from 60 to 120 cm per year mainly as rain. Grasses do not generally go dormant during winter. Some cool-season grasses such as Kentucky bluegrass (*Poa pratensis*) perform poorly over time. Warm-season grasses often survive here but compete poorly due to the mild summers.

Zone 3—Transition Climates

Located at transition points where winters are too cold for warm-season grasses to survive reliably and summers are too warm for cool-season grasses to thrive. Summers are generally hot and often humid. Precipitation is variable, ranging from 8 to 48 inches per year (20 to 120 cm per year). In humid transition zones, rain falls primarily during summer with additional precipitation falling as snow in winter. This is a difficult area to grow healthy lawns and is noted for high populations of weeds, insects, and diseases.

Zone 4—Warm Temperate Continental/Marine Climates

This primarily warm-season grass zone has milder winters than the transition zone, with summers reliably long and hot and ranging from low to high in humidity. Precipitation is similar to the transition zone. Only the most sensitive warm-season grasses are injured in winter, and the primary cool-season grass used in cooler parts of the zone is tall fescue (*Schedonorus arundinaceus*).

Zone 5—Tropical Climates

The true warm-season grass climates where winter cold is not an issue. Growing seasons are very long, moisture is ample, and insects and diseases are prevalent. Except at high altitudes, cool-season grasses are not suited to this zone.

Zone 6—Cold or Alpine Climates

This zone includes areas with short, generally mild summers and very long, very severe winters. Only the most cold-tolerant cool-season grasses can survive. Dominant grasses are often indigenous alpine grasses. These areas are not suited to conventional lawn culture.

*Descriptions are based on zones delineated by Brede (2000) and modified based on the authors' observations.

Asia, the northern half of the United States, Canada, much of New Zealand, southern Australia, northern Japan, the southern tip of South America, and higher elevations in many tropical and subtropical climate zones. Warm-season grasses thrive in tropical and warm temperate continental or marine climates typical of the southern parts of the United States, Central America and much of South America, Spain, Africa, India, China, East Asia, and most of Japan and Korea.

Climatic regions where temperate climates meet subtropical climates result in transition zones where both cool- and warm-season grasses are found, with cool-season grasses performing best during the cool times of the year and warm-season grasses performing best during hotter periods. Notable transition regions worldwide include an elongated area running from Washington, DC, to El Paso, Texas, in the United States; the southern part of France; parts of Italy; and parts of Japan and China. In humid transitional zones, it is often very difficult to produce healthy lawns because neither cool-season grasses nor warm-season grasses are well adapted. Brede (2000) proposed a six-zone scheme to characterize major worldwide adaptation of lawn grasses. The zones are described with some modifications in Table 9-1. For more detailed information and other views on climate zones and grass adaptation, see Beard and Beard (2005), Brede (2000), Cook and Ervin (2010), and Turgeon (2008).

In theory, grasses and dicots for a specific site should be selected for how well they are adapted to that site. On a given property, a range of plants might be used to account for shade, fertility management, and irrigation strategies. Sodded lawns would be selected in the same way as grass seed. In reality, both seed and sod choices are limited based on local availability. Seed choices have become largely standardized, resulting in single-species blends (two or more cultivars of one species), all-purpose mixes (two or more species), and heavy-wear mixes or blends. Sod choices are even more restricted in most areas. The result is that grasses are largely selected according to what is available from suppliers, and allowances are rarely made for unique site requirements. Dicot plants have only recently come back into favor as acceptable components of lawns in cool temperate marine climates such as the Pacific Northwest and parts of New England. With industry standards slanted toward elite dark-green grass cultivars that perform best under medium to high fertility and regular irrigation, landscape managers have been forced to tailor their maintenance strategies to accommodate these elite grasses.

IMPACT OF GRASS BREEDING PROGRAMS

Breeding for most lawn grasses started in earnest in the 1960s and led to a major shift in grasses for lawns from upright common types to compact selections and hybrids. Dramatic improvements in cool-season grasses such as Kentucky bluegrass (*Poa pratensis*), perennial ryegrass (*Lolium perenne*), fine fescues (*Festuca* spp.), and tall fescue (*Schedonorus arundinaceus/Festuca arundinacea*) reshaped the vision of what lawns could look like. Almost from the beginning, breeding and selection goals in the United States focused on developing dark-green, fine-textured, and dense-growing cultivars of tall fescue, perennial ryegrass, fine fescues, and Kentucky bluegrass. Breeders have more recently incorporated endophytic fungi into fine and tall fescues and perennial ryegrass as a means of repelling some common foliar feeding insects and improving turf performance during high-temperature stress periods.

The American vision of the "acceptable" appearance of lawns changed in the 1970s due to the efforts of breeders, the opinions of turf experts, and the marketing campaigns of seed companies. The new standard was irrigated dark-green grass free of all controllable dicot weeds and annual grasses, tolerant of a wide range of diseases, and free of insect pests. For better or worse, this point of view has been widely adopted by the lawn care industry. In contrast to the American color preferences, Canadian and European standards for acceptable lawn grasses have historically favored lighter-green grasses.

More recently, breeders throughout the world have realized that it is possible to make grasses too fine and too dense, resulting in increased disease problems (e.g., increased large brown patch in newer tall fescue cultivars). Breeding and selection work has expanded into warm-season grasses with the goal of improving seeded cultivars of Bermudagrass (*Cynodon* spp.) and zoysiagrass (*Zoysia* spp.). Vegetative selection and breeding work has also improved Saint Augustinegrass (*Stenotaphrum secundatum*), American buffalograss (*Buchloe dactyloides*), and seashore paspalum (*Paspalum vaginatum*). Opportunities for improving warm-season grasses are immense. Common grasses used for turf in various parts of the world are listed in Table 9-2.

TABLE 9-2 Cool- and Warm-Season Domesticated and Volunteer Lawn Grasses Suitable for Lawns

Cool-Season Grass Species

Agrostis, bentgrass

- *A. canina* L., velvet bentgrass
- *A. capillaris* L. [*A. tenuis* Sibth.], colonial bentgrass, browntop
- *A. castellana* Boiss. & Reut., dryland bentgrass, highland bentgrass
- *A. idahoensis* Nash, Idaho redtop
- *A. stolonifera* [syn. *A. palustris* Huds.], creeping bentgrass

Festuca, fine fescue

- *F. ovina* L. ssp. *hirtula* (Hackel ex Travis) Wilkinson, sheep fescue
- *F. rubra* L. ssp. *commutata* Gaudin, Chewings fescue
- *F. rubra* L. ssp. *mediana* (Pavlick) Pavlick [syn. ssp. *litoralis*], slender creeping red fescue
- *F. rubra* L. ssp. *rubra* Gaudin, strong creeping red fescue
- *F. trachyphylla* (Hack.) Krajina [syn. *F. brevipila* Tracey], hard fescue

Lolium, ryegrass

- *L. multiflorum* Lam., annual ryegrass
- *L. perenne* L., perennial ryegrass

Poa, bluegrass, meadowgrass

- *P. annua* L. ssp. *reptans*, annual bluegrass, annual meadowgrass
- *P. pratensis* L., Kentucky bluegrass, smoothstalk meadow grass
- *P. supina* Schard., supina bluegrass
- *P. trivialis* L., roughstalk bluegrass, roughstalk meadow grass

Schedonorus, tall fescue

- *S. arundinaceus* (Schreb.) Dumort. [syn. *Schedonorus* phoenix (Scop.) Holub, *Lolium arundinaceum* (Darbyshire), *Festuca arundinacea* (Schreb.)], *tall fescue*

Miscellaneous Cool-Season Grass Species:

- *Agropyron cristatum* (L.) Gaertn., crested wheatgrass
- *Bromis inermis* Leyss., smooth bromegrass
- *Dactylis glomerata* L., orchardgrass, cocksfoot
- *Elymus lanceolatus* ssp. *riparius* (Scribn. & J. G. Sm.) Barkworth, streambank wheatgrass
- *E. repens* (L.) Gould, quackgrass
- *Holcus lanatus* L., velvetgrass, Yorkshire fog
- *H. mollis* L. ssp. *mollis*, creeping velvetgrass, German velvetgrass
- *Pascopyrum smithii* (Rydb.) Barkworth & D. R. Dewey, western wheatgrass
- *Vulpia myuros* (L.) C. C. Gmel. (winter annual), rattail fescue

Warm-Season Grass Species

Axonopus, carpetgrass

- *A. compressus* (Sw.) Beauv. var. *australis* G. A. Black, tropical carpetgrass
- *A. fissifolius* (Raddi) Kuhlm. [syn. *A. affinis* Chase], common carpetgrass

Bouteloua, grama

- *B. gracillis* (Kunth) Lag. ex Griffiths, blue grama

Buchloe, American buffalograss

- *B. dactyloides* (Nutt.) Engelm.

Cynodon, Bermudagrass, couchgrass

- *C. dactylon* (L.) Pers. var. *dactylon*
- *C. transvaalensis* Burtt-Davy
- *Cynodon* hybrids

Eremochloa, centipedegrass

- *E. ophiuroides* (Munro) Hack.

Paspalum
- *P. notatum* Flugge, bahiagrass
- *P. vaginatum* Swartz., seashore paspalum

Pennisetum, kikuyugrass
- *P. clandestinum* Hochst. ex Chiov.

Stenotaphrum, Saint Augustinegrass, tropical buffalograss
- *S. secundatum* (Walt.) Kuntze

Zoysia, zoysiagrass
- *Z. japonica* (Steud.), Japanese lawngrass
- *Z. matrella* (L.) Merr., Manilagrass
- *Z. tenuifolia* Willd. ex Trin.
- *Zoysia* hybrids

SPECIES FOR SUSTAINABLE LAWNS

Sustainable lawns need to be built around species with a specific set of characteristics, which include the following:

- Have the ability to persist over time.
- Maintain adequate density with modest inputs of water and fertilizer.
- Be adapted to local soil conditions.
- Survive significant drought stress.
- Have a minimum of insect and disease problems.
- Blend well with other grasses and dicot plants.
- Produce manageable amounts of thatch.

Because no single species possesses all of these traits, choosing grasses and dicots for lawns can be challenging.

The biggest stumbling block to sustainable lawns may be changing the public's expectations about what lawns should look like. Not every lawn needs to be a perfect monoculture of a single species of grass free of all contaminants. While there are situations where perfect, pure grass lawns are congruent with the overall landscape design, there is also a place for a variety of levels of lawn quality.

In commercial landscapes, for instance, the key to creating a sustainable landscape is to use common sense in differentiating between the needs of the main entrance to the headquarters building and the service area behind the warehouse. The following sections describe several cool- and warm-season grasses and dicot plants with regard to their general suitability for sustainable lawns. Many factors (e.g., soil type, annual precipitation, winter and summer temperatures, and humidity levels) will impact the success of each species. Before selecting a species or cultivar for a particular site, it is important to carefully evaluate the site conditions and consult with local experts to ensure the appropriate selection is made.

Cool-Season Grasses for Sustainable Lawns

Bentgrass, Agrostis *spp.*

Colonial bentgrass (*Agrostis capillaris*) and dryland bentgrass (*Agrostis castellana*) are excellent low-input grasses in areas where they are adapted. These are two of the most common subclimax grasses, along with wild-type creeping bentgrass (*Agrostis stolonifera*) and natural hybrid bentgrasses (*Agrostis* hybrids) found in old lawns. Some important cultivars of colonial and dryland bent grasses are listed in Table 9-3.

SUCCESSION IN LAWNS

In nature, plant communities go through a series of successions over time until they reach the terminal (climax) stage plant community, which makes maximum use of the available resources at that site (Ashby 1969). Any continuous factor that holds up the progress of succession at a specific stage results in a subclimax plant community. Mowing is the continuous factor that produces subclimax lawns.

TABLE 9-3 BENTGRASS CULTIVARS SUITED TO LOW-INPUT LAWNS*

Colonial Bentgrass, Browntop: *Agrostis capillaris* L. (*A. tenuis* Sibth.)
All produce modest numbers of rhizomes and stolons.
Alister
Bardot
Barking
Glory
Heriot
SR 7100
SR 7150
Tiger
Tiger II
Dryland Bentgrass, Highland Bentgrass: *Agrostis castellana* Boiss. & Reut.
Strongly rhizomatous with limited stolon development.
Exeter[†]
Highland

*No named cultivars of *A. stolonifera* or *A. canina* are suited for use in low-input lawns due to poor performance at typical lawn mowing heights. Wild types of *A. stolonifera* and hybrids with *A. capillaris* often produce acceptable lawn grasses.

[†]Historically considered to be *A. capillaris* but more recently recognized as *A. castellana* type.

Bentgrasses thrive in the cool temperate marine climates typical of coastal New England north to coastal Canada, the west coast of North America from Vancouver to the San Francisco West Bay area, New Zealand, the United Kingdom, and northern Europe. The strongest traits of bentgrasses are their ability to thrive in a wide range of soils and to persist under very low fertility conditions (Figure 9-1). They are competitive by nature and generally, where adapted, will dominate all temperate-zone grasses in mixtures maintained with low cultural inputs. Because they are either native or naturalized in the zones mentioned previously, they are common in soil seed banks and frequently appear in newly planted lawns within a year or two after planting (Figure 9-2). Once established, they survive drought by going dormant (meaning they turn brown) under summer water stress conditions, recovering during milder, wetter weather associated with fall, winter, and spring.

Figure 9-1 In time, locally adapted grasses will dominate most lawns as seen in this photo of bentgrass (*Agrostis* spp.) in a cool temperate marine climate.

Fine Fescues, Festuca *spp.*

The fine fescues are composed of several different *Festuca* species and subspecies. All are fine textured compared to most other commonly planted turfgrasses. Fine fescues are adapted in all cool

Figure 9-2 Bentgrass (*Agrostis* spp.), the lighter-colored grass, has invaded this lawn and will soon dominate the stand.

temperate continental and cool temperate marine climates. They have long been used in mixtures with other grasses and, in recent years, have received attention as low-input, environmentally sustainable grasses. Most retail lawn mixtures contain at least some fine fescue. Recently, breeders have incorporated endophytic fungi (see Chapter 10) into many newer cultivars.

In general, strong creeping red, hard, and sheep fescues are good choices for a sustainable lawn due to their modest growth rates and ability to produce functional turf under low fertility and minimal irrigation in climates where they are adapted. Table 9-4 lists cultivars of strong creeping red, hard, and sheep fescues with sustainable characteristics.

TABLE 9-4 Selected Hard, Sheep, and Strong Creeping Red Fescues Suited for Low-Input Lawns*

2003 NTEP Fine Fescue Trial Data from All Sites

Cultivar	Type[0]	Turf Quality[1]	Drought Resistance[2]	Red Thread[3]	Combined Score[4]
'Spartan II'	HF	6.2	9	7.7	22.9
'Reliant IV'	HF	5.8	8.7	7.8	22.3
'Gotham'	HF	6	8.3	7.9	22.2
'Predator'	HF	5.8	8.7	7.6	22.1
'Firefly'	HF	5.7	8.7	7.7	22.1
'Berkshire'	HF	5.6	7.7	7.8	21.1
'Oxford'	HF	5.8	7.3	7.7	20.8
'Epic'	SCRF	6	7.3	7.4	20.7
'SR 3000'	HF	5.2	7.7	7.4	20.3
'Wendy Jean'	SCRF	5.8	7	7.1	19.9
'PST 8000'	SCRF	5.5	7	6.9	19.4
'Fortitude'	SCRF	5.9	5.7	7.7	19.3
'Scaldis'	HF	4.8	7.3	7	19.1
'Cardinal'	SCRF	5.7	6	7.3	19
'Garnet'	SCRF	5.7	6.3	6.9	18.9
'Class One'	SCRF	5.6	6.3	6.9	18.8

*Data gleaned from NTEP turf trials conducted in the United States.

[0] HF = hard fescue; SCRF = strong creeping red fescue.

[1] 1 = worst-possible turf quality; 9 = best-possible turf quality (national average from 2004 to 2007).

[2] 1 = dormant turf; 9 = green turf no sign of dormancy (average from one site on one date).

[3] 1 = severe disease activity; 9 = no sign of disease (national average for all sites 2004–2007).

[4] Combined scores from quality, drought, and red thread disease. Only cultivars with scores above 18.5 are listed.

(Continued)

TABLE 9-4 (Continued)

1998 NTEP Fine Fescue Trial Data from Low-Input Sites

Cultivar	Type[0]	Turf Quality[1]	Drought Resistance[2]	Red Thread[3]	Combined Score[4]
'Berkshire'	HF	5.8	7.7	7.6	21.1
'Viking'	HF	5.7	7.7	7.5	20.9
'Stonehenge'	HF	5.5	8	7.1	20.6
'Eureka II'	HF	5.4	7.3	7.5	20.2
'Nordic'	HF	5.6	7	7.4	20
'Oxford'	HF	5.7	7	7.2	19.9
'Scaldis II'	HF	5.2	7.7	6.9	19.8
'Hardtop'	HF	5.6	7	7.1	19.7
'Cindy Lou'	SCRF	5.6	6.7	7.3	19.6
'Chariot'	HF	5.5	6.7	7.3	19.5
'Bighorn'	SF	5.2	7.3	7	19.5
'Osprey'	HF	5.4	6.7	7.3	19.4
'Scaldis'	HF	5.2	7	6.9	19.1
'Reliant II'	HF	5.4	6.3	7.3	19
'Pathfinder'	SCRF	5.4	7.3	6.1	18.8
'Minotaur'	HF	5.3	6	7.2	18.5
'Salsa'	SCRF	5.2	8	5.3	18.5

*Data gleaned from NTEP turf trials conducted in the United States.

[0] HF = hard fescue; SCRF = strong creeping red fescue, SF = sheep fescue.

[1] 1 = worst-possible turf quality; 9 = best-possible turf quality (national average from 1999 to 2002).

[2] 1 = dormant turf; 9 = green turf no sign of dormancy (average from one site on one date).

[3] 1 = severe disease activity; 9 = no sign of disease (national average for all sites 1999–2002).

[4] Combined scores from quality, drought, and red thread disease. Only cultivars with scores above 18.5 are listed.

Tall Fescue, Schedonorus arundinaceus *(Schreb.) Dumort. [syn.* Schedonorus phoenix *(Scop.) Holub,* Lolium arundinaceum *(Darbyshire),* Festuca arundinacea *(Schreb.)]*

Tall fescue is widely adapted to cool temperate continental climates throughout the world and is particularly well suited for transition-zone climates. It is very common in cool temperate marine climates and is somewhat adapted in warm temperate continental or marine climates. It has better heat and drought tolerance than other commonly planted cool-season lawn grasses.

In transition-zone climates, tall fescue is one of two grasses that stand out from a sustainable perspective. In cold winter temperate climates, it often is injured in winter and does not compete well with better-adapted grasses. In warm temperate and tropical climates, it is not competitive with warm-season grasses. Its strength lies in climates that are too hot for other cool-season grasses to thrive and too cold for warm-season grasses to thrive. It is not very competitive in mixtures and will usually be reduced to isolated clumps when competing against other cool-season or warm-season grasses. In most cases, tall fescue should be planted alone or in blends of three tall fescue cultivars. Some turf experts advocate mixing tall fescue with small percentages of Kentucky bluegrass or hard fescue in transition climates.

Tall fescue is best suited to areas where soils are deep and irrigation is available or rainfall is normally consistent during summer. In arid climates, tall fescue will go dormant just like other grasses when irrigation is withheld or water is unavailable (Figure 9-3). Table 9-5 lists some of the top tall fescue cultivars for the transition zone in the United States based on National Turfgrass Evaluation Program trials (www.ntep.org).

Figure 9-3 Tall fescue (*Schedonorus arundinaceus*) is unable to stay green for the entire growing season without irrigation. This lawn was not irrigated for the entire summer in a dry cool temperate climate.

Warm-Season Grasses for Sustainable Lawns

Tropical Carpetgrass, Axonopus compressus *(Sw.) Beauv.*

In moist tropical areas, tropical carpetgrass (*Axonopus compressus*) is the default choice for sustainable lawns along with Manila grass (*Zoysia matrella*). Carpetgrass dominates in acidic soils, under low fertility, and under low light conditions. Requiring only occasional mowing, this stoloniferous grass often attains almost pure stands under low-input conditions. It is very common in commercial landscapes, where it is seldom bothered by diseases or insects in areas where it does not go dormant (M. Woods, pers. comm.). Turf quality is average, and no improved cultivars are available.

American Buffalograss, Buchloe dactyloides *(Nutt.) Engelm.*

Native to the Great Plains of North America from Canada to Mexico, this dioecious stoloniferous warm-season perennial grass shows great promise as a sustainable lawn grass. It is particularly well suited to drier regions of cool temperate and warm temperate continental and warm marine climates. It has been used successfully for lawns outside the Great Plains in eastern regions of the United States, California, Canada, Mexico, Australia, and China. For a warm-season grass, it has exceptional cold tolerance. Native types have slow vertical growth rates and very low fertility requirements. Coupled with excellent drought resistance, these traits make buffalograss the ultimate low-input grass in climates where it is adapted.

Breeding and selection for improved cultivars of buffalograss has occurred only in recent years. Newer cultivars have improved density and dark color. The fertility and water requirements of buffalograss are lower than those of all other turfgrasses. Currently available cultivars are listed in Table 9-6.

TABLE 9-5 Selected Tall Fescue Cultivars Suited for Transition-Zone Lawns*

2001 NTEP Tall Fescue Trial Data from Transition-Zone Sites

Cultivar	Turf Quality[1]	Drought Resistance[2]	Brown Patch[3]	Combined Score[4]
'Blackwatch'	6.1	7	6.4	19.5
'Avenger'	6.1	7	6.2	19.3
'Finelawn Elite'	6.2	6	6.8	19
'Solara'	6.2	6.3	6.4	18.9
'Fidelity'	6.2	6.3	6.4	18.9
'Falcon IV'	6.3	5.7	6.5	18.5
'Rebel Exeda'	6.1	5.7	6.6	18.4
'Turbo'	6.1	5.7	6.3	18.1
'Titanium'	6.1	5	6.8	17.9
'Apache III'	6.1	5.3	6.5	17.9
'Houndog 6'	6.1	5.7	6.1	17.9
'Justice'	6.3	5	6.5	17.8
'Padre'	6.1	5	6.7	17.8
'Masterpiece'	6.1	5	6.4	17.5
'Davinci'	6.1	4.7	6.5	17.3
'2nd Millenium'	6.1	4.7	6.4	17.2
'Cayenne'	6.1	4.3	6.6	17
'Inferno'	6.1	4.7	6.2	17
'Lexington'	6.1	4.7	6.2	17

*Data gleaned from NTEP turf trials conducted in the United States.

[1] 1 = worst-possible turf quality; 9 = best-possible turf quality (national average from 2002 to 2005).

[2] 1 = wilted turf; 9 = green turf no sign of wilting (one site reporting).

[3] 1 = severe disease activity; 9 = no sign of disease (national average for all sites 2002–2005).

[4] Combined scores from quality, drought, and brown patch disease. Only cultivars with scores of 17 or above are listed.

TABLE 9-5 (Continued)

1996 NTEP Tall Fescue Trial Data from Transition-Zone Sites

Cultivar	Turf Quality[1]	Drought Resistance[2]	Brown Patch[3]	Combined Score[4]
'Rembrandt'	6.3	5.7	6.6	18.6
'Olympic Gold'	6	5.4	6.6	18
'Jaguar 3'	6	5	6.7	17.7
'Crossfire II'	5.9	5.1	6.6	17.6
'Millenium'	6.1	5.2	6.3	17.6
'Mustang II'	5.9	5.2	6.4	17.5
'Plantation'	6.2	5	6.3	17.5
'Scorpio'	6	5.2	6.3	17.5
'Durana'	5.9	5	6.5	17.4
'Dominion'	6	5.1	6.3	17.4
'Masterpiece'	6.1	4.9	6.3	17.3
'Tarhee'	5.9	4.8	6.6	17.3
'Wolfpack'	5.9	4.8	6.5	17.2
'Oncue'	5.9	4.7	6.5	17.1
'Arid 3'	5.9	4.8	6.4	17.1
'Dynasty'	6.1	4.7	6.3	17.1
'Redcoat'	5.8	5	6.3	17.1

[*] Data gleaned from NTEP turf trials conducted in the United States.

[1] 1 = worst-possible turf quality; 9 = best-possible turf quality (national average from 1997 to 2000).

[2] 1 = dormant turf; 9 = green turf no sign of dormancy (average of three sites).

[3] 1 = severe disease activity; 9 = no sign of disease (national average for all sites 1997–2000).

[4] Combined scores from quality, drought, and brown patch disease. Only cultivars with scores of 17 or above are listed.

Centipedegrass, Eremochloa ophiuroides *(Munro) Hack.*

This warm-season stoloniferousgrass is native to China and suited to tropical and warm temperate continental and warm marine climates where soils are acidic and rainfall exceeds 40 inches per year (100 cm per year). Centipedegrass is commonly planted in the West Indies, South America, and parts of the west coast of Africa (Duble 1996). Wiecko (2006) considers it a popular grass throughout tropical Asia and in tropical Pacific Islands. It thrives in sandy soils and has moderate shade tolerance. Its primary strengths as a sustainable grass are its acceptable turf quality under minimal inputs. On many sites, it will thrive without added fertilizer, require only modest supplemental irrigation, compete well with weeds, and be

TABLE 9-6 American Buffalograss Cultivars for Lawn Use*

Cultivar Name	Sex	U.S. Zones†	Propagation
Bison	M/F	N/T	Seed
Bowie	M/F	N/T	Seed
Cody	M/F	N/S/T	Seed
Density	F	S/T	Vegetative
Frontier Turffalo	M/F	S/T	Seed
Legacy	F	N/T	Vegetative
Plains	M/F	S/T	Seed
Prairie	F	S/T	Vegetative
Sharp's Improved	M/F	N/T	Seed
Stampede	F	S/T	Vegetative
Texoka	M/F	N/T	Seed
Topgun	M/F	S/T	Seed
118	F	S/T	Vegetative
315	F	N/T	Vegetative
378	F	N/T	Vegetative
609	F	S/T	Vegetative

*For a detailed guide to cultivars, see Shearman et al. (2004).

†N = northern United States; S = southern United States; T = transition zone.

free of any serious insect or disease pests. Most of its problems are associated with excess fertilizer and iron deficiency when grown on high-pH soils. There has been little selection and breeding work to improve the species, and the most widely planted type is common centipedegrass.

Zoysiagrass, Zoysia japonica *(Steud.),* Zoysia matrella *(L.) Merr.* Zoysia *Hybrids*

Zoysia japonica (Korean lawngrass or Japanese lawngrass) is a relatively slow growing warm-season grass native to Asia and adapted to tropical, warm temperate continental, warm marine, and transition climates worldwide. It spreads via rhizomes and stolons. It is adapted in the United States in coastal areas from New England to Texas and in parts of California (Duble 1996). It has a special niche in the transition zones and will survive in many cool temperate continental and cool temperate marine climates, but it is not generally competitive with indigenous cool-season grasses in those climates and is dormant for up to six to eight months per year where winters are cold.

Zoysia japonica has excellent cold hardiness for a warm-season grass and is moderately shade tolerant, salt tolerant, and drought tolerant, often producing acceptable turf without irrigation where annual rainfall is in the range of 25 to 30 inches (70 to 80 cm) (White et al. 1993). In addition to these qualities, it grows slowly, has a minimal fertility requirement for lawn purposes, and is relatively free of pest problems, except for rust (*Puccinia zoysiae* Diet.), *Rhizoctonia* diseases, and white grub insects (Duble 1996).

Breeding and selection of zoysiagrass has produced numerous vegetative and, more recently, a few seed-propagated cultivars. Table 9-7 provides a detailed assessment of available zoysiagrass cultivars and their use in several different climate zones.

Other Commonly Planted Grasses

The previous discussion of sustainable grasses focused on those grasses that have qualities associated with sustainability, including moderate to slow growth rates, relatively good drought tolerance, low fertility requirements, and better-than-average pest resistance. Some of the most widely planted grasses such as Kentucky bluegrass, perennial ryegrass, Bermudagrass, and Saint Augustinegrass were excluded for various reasons.

Kentucky bluegrass has a moderately high fertility requirement and is prone to excessive thatch buildup, which reduces its drought tolerance because fewer roots are growing in the soil (Figure 9-4). Excessive thatch buildup forces managers into periodic dethatching and coring (labor intensive) or consistent overirrigation to prevent development of localized

TABLE 9-7 Zoysiagrass Cultivars Suited to Several Different Climate Zones*

Transition Zones with Cold Winters	Humid Transition Zones	Warm Humid Zones
Belair	Cavalier	Cashmere
Chinese Common	Emerald	Cavalier
Meyer	El Toro	Crowne
Zenith	Himeno	Emerald
Zeon	Meyer	El Toro
Zorro	Zenith	Empire
	Zeon	GN-Z
	Zorro	JaMur
		Palisades
		PristineFlora
		Shadow Turf
		UltimateFlora
		Zeon
		Zorro
		Zoyboy

*For detailed information on cultivar selection, see Patton (2009).

Figure 9-4 Kentucky bluegrass (*Poa pratensis*) is prone to thatch buildup. Excess thatch reduces drought tolerance.

dry spots. Perennial ryegrass has the highest fertility requirement of any of the cool-season grasses. Under low nitrogen fertility, it is prone to several diseases that disfigure the stand and facilitate encroachment of other grasses. Bermudagrass is very drought tolerant but has a high fertilizer requirement and, when vigorous, produces excessive clippings. Saint Augustinegrass has many characteristics similar to centipedegrass but has more insect problems under low fertility and requires frequent mowing due to rapid vertical growth.

The reality is that maintenance contractors simply have to find ways to reduce maintenance inputs on whatever grass has been planted on the site. Wholesale regrassing of lawns to more sustainable species at most sites is likely prohibitive due to the costs involved. Therefore, the manner in which existing lawns are maintained will generally have a greater impact on sustainability than the type of grass growing in the lawn.

Grass-Dicot Combinations for Sustainable Lawns

Historically, turf researchers, professional landscape managers, and homeowners have held to the notion that lawns can only be composed of pure stands of grass. Most lawns have chronic infestations of many types of broadleaf (dicot) plants, and many of these species are well adapted to the rigors of regular mowing. A quick look around the world indicates that lawns commonly contain a wide diversity of species. In New Zealand, for example, Horne et al. (2005) found 139 plant species among 350 lawns they examined in Christchurch. In Germany, 83 plant species were observed in lawns throughout western parts of the country (Muller 1990). In the United Kingdom, Thompson et al. (2004) counted 159 different species. Given that most mature lawns do indeed contain noticeable populations of dicots and the lawns function just fine, the idea that lawns should start out with more than just grasses is not unreasonable. Some dicot species may be objectionable because they disrupt the surface or destroy the uniformity of the lawn. But other species actually blend well with grass and when uniformly mixed have essentially no undesirable impact on the appearance of lawns.

It is possible to assemble mixtures of grasses and dicots that complement each other and produce functional and aesthetically acceptable lawns. Irrigation requirements can be reduced by combining drought-resistant dicots with grasses because the dicots stay green longer than the grass under prolonged drought, resulting in a satisfactory appearance to the lawn. Fertilizer inputs can be reduced by combining legumes that fix atmospheric nitrogen together with grasses. While this broader vision of lawns may require fewer inputs and is more sustainable than traditional lawns, it will require a significant shift in the public perception of what lawns should look like, and it may not work in all climate zones.

DESIGNING LOW-INPUT GRASS-DICOT MIXTURES

Starting in the 1980s, researchers at Oregon State University began looking at mixtures of grasses and selected dicots for use in cool temperate marine climates. The goal was to determine if acceptable lawns could be created that had minimal fertility requirements and were more drought resistant than straight grass lawns. After selecting appropriate dicots and finding commercial sources of seed for the dicots, mixes were assembled using a "best guess" approach, and various grass-dicot combinations were planted. After several years under minimal irrigation and mowing, it became apparent that certain mixes looked better than others, and additional research was conducted with those mixes. The final mixes were fairly simple and have worked surprisingly well (Color Plate 9-1).

Suitable Grass-Dicot Mixes

Under cool temperate marine climate conditions, the mixes that have shown the most promise have a base of perennial ryegrass or perennial ryegrass and hard fescue. While it seems counterintuitive to use perennial ryegrass, which has a high nitrogen fertility requirement for a low-input lawn, it works because, under low fertility, ryegrass is not overly competitive so the stand stays in equilibrium. The most frequently used dicots in dicot-grass mixes include common yarrow (*Achillea millefolium*), strawberry clover 'Fresa' (*Trifolium fragiferum*), micro white clover 'Pipolina' (*Trifolium repens*), and English daisy (*Bellis perennis*). Some mixes contain all of these, while others contain only yarrow and clover or even just yarrow.

On silty clay loam soils, grass-dicot mixtures have provided aesthetically acceptable green lawns. These mixtures are sustainable because they persist with only one-half to two-thirds as much irrigation as pure grass lawns. Partially green lawns were achieved with as few as three irrigations per year. The lawns only required mowing every two to three weeks at 2 inches (5 cm), and required no more than one fertilizer application per year on established stands (Cook 1993). Most of the year the mixes look much like conventional lawns except during spring when daisies flower and in midsummer when the clovers flower. Mixtures with grass and yarrow look just like conventional grass lawns as yarrow does not normally flower under regular mowing. The stands tend to be dominated by grass in the mild rainy winters and by clover and yarrow in summer (Color Plate 9-2). Domesticated English daisies tend to be short lived in mixtures. The potential use of dicots with warm-season grasses has not been evaluated to date. Several commercially available cool-season mixtures are described at http://www.protimelawnseed.com/products-page/?product_id=21.

Table 9-8 provides an annotated list of dicots with potential for use in grass-dicot mixtures in cool temperate marine climates. Most plants in Table 9-8 are commonly considered weeds today, but all have

TABLE 9-8 Some Lawn-Compatible Dicot Species

Drought Tolerant

Achillea millefolium, common yarrow

Blends well with grass. Spreads via rhizomes. Will stay green under prolonged drought. Tolerates a wide range of climates.

Bellis perennis, English daisy

White or pink flowers in spring. Drought tolerant but will go dormant under prolonged dry periods. Wild types are hardier than domesticated cultivars.

Galium verum, lady's bedstraw

The most drought resistant lawn dicot. Very compatible with grasses. Spreads via rhizomes but not invasive. Produces yellow flowers in summer.

Prunella vulgaris, heal-all, self-heal

Quite drought tolerant in mild temperate climates. Tends to form dense tight patches. Produces purple flowers at mowing height.

Trifolium fragiferum, strawberry clover

Very drought tolerant. 'Fresa' cultivar is dense and low growing. Flower period is shorter than that of white clover. Blends well with grass.

Trifolium repens, white clover

Very drought tolerant. Wild types are variable in growth and flowering. 'Pipolina' cultivar is lower growing than common types.

Wet and/or Shade Tolerant

Glechoma hederacea, ground ivy, creeping Charlie

Handles shade well. Low growing. Foliage is somewhat coarse but blends fairly well with grass.

Ranunculus repens, creeping buttercup

Tolerates wet soils and moderate shade well. Vigorous spreader. Yellow flowers in spring at mowing height. Foliage somewhat coarse.

Veronica spp., perennial speedwells

Perform well in wet areas and in shady areas. Stay low growing at all times. Produce blue flowers in spring.

Broad Adaptation

Anthemis nobilis, chamomile

Blends well with grass. Similar to yarrow but lighter green and not as drought tolerant. Emits lemon fragrance when mowed. Not as persistent as other dicots under regular mowing.

Oxalis spp., wood sorrel

Behaves as an herbaceous perennial, often dying back to the ground in winter. Mixes with grass much like clover. Produces yellow flowers at mowing heights.

Viola spp., lawn violets

Leaves are coarser in texture and do not entirely mix well with grass. Spreads slowly and produces purple to pink flowers in early spring. Common in shady, low-fertility lawns.

Dicots Best Used Alone

Dichondra spp.

Dense growing, competitive, and thatch prone. Does not mix well with grass and performs best when planted alone. Tolerates low mowing.

Leptinella spp. (Hook. f.) (formerly *Cotula* sp.), cotula

Extremely dense growing. Does not mix well with grass and performs best when planted alone. Tolerates low mowing.

adaptive qualities that make them well suited for lower-input lawns (Color Plate 9-3). With breeding and selection work, there are great opportunities for improvement. The driving force for increasing the use of dicots in lawns will be restrictions on water use in landscape settings and restrictions on the use of herbicides on lawns merely for aesthetic purposes.

Grass-dicot mixtures are not a panacea and, at the present time, are suited only for several niche markets. In the future, they will likely find a place in lawns that are viewed at a distance or as "drive-by lawns," those that are not subject to heavy wear, and those not fertilized or watered intensively. In the world of perfect turf, they will never be accepted, but, when used appropriately, they provide another tool in the quest for sustainability. For differing views on the lawn aesthetic and attitudes regarding the use of dicots with grasses, see Bormann, Balmori, and Geballe (2001) and Brede (2000).

SUSTAINABLE MAINTENANCE STRATEGIES

Basic maintenance practices include mowing, irrigation, fertilization, and pest control. These are aided by coring and thatch management as auxiliary practices to enhance growing conditions. This section will discuss mowing, irrigation, and fertilization with brief mention of coring and dethatching. Pest management is addressed in Chapter 10.

Mowing Strategies

Lawns are defined by mowing. From the invention of the reel mower in 1830 to the present, mowing has been the primary lawn care activity. Manufacturers have produced a wide array of equipment to improve the speed and efficiency of mowing and more effective technology for handling clippings. This section will address four mowing variables that can be manipulated in the quest for more sustainable lawns: mowing frequency, mowing height, clipping management, and choice of mowing equipment.

Mowing Frequency

The standard target frequency for commercial lawn mowing is once per week on irrigated sites, and it is rare that these sites are mowed more than once per week. The recommendation to mow often enough so you never remove more than one-third of the total height of the grass is largely unrealistic. In commercial maintenance, the realities of scheduling dictate mowing according to the calendar and not the needs of the grass.

To reduce the frequency of mowing and still maintain groomed lawns, the primary options include:

- Reducing the growth rate by reducing irrigation
- Reducing the growth rate by applying less nitrogen fertilizer
- Planting slower-growing grasses
- Applying chemical growth regulators to suppress growth (this has some merit on golf courses but is largely impractical in commercial maintenance scenarios)

Mowing Height

Mowing height is a major variable to consider when striving for sustainability. The standard mantra is "mow as high as possible." This is fine when dealing with naturally erect-growing grasses such as tall fescue, Kentucky bluegrass, perennial ryegrass, fine fescues, bahiagrass (*Paspalum notatum*), or Saint Augustinegrass. But it doesn't work very well for naturally low-growing grasses such as bentgrass, *Zoysia japonica* 'Meyer', *Zoysia matrella*, zoysiagrass hybrids, or Bermudagrass. The big question for every type of grass is what constitutes mowing too low and what constitutes the optimum high-mowing-height range.

The most universally recommended mowing heights for erect grasses are in the range of 2 to 3 inches (5 to 7.5 cm), with extreme heights in the range of 4 to 5 inches (10 to 12.5 cm) (Baxendale and Gaussoin 1997; Christians 1998; Dunn and

THE BENTGRASS DILEMMA

Currently available bentgrasses look their best when mowed with reel mowers at lower rather than higher heights. While they will tolerate lawn mowing heights as low as 0.4 inches (1cm), they are more easily maintained at 0.75 to 1.5 inches (2 to 4 cm). Above 1.25 inches (3.5 cm), they are prone to false crowning, which results in scalping and poor turf quality.

Because much of commercial maintenance is done with rotary mowers set at or above 2 inches (5 cm) for erect-growing grasses such as Kentucky bluegrass, tall fescue, or perennial ryegrass, bent grass is generally considered a weed when it first appears in these lawns. This creates a dilemma for turf managers. If they continue to mow with rotary mowers set high, the quality of the lawn will deteriorate as bent grass spreads and dominates the site (Figure 9-5a). The sustainable strategy involves mowing lower with rotary mowers or switching to reel mowers set lower. It also involves reducing fertilizer nitrogen to levels suited to bentgrass. At optimum fertility levels and proper mowing heights, bentgrasses produce relatively little thatch and are remarkably easy to maintain (Figure 9-5b).

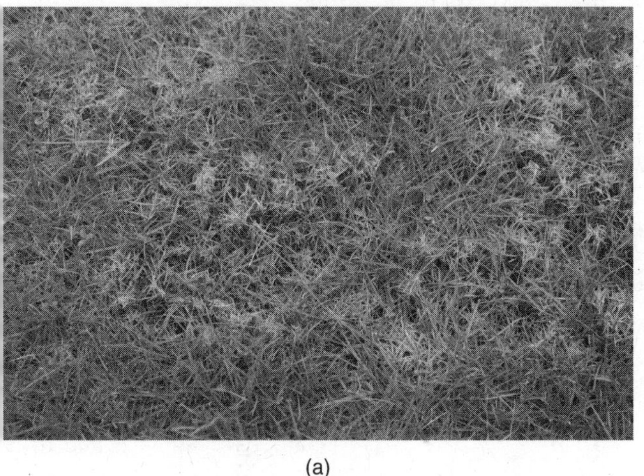

(a)

(b)

Figure 9-5 (a) When bentgrass (*Agrostis* spp.) is mowed at 2 inches (5 cm) or higher, it produces false crowns, which ruin the appearance of the lawn. (b) When mowed below 1.25 inches (4 cm), it looks very good.

Diesburg 2004; Ruppert and Black 1997; Wiecko 2006). Except possibly in transition-zone climates, it is hard to argue for mowing cool-season grass lawns above 3 inches (7.5 cm).

When erect growing grasses are mowed at heights above 3 inches (7.5 cm), the grass competes better against weeds like crabgrass (*Digitaria* spp.) and performs better in the shade. Because the plants are bigger and have more robust root systems, they may also withstand drought and heat stress better. On the downside, tall grass uses significantly more water than shorter-cut grass (Sheard 2000). Also, at extremely high mowing heights, lawns begin to look like pastures and lose their groomed appearance. Because of high temperatures during the summer, some experts recommend mowing higher in summer than in spring or fall (Baxendale and Gaussoin 1997). Examples of commonly recommended mowing heights for cool- and warm-season grasses are presented in Table 9-9.

TABLE 9-9 Mowing Heights for Common Turfgrasses and Grass-Dicot Mixtures in Low-Input Lawns Mowed Weekly

		Commonly Reported Mowing htranges (centimeters)**				
Law Species	**Climate Zones***	**Spring**	**Summer**	**Fall**	**Preferred Mower Types/s**	**Comments**
Agrostis capillaris, Colonial bentgrass	Zone 2		2.5–5.0		Reel or rotary	Visual quality is better when cut with reel mowers.
Agrostis castellana, Dryland bentgrass	Zone 2		2.0–4.0		Reel or rotary	Visual quality is better when cut with reel mowers.
Agrostis idahoensis, Idaho bentgrass	Zone 2		2.5–5.0		Reel or rotary	Visual quality is better when cut with reel mowers.
Axonopus spp. Carpetgrass	Zone 5		2.5–5.0		Rotary	Rotary mowers remove flower stalks.
Buchloe dactyloides, American buffalograss	Zone 3 and 4		2.5–5.0 (vegetative cultivars)		Rotary	Some nonirrigated low-maintenance sites may not require regular mowing.
			5.0–7.5 (common types)			
Cynodon dactylon, bermudagrass	Zone 3—Transition		2.5–5.0	5.0	Reel or rotary	High fall mowing height in fall may improve winter survival.
	Zones 4 and 5		2.5–5.0		Reel or rotary	
Elymus lanceolatus, streambank wheatgrass	Zone 1—semiarid regions	7.5	7.5–10.0	7.5	Rotary	
Eremochloa ophiuroides, Centipedegrass	Zone 4 and 5		2.5–5.0		Reel or rotary	
Festuca spp., creeping, hard, and sheep fescues	Zone 1	5.0	7.5	5.0	Rotary	Raising height of cut in summer may enhance summer performance.
	Zone 2	5.0	5.0	5.0	Rotary	
Lolium perenne, Perennial ryegrass	Zone 1	5.0	5.0–7.5	5.0	Rotary	Raising height of cut in summer may enhance summer performance.
	Zone 2	5.0	5.0	5.0	Rotary	
Lolium + dicot mixtures	Zones 1 and 2	5.0–7.5	5.0–7.5	5.0–7.5	Rotary	Target frequency is once every 2–4 weeks, more often in spring if needed.
Pascopyron smithii, western wheatgrass	Zone 1—semiarid regions	7.5	7.5–10.0	7.5	Rotary	
Paspalum notatum, bahiagrass	Zones 4 and 5		5.0–10.0		Rotary	Requires weekly mowing to minimize development of flower stalks.

Pennisetum clandestinum, Kikuyugrass	Zones 4 and 5		2.5–5.0		Reel	Turf performance is better at lower mowing heights and regular vertical mowing
Poa pratensis, Kentucky bluegrass	Zone 1	5.0	5.0–7.5	5.0	Rotary	Raising height of cut in summer may enhance summer performance.
P. supina, supina bluegrass	Zones 1 and 2	2.5–4.0	2.5–4.0	2.5–4.0	Reel or rotary	
P. trivialis, roughstalk bluegrass	Zone 1—shade only	2.5–5.0	2.5–5.0	2.5–5.0	Reel or rotary	
	Zone 2—sun and shade	2.5–5.0	2.5–5.0	2.5–5.0	Reel or rotary	
Schedonorus arundinaceus, tall fescue	Zone 1	5.0–7.5	7.5	5.0–7.5	Rotary	
	Zone 3 and 4	7.5	7.5–10.0	7.5	Rotary	Marginally adapted in zone 4.
Stenotaphrum secundatum, Saint Augustinegrass	Zones 4 and 5		5.0–10.0		Rotary	Lower mowing heights may require more frequent mowing.
Zoysia japanica, zoysiagrass	Zone 3—Transition		2.5		Reel	'Meyer' is best mowed at 2.5 cm.
	Zones 4 and 5		2.5–5.0		Reel or rotary	Common types handle higher mowing heights well.
Z. matrella, Manilagrass	Zones 4 and 5		1.25–2.5		Reel	

* Climate zones from Brede (2000).

** Mowing heights assimilated from Turgeon (2008), Wiecko (2006), Dunn and Diesburg (2004), Fry and Huang (2004), Christians (1998), Baxendale and Gaussoin (1997), and Duble (1996).

Clipping Management

Grass type, irrigation, and fertilizer all impact the quantity of clippings. The goal is to manipulate all of these factors to reduce clipping production, which, in turn, will speed up mowing and reduce fuel consumption. For cool-season grasses, the goal is to avoid stimulating excess growth with fertilizer and irrigation in spring and fall when lawns are naturally vigorous. For warm-season grasses, the goal is to minimize growth in summer when they are naturally most vigorous.

Clipping management has always been problematic in commercial lawn care. The majority of lawns mowed with small [21-inch (55- cm)] walking rotary mowers have clippings removed. As mowers become wider [more than 48 inches (125 cm)] and lawns become larger, there is a break-even point, where many maintenance companies begin to return clippings. Historically, clippings removed during mowing were disposed of in landfills. The result was a major waste issue and a fertilizer problem, because nutrients removed in clippings had to be replaced by additional fertilizer applications. Today, clippings are still largely removed from medium to small lawns and are sent to composting facilities rather than landfills. The primary concern now is increased fertilizer needs resulting from clipping removal. From a sustainable perspective, clipping removal is among the least desirable practices in commercial mowing.

Choice of Mowing Equipment

The obvious solution for the clipping problem is to use mulching mower technology to return clippings, thus solving the disposal problem and reducing fertilizer requirements at the same time (Figure 9-6). For many contractors, this is an "easier said than done" situation. The problem is that with current maintenance standards for commercial work (e.g., regular fertilizer, regular irrigation, and weekly mowing), there is often too much growth to mulch clippings with rotary mowers and obtain aesthetically pleasing results. The mowers can handle the workload, but lawns look messy with clumps of mulched clippings and grass stains on sidewalks. The best scenario for using mulching mowers involves reducing fertilizer and water applications to reduce weekly growth to a

(a)

(b)

Figure 9-6 (a) Mulching mowers offer one approach to returning clippings to lawns. (b) Straight blade at top is designed to pick up clippings while X shaped mulching blade at bottom is designed to cut clippings multiple times before they sift down into the canopy.

point where mowers can effectively mulch clippings without producing a mess. Mulching clippings may still not be feasible in spring on cool-season grasses or during peak summer growth for warm-season grasses because of the high growth rate. Since the ultimate goal is to reduce the amount of clippings removed from the site, contractors may have to continue removing clippings on high-profile sites during periods of peak growth but may be able to return clippings during times of slower growth. All possible options should be explored to find ways to return clippings on amenity lawns when possible and on larger lawns most of the time since appearance standards there are not as high.

Irrigation Strategies

One of the major complaints about lawns is the amount of irrigation required to produce aesthetically acceptable turf. The perception that lawns are water hogs is due largely to indiscriminate and mindless watering that is apparent wherever lawns are irrigated. In reality, lawns require less water than they often receive and often require no more water than other common landscape plantings. Because irrigation in the context of commercial landscape maintenance is a very public process, it requires a great deal more thought than it generally receives.

One barrier to sustainability for professionally maintained landscapes is how they are designed. Many commercial sites include lawns at the edge of roads, in median strips, as part of narrow street tree plantings, and on steep slopes. These are all difficult to irrigate without overwatering and without overspray on roads, which can lead to water running down the street gutters to the nearest storm sewer (Figure 9-7). Further, odd-shaped areas do not lend themselves to efficient irrigation because it is impossible to properly space heads, thus forcing contractors to grossly overirrigate to create the illusion of uniform coverage.

The failure to analyze and modify zones and sprinkler heads as the landscape develops and changes makes aging systems less and less effective. Failing to repair broken heads in a timely manner (Figure 9-8), replacing damaged heads with heads that do not match the originals (Figure 9-9), failing to use proper nozzles to achieve matched precipitation, and not auditing and adjusting zones regularly to improve coverage all contribute to irrigation problems. Finally,

Figure 9-7 Poorly adjusted sprinklers often result in wasted water, as noted here, where water is running down the street due to sprinkler overthrow.

Figure 9-8 Broken heads may go unnoticed until parts of the lawn start to turn brown from drought.

Figure 9-9 Mixing heads with different gpm (lpm) rates on the same zone makes it impossible to achieve uniform precipitation.

operating systems at windy times of the day, turning systems on too early in the spring, running them too late into fall, and setting run times by feel rather than by using real knowledge of precipitation rates for specific zones all contribute to wasting water. Clearly, there is plenty of room for improvement to manage lawn irrigation sustainably.

Sustainable Lawn Irrigation

Sustainable lawn irrigation requires a systematic approach. The five critical steps in this approach are summarized below:

1. *Prioritize areas according to irrigation needs.* The easiest way to reduce water use is not to water areas that do not need to be irrigated. Many lawns can be divided into nonirrigated, occasionally irrigated, and regularly irrigated areas as noted in Color Plate 9-4.
2. *Analyze the mechanics of the irrigation system and perform regular audits.* Efficient irrigation requires a system that applies water uniformly and at a known precipitation rate. Landscape managers should:

Drought stress has different meanings depending on the region. In the cool temperate marine climates of western North America, drought is a constant during the dry summer months. In the cool temperate and warm temperate arid zones of North America, drought is a year-round phenomenon. In much of the cool temperate continental climates of North America and Europe, frequent summer rain is common so three weeks without precipitation is a significant period of drought.

When researchers refer to "drought tolerance," they are usually referring to "drought resistance," which is the ability of plants to stay green when subjected to short-term drought stress. Tall fescue, hard and sheep fescue, and, to a lesser degree, perennial ryegrass are cool-season grasses with good drought resistance. Bermudagrass, zoysiagrass, and American buffalograss are warm-season grasses with good drought resistance. When drought is severe and prolonged, most grasses will go dormant and turn brown. Grasses that lack the ability to go dormant will simply die. Figure 9-10 shows how lawn grasses survive short- and long-term drought.

Determine if current zones are still appropriate.

Adjust head spacing to achieve head-to-head coverage.

Straighten heads.

Raise or lower heads.

Adjust the arc on partial-circle heads.

Determine that nozzle sizes are matched properly.

Optimize water throw via pressure-compensating heads or valve pressure regulators.

Measure zone precipitation rates.

Make sure controllers are operating properly.

3. *Optimize irrigation with proper turf cultural practices.* A perfectly designed and

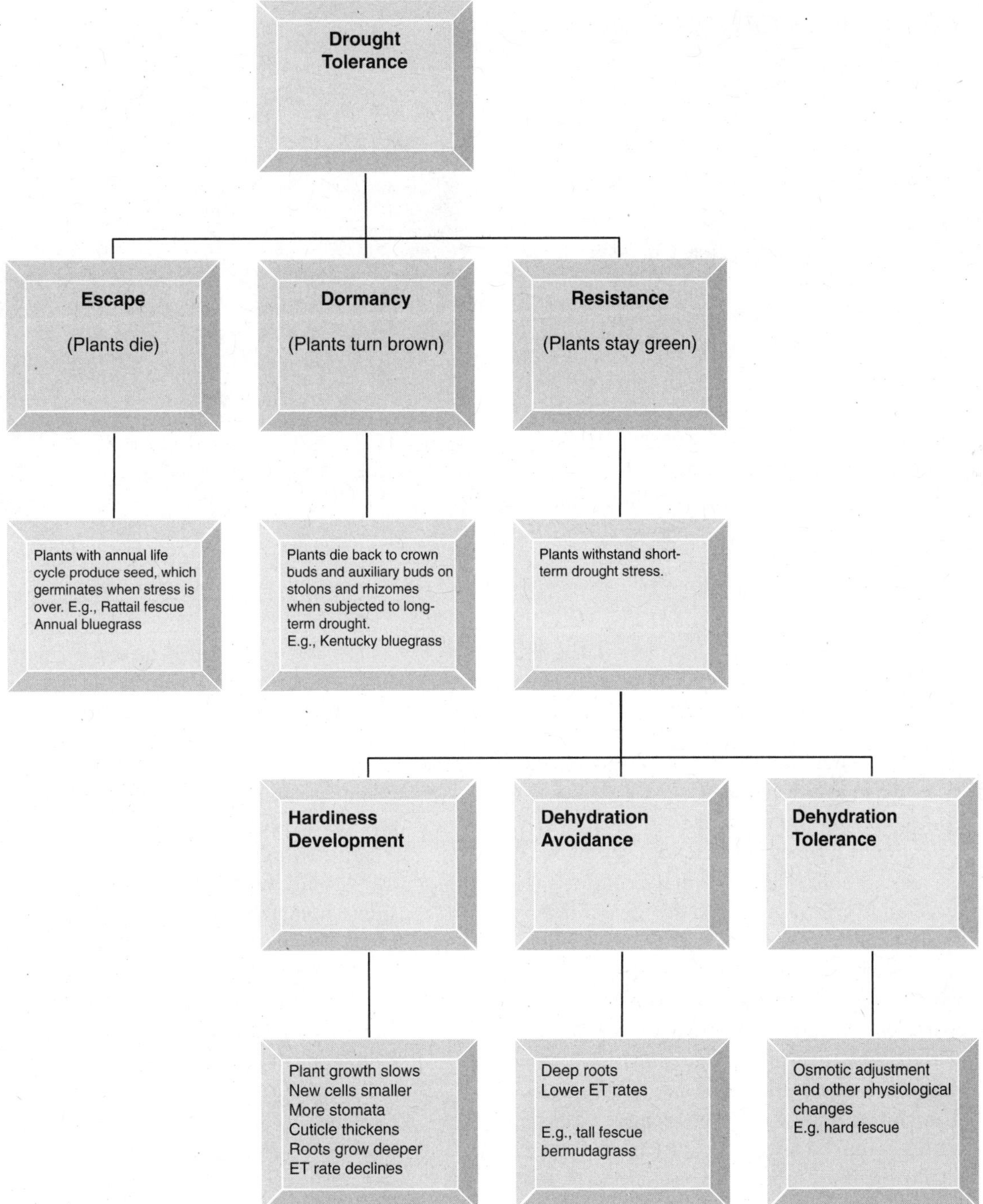

Figure 9-10 How lawn grasses survive short- and long-term drought.

USING CAN TESTS CAN SAVE MONEY

After observation of countless irrigation systems, it is clear that many irrigators do not appear to understand the concept of matched precipitation or the importance of uniform application of irrigation water.

Can tests are the only way to accurately determine zone precipitation rates and precisely where coverage problems occur. A can test involves placing small containers throughout a zone, collecting water from the irrigation system, computing the precipitation rate, determining the distribution uniformity, and calculating the scheduling coefficient (Figure 9-11). Making the necessary system adjustments based on the can test results can pay off in big water savings. While nozzle manufacturer precipitation rate charts are available, they only approximate precipitation rates.

Figure 9-11 Can tests start with cans laid out on a grid. The system is run for a given amount of time, and the water collected in the containers is used to compute the precipitation rate, the distribution uniformity, and the scheduling coefficient. Adjustments are made as needed to improve coverage.

adjusted irrigation system cannot make up for variable soil types, compacted areas, or excess thatch accumulation. Variation in soil types may require changing the irrigation zone configuration in order to allow proper irrigation run times for sites with sandy versus clay soils. Clay soils may require a cycle-and-soak approach to avoid runoff due to slow infiltration rates. Compaction, which reduces infiltration and promotes runoff, may be one of the biggest contributors to inefficient irrigation. One remedy is aerifying with hollow tines in spring to enhance infiltration and facilitate deeper root growth. Thatch control is important because excess thatch results in lawn root systems that are shallow and, in some cases, contained entirely in the thatch layer. This is particularly common in Kentucky bluegrass and fine fescue lawns in cool temperate climates.

4. *Determine water requirements.* Until recently, lawn water requirements were largely determined by trial and error. When the lawn looked dry, run times were increased; when a lawn looked good, irrigation was considered about right. Unfortunately, the trial-and-error approach almost invariably led to overirrigated lawns. To move beyond trial and error, the industry has embraced the concept of irrigation based on evapotranspiration (ET). With ET, irrigators have a more reliable means of determining lawn water use, but there are still numerous problems. ET estimates are most reliable in the summer when soils are predictably dry and water use is strongly related to weather conditions. There is a tendency for meteorologically based formulas to err on the side of overwatering. Blindly

following ET estimates will still result in overirrigation. ET values should be used as starting points and then be adjusted by trial and error to reduce applied water.

5. *Develop a strategy for the irrigation year.* Irrigation needs vary during the growing season. Unfortunately, a common strategy is often to activate the system in early spring, adjust the run times to meet mid-summer conditions, set the system to operate daily for run times that are not based on environmental conditions, and run it until late fall when the irrigation system is shut down and winterized. This is a recipe for gross overirrigation.

   A better approach begins with starting up the system in early spring and straightening, adjusting, repairing, and replacing heads as needed. Conduct a complete water audit on several zones each year, focusing on the most important zones first or those zones that have had coverage problems in the past. Once the system is tuned up, it is advisable to wait as long as possible before initiating regular irrigation for the season as well as selecting an irrigation frequency that is appropriate for the site. In most cases, the frequency will range from two to four irrigations per week. Partitioning irrigation into two to four applications spread throughout the week will generally produce optimum quality turf without overwatering, provided the system is applying water uniformly (Minner 1987). As summer turns into fall, a sustainable lawn irrigation approach prescribes cutting back or stopping irrigation as soon as possible.

   Starting irrigation as late as possible in spring, irrigating conservatively with a properly tuned system during the summer, and taking advantage of technology to further minimize overwatering will allow acceptable turf without wasting water.

DETERMINING IRRIGATION FREQUENCY

A low-tech strategy for determining the fewest number of irrigations needed in an average week involves setting the system to irrigate seven days per week and estimating the best daily run times. After the system has run for a week or two, shut off one day. A week later, shut off another day at a different time of the week. Continue this process until the fewest number of days that particular zone needs to run to produce acceptable turf can be determined. During hot spells, make changes by adding days. If this exercise allows cutting back to two or three irrigations per week, then the system has better-than-average coverage and estimated run times are fairly accurate. The net impact is that the amount of water applied has been reduced by over half. If the system has to be run five or six days per week, either the estimated run times are too low or the zone has poor coverage and a full audit on the zone will be needed so the problem can be corrected.

Fertilization Strategies

Managing lawn fertility sustainably requires a multifaceted approach. Some considerations include the aesthetic expectations for the lawn and clipping management, discussed earlier in this chapter. Additional considerations include soil testing, fertilizers, fertilizer application rates and timing, and fertilizer application procedures. This section will discuss how these factors interact to facilitate a sustainable fertilization strategy.

Soil Testing

Regular soil testing provides a snapshot of soil fertility at the time of the test and provides a picture of how fertilizer programs affect soil fertility over the years. Basic soil tests generally provide information on organic matter content, estimated nitrogen release, soil pH, calcium, magnesium, phosphorus, potassium, sodium, and, in some cases, sulfate-sulfur. When soil testing labs are provided with appropriate information, most will provide fertilizer application recommendations. This section will discuss soil pH, phosphorus, potassium, and nitrogen, because they are the most important for planning basic fertilizer programs for lawns. For a more detailed discussion of soil fertility management and all factors related to soil testing, consult Carrow, Waddington, and Rieke (2001).

Soil pH

Soil pH gives a fairly accurate picture of the amount of active acidity in the soil. As the pH goes down, the acidity increases, and as the pH goes up, the acidity decreases. Based on a scale of 1 to 14, where 7 is neutral, most grasses will grow acceptably at a pH between 5 and 8, with the ideal range between 6 and 7. The goal, then, is to maintain the pH in that range. If soil is too acidic, lime can be applied to raise the pH. If the pH is too high, the soil can be acidified by adding sulfur. Soil pH is important because it affects the retention and availability of nutrient cations. Excessively acidic soils (pH below 5) tend not to retain nutrients and may result in excessive aluminum availability, which can be toxic to many grasses. Excessively alkaline soils (pH above 7.5) tend to reduce the availability of nutrients such as iron and phosphorus.

Phosphorus

Phosphorus is easily measured with soil tests, and research has shown reasonably good correlations between phosphorus levels and plant health. Overapplication of phosphorus is a concern because it tends to accumulate in soil and can build up beyond levels needed for healthy plant growth. Phosphorus that washes into lakes and streams due to surface runoff, soil erosion, and direct application into roadways and waterways from rotary spreaders causes eutrophication (excess algae growth due to nutrient enrichment). This threat has led to some states banning phosphorus fertilizers for lawn use (see Chapter 6). Phosphorus should only be applied to landscapes if soil tests indicate levels are below the adequate range.

Potassium

Potassium is also easily measured with soil tests and, except in very sandy soils, is rarely lacking. Historically, there has been a tendency to overapply potassium fertilizers due partly to a lack of soil testing and partly to perceived enhanced stress tolerance of grasses fertilized heavily with potassium. Unnecessary potassium applications can be eliminated by monitoring soil levels at two- to three-year intervals. Based on this information, applications can be adjusted to keep potassium in the range for healthy turf growth.

Nitrogen

The most important nutrient for lawn fertilization is nitrogen. However, it is also one of the few essential elements for which soil tests fail to provide reliable information (see Carrow, Waddington, and Rieke 2001 for a detailed explanation). Nitrogen fertilization is ultimately based on aesthetic expectations for the lawn, soil type (i.e., sand versus clay), grass requirements, and clipping management practices. Because nitrogen applications make lawns darker green, stimulate shoot production, and increase leaf elongation, applications need to be managed carefully and with restraint. In general, mature lawns growing on heavier-textured soils rather than sandy soils, with moderate irrigation and clippings returned, will require the least amount of supplemental nitrogen. For spring applications, products that are either quick release (i.e., blood meal or urea) or whose release is less temperature dependent (i.e., sulfur-coated urea or short-chain methylene ureas) are generally more effective than other slow-release materials.

Fertilizer Selection

The goal of a sustainable fertilization program is to produce healthy lawns that are dense enough to compete against weeds, have acceptable color, and produce the least amount of clippings possible. On golf course putting greens, minimal growth is achieved with frequent applications of soluble nitrogen at low rates of 0.1 pound N/1000 square feet/application (0.5 g N/m^2/application). Logistics make this approach impossible for commercially maintained lawns. Instead, applications are typically spread throughout the growing season, and mixtures of soluble and slow-release nitrogen fertilizers are used to ensure moderate growth.

Ultimately, the key is to find fertilizer materials that are affordable, available, and suitable for the level of quality required at commercial sites. Because workers have to apply fertilizers, it is also important to use products with high enough analyses to reduce the amount of bulk, select products with minimal odor problems, and avoid products that are overly dusty.

Fertilizer analysis refers to the relative amount of nitrogen (as N), phosphorus (as P_2O_5), and potassium (as K_2O). Fertilizer with a 15-5-10 analysis contains 15 percent nitrogen, 5 percent P_2O_5, and 10 percent K_2O. Because nitrogen is the most important element for plant growth, applications are based on it. Table 9-10 lists common fertilizer sources and their N-P_2O_5-K_2O analyses.

TABLE 9-10 Common Natural and Synthetic Nitrogen Fertilizer Sources

Source	N	P_2O_5	K_2O	Response Rate
Activated sewage sludge	6	2	0	Slow
Blood meal*	12–13	0	0	Fast
Corn gluten meal*	9–10	0	0	Intermediate
Cottonseed meal*	5	2	1	Slow
Dried poultry waste*	4	3	3	Slow
Feather meal*	12	0	0	Slow
Fish meal*	10	4	0	Slow
Soybean meal*	7	2	1	Slow
Ammonium nitrate	33	0	0	Fast
Ammonium sulfate	21	0	0	Fast
Urea	46	0	0	Fast
Urea-formaldehyde products	38	0	0	Slow
Methylene ureas	40	0	0	Intermediate
Sulfur-coated urea	32	0	0	Intermediate
Polymer-coated urea	39–44	0	0	Slow
Polymer-coated, sulfur-coated urea	40	0	0	Intermediate

*Percentages will vary based on actual processing techniques.

Many people assume sustainable fertility management simply involves switching from synthetic to natural nutrient sources, but this may not be true once all factors are considered. For example, natural products are often generated from waste products from factory farms or slaughterhouses, are formulated and processed using significant inputs of natural gas for drying and granulating (e.g., Milorganite), and may be shipped great distances from production sites to end users. In some cases, there may be little difference in energy costs to produce and distribute organic and synthetic fertilizers. Further, some organic fertilizers have inordinately high levels of phosphorus in proportion to nitrogen so regular applications will eventually result in excessive phosphorus levels.

Fertilizer Application Rates and Timing

The standard rate per application for nitrogen is nominally 1 pound N/1000 square feet, which is approximately equal to 5 g N/m^2. The range of rates normally considered for application runs from 0.5 pound N/1000 square feet to 2 pounds N/1000 square feet (2.5 g N/m^2 to 10g N/m^2). Low rates are suitable for dense healthy lawns that just need a slight color boost or for maintenance of growth, but are generally not adequate to stimulate significant tillering or a prolonged color response. Rates of 1.5 to 2 pounds N/1000 square feet (7.5 to 10 g N/m^2) are intended to push growth and increase shoot density. These rates are useful for thickening thin stands of grass or when the material being applied is a slow-release product containing little soluble nitrogen. Mixed products containing both quick-release and slow-release nitrogen are commonly applied at 1 to 1.5 pounds N/1000 square feet (5 to 7.5g N/m^2).

Historically, phosphorus and potassium have been applied along with nitrogen in mixed fertilizers at standardized ratios based loosely on tissue analysis of common turfgrass species. Common fertilizer ratios range between 3-1-2 and 6-1-4 (N-P_2O_5-K_2O). Used regularly, these ratios will ultimately overapply phosphorus and potassium on many mineral soils. From a sustainable perspective, N-P_2O_5-K_2O ratios on soils without known deficiencies of phosphorus or potassium should probably be in the 10-1-2 range. When deficient levels are documented, targeted applications should not exceed 1 pound P_2O_5 or K_2O/1000 square feet/application (5 g P_2O_5 or K_2O/m^2/application).

The timing of lawn fertilizer applications should be adapted to the local climate and the specific goals of the fertilizer program. Usually, most landscape maintenance contractors adhere to fall or spring applications for cool-season grasses and summer applications for warm-season grasses under transition conditions. Study local recommendations whenever possible, because these are generally based on extensive local experience.

Fertilizer Application Procedures

When fertilizing lawns, it is important to keep fertilizer on the lawn and away from hard-surface areas where it might be washed into storm drains or into surface waters (e.g., lakes and streams). One of the most common sources of fertilizer pollution is overthrow from rotary spreaders (Figure 9-12). It is difficult to keep fertilizer on a 6 foot (2 m) wide parking strip with a spreader that throws 15 feet (5 m). The easiest solution to avoid overthrow from rotary spreaders is to use rotary spreaders with adjustable drop-down guards that convert full-throw to half-throw. These spreaders certainly reduce overthrow but are not totally effective and suffer an additional drawback of pattern distortion caused by the deflector. A better solution for dry products is to apply fertilizer with drop spreaders (Figure 9-13). These spreaders are very accurate and with care will virtually eliminate overthrow. Unfortunately, drop spreaders are a bit cumbersome to use and are prone to skips when not operated correctly.

Liquid fertilizer applied with a gun nozzle is attractive because a skilled operator can "paint" directly to the edge of a lawn without any overthrow (Figure 9-14). Unfortunately, it is difficult to apply slow-release products with this system, and it also precludes using natural granular products.

(a)

(b)

Figure 9-12 (a) Rotary spreaders tend to throw fertilizer on beds, sidewalks, parking lots, and roads, resulting in (b) fertilizer prills scattered on impervious surfaces.

Using blowers to remove fertilizer from roadways and parking lots is commonly done but is often ineffective because curbs simply guide fertilizer into storm sewers. Another strategy involves collecting overthrow material with a vacuum. This, too, sort of solves the problem but requires more equipment and more time. The sustainable alternative to avoid the overthrow problem is to use the proper equipment and fertilizer.

Figure 9-13 Drop spreaders can apply fertilizer right up to the edge of the sidewalk, parking lot, or road, without spreading fertilizer on impervious surfaces.

Figure 9-14 Liquid fertilizers allow applicators to "paint" right to the line without any overthrow. In this case, the technician had to spray around the front ends of several parked cars, resulting in yellow grass where no fertilizer was applied.

SUSTAINABLE FERTILIZATION TIPS

Strategiès for making fertilization programs more sustainable include the following:

- Avoid designing lawns for awkward areas such as narrow median strips or along waterways.
- For new lawns, select grasses or grass-dicot mixtures with low fertility requirements.
- For existing lawns, find ways to reduce nitrogen fertilizer applications such as altering aesthetic expectations; returning clippings; using slow-release nitrogen (synthetic or natural); and prioritizing areas as high-, medium-, or low-nitrogen sites.
- Apply fertilizers at the lowest effective rate per application and target applications seasonally at times when grasses are most responsive.
- Use consistent periodic soil tests to monitor and guide applications of phosphorus and potassium and to determine liming or acidification needs. Avoid indiscriminate use of products with high phosphorus and potassium levels (e.g., 16-16-16).
- Develop application procedures that do not throw fertilizer directly into roadways or waterways and remove fertilizer that accidentally finds its way into these areas.
- Avoid applying fertilizer prior to forecasted heavy rainfall events.

SUMMARY

A sustainable lawn begins with selection of the most appropriate grass or grass-dicot mixture for the specific location in the landscape, with an emphasis on cultivars that have slower growth rates, lower nutrient requirements, and superior drought tolerance. In order to better contribute to sustainable landscapes, grass breeders need to focus on grasses with sustainable qualities suitable for low-input situations (not just on those that are darker green and exhibit a finer texture). Lawn areas should include a range of lawn types from intensively maintained areas to intermediate maintenance and, finally, to areas mowed only two or three times per year. Maintenance contractors should develop strategies that reduce regular removal of clippings from lawns and discourage calendar approaches to fertilization and irrigation. By using regular soil testing, nutrients can be applied more efficiently. Traditional problems with irrigation systems can be solved with an improved effort in design, system maintenance, and irrigation decision making. Mowing technology needs to continue moving toward mulching and improved clipping dispersal and away from clipping harvesting systems as this will largely eliminate the waste stream and significantly reduce fertilizer needs.

STUDY QUESTIONS

1. What qualities determine the sustainability of a given grass?
2. What grasses would be the best choice for sustainable lawns in the following cities?
   a. Seattle, Washington
   b. Washington, DC
   c. Tuscaloosa, Alabama
   d. Berlin, Germany
   e. Rome, Italy
   f. Tokyo, Japan
   g. Christchurch, New Zealand
3. How have grass breeders made grasses more sustainable?
4. From a sustainable perspective, what are the advantages of mixing broadleaf plants with lawn grasses?
5. What is wrong with the common advice, "Mow all lawns at least 3 inches (7.5 cm) high"?
6. What is an acceptable height for each of the following grasses?
   a. Tall fescue
   b. Saint Augustinegrass

   c. Strong creeping red fescue
   d. Colonial bentgrass
7. In commercial mowing, does it make sense to mow frequently enough so you never remove more than one-third of the total grass height? Explain.
8. Why do landscape maintenance companies commonly not use mulching rotary mowers to manage lawn clippings? Are there problems with the mowers?
9. Lawns are often accused of being "water hogs." Do lawns really require as much water as the public imagines? Explain.
10. What role does site design play in problems associated with irrigating lawns?
11. Explain a sustainable approach to developing an irrigation plan for a commercial landscape with green lawns and healthy bed plantings.
12. Explain what will happen to a lawn located in each of the following cities if it is not irrigated:
    a. London, England
    b. Salt Lake City, Utah
    c. Orlando, Florida
    d. Sydney, Australia
13. How would soil testing help to devise a fertilizer strategy for lawns at a commercial site? What can be learned from soil tests to guide a determination of how much nitrogen to apply each year?
14. What problems are associated with using rotary fertilizer spreaders?
15. What are the major differences between conventional lawn care and sustainable lawn care?

chapter 10

Sustainable Pest Management

INTRODUCTION

The goal of sustainable pest management is to minimize the need for pesticides in the landscape, thereby reducing their use. Research shows significant reductions in pesticide use when managers initiate well-planned integrated pest management (IPM) programs (Funk 1988; Holmes and Davidson 1984; Raupp, Koehler, and Davidson 1994; Raupp and Noland 1984; Schultz and Sivyer 2006). In some cases, pesticide use has been completely eliminated.

This chapter will discuss the following:

- Definition of integrated pest management
- Components of integrated pest management
- Insect control strategies
- Disease control strategies
- Weed control strategies

DEFINITION OF INTEGRATED PEST MANAGEMENT

The U.S. Environmental Protection Agency defines IPM as follows:

> Integrated Pest Management (IPM) is an effective and environmentally sensitive approach to pest management that relies on a combination of common-sense practices. IPM programs use current, comprehensive information on the life cycles of pests and their interaction with the environment. This information, in combination with available pest control methods, is used to manage pest damage by the most economical means, and with the least possible hazard to people, property, and the environment.

Key elements in this definition include common sense, knowledge, economy, and safety. Common sense implies that managers will use good judgment and avoid routine pesticide applications. Knowledge of pests and the local environment enable managers to avoid unnecessary pesticide treatments and to properly time treatments when needed. Economy means eliminating needless treatments and minimizing the number of applications. Safety starts with selecting the least environmentally toxic products and making thoughtful decisions about timing to minimize exposure of wildlife and humans. Integrated together, they provide a highly effective approach to sustainable pest management.

COMPONENTS OF INTEGRATED PEST MANAGEMENT

This section will focus on the specific components of IPM and how they are applied in the landscape:

Preconstruction planning

Analysis of existing landscapes

Key plants and key pests

Developing action thresholds

Selecting resistant plants

Preconstruction Planning

Ideally, a great deal of effort goes into plant selection for new landscapes. After preliminary designs and plant selection, a detailed horticultural review should determine what diseases and insect pests are likely to affect the plant choices or placement at the intended site. For example, in climates where tulip poplar (*Liriodendron tulipifera*) trees are consistently attacked by tulip tree aphids (*Illinoia liriodendri*), placement of the trees within the landscape becomes a major consideration. Planting away from sidewalks or as part of a mixed grouping of background plants may allow site managers to ignore the problem. If the tree is placed in a key spot by the front entrance of a building, it will very likely have to be treated regularly to control the aphids.

Often the best information on potential problem plants is found from local sources, including landscape maintenance contractors and spray services. Additional information can be found on-line and in pathology and entomology textbooks. Unfortunately, ornamental plant books rarely offer much detailed information on pests, and what little information they do include is often generic and doesn't include lists of resistant cultivars (Dirr 1997; Grant and Grant 1990). To date, priorities for selecting plants for landscapes have tended toward size, flower color, foliage, and fall color. In sustainable landscapes, resistance to pests will be an important part of the selection process. As part of a sustainable design process, landscape designers should submit a "pest analysis impact statement" with each design to demonstrate that they have selected resistant plants when possible and have justified the use of pest-prone plants. The combination of poor soils, compaction, and thoughtless plant selection increases plant health problems later and predisposes plants to pests.

Analysis of Existing Landscapes

In working with existing sites, the first step in developing an IPM plan is to identify unhealthy planting situations. The designer should look for red flags such as shrubs in wet soils, trees in severe locations, or lawns in deep shade (Color Plate 10-1). Recommendations should be made to change plants, eliminate problem lawns, improve drainage, or aerate soils to give plantings a fighting chance to grow in a healthy environment. Often there is a tendency to accept the status quo and find ways to nurse plantings along with fungicides and insecticides rather than address the fundamental causes of the problems.

Key Plants and Key Pests

From a pest management perspective, key plants are those most prone to insect or disease problems that diminish their value in the landscape. In other words, they are the plants that need regular monitoring. An effective IPM program focuses on key plants to streamline monitoring activities.

Raupp et al. (1985) studied plant pest problems in the Mid-Atlantic region of the United States. This study concluded that the same plants experienced the majority of pest problems at a wide range of locations. They also identified many plants common throughout the study area that exhibited very few pest problems. They identified crab apple (*Malus* spp.), firethorn (*Pyracantha* spp.), dogwood (*Cornus* spp.), cherry (*Prunus* spp.), and rose (*Rosa* spp.) as the most problem-prone plants. Viburnum (*Viburnum* spp.), yew (*Taxus* spp.), arborvitae (*Thuja* spp.), holly (*Ilex* spp.), and forsythia (*Forsythia* spp.)

were never found among the problem-prone plants. Their study emphasized the need to re-evaluate plant choices to consciously avoid planting problem-prone plants. Because every climate zone has its own unique pests, expect to find different problem plants in different zones. Plants that are trouble-free in one climate may be major problem plants in another.

The key plant/key pest concept is important because there are a modest number of problem plants and a modest number of important pests found in any given landscape. Raupp, Koehler, and Davidson (1994) concluded that while there is a large diversity of potential pests, a relative few are responsible for most of the damage. In an earlier report by Raupp and Noland (1984), the 10 most common insect and mite pests of trees and shrubs in community landscapes in Maryland accounted for 83 percent of the pest activity out of 913 identified potential pests. In a college campus setting, they found notable differences in plant composition compared to home landscapes. In the college setting with a different group of pests, the top 10 insect and mite pests were responsible for 97 percent of the total pest activity out of a total of 1262 identified potential pests. Identifying key plants and key pests is critical in developing an effective IPM program.

Monitoring

Knowing key plants and key pests in a landscape allows development of a monitoring plan. Regular monitoring is what drives IPM. Monitoring helps determine whether pests are present and whether damage is significant enough to warrant treatment.

In its simplest form, monitoring involves visual inspection of plants for signs of pests or pest damage. This may involve looking at plants from a distance, carefully examining leaves, or counting affected shoots. Quantifying the number of pests or the extent of damage helps determine if damage is increasing to the point where control measures are needed to prevent unacceptable injury. Monitoring normally starts in spring as growth begins. Inspections every two weeks are often adequate to determine what is present and how much damage is occurring (Raupp 1985). It is important to build monitoring schedules around expected pests so that the stages of development can be observed in a timely manner. An important part of monitoring involves keeping accurate records and developing an effective database for each landscape to help make decisions. Keeping records from previous years allows fine-tuning of critical monitoring methods and dates.

Speed is essential if monitoring is going to be economically feasible. IPM practitioners have become very savvy and have learned through experience how to work fast and still see important changes. Knowledge of pest life cycles, critical life stages, and practical thresholds has facilitated cost-effective monitoring. Familiarity with a given site also speeds up the process as practitioners know just where to look and when.

More sophisticated monitoring techniques are available when needed. Insect pheromone traps with sticky paper attract insects and allow landscape managers to track the movement of adults of important insects like gypsy moth (*Lymantria dispar*) and Japanese beetle (*Popillia japonica* Newman). Traps also allow quantification of beneficial insect predators (Raupp 1985).

Another method of monitoring is using degree-day models, which predict insect life stages based on accumulated temperature degree-days. With practice, degree-day calculations can be made fairly easily and can become another tool for gauging what pests to look for and when (see the suggested reading at the end of this chapter).

Developing Action Thresholds

Monitoring quantifies how many leaf spots are present or the number of insect larvae attacking leaves or stems, but that alone does not help with decisions on whether or not action is required. Action thresholds are the standards that inform landscape managers either to do nothing or to start treatment.

CASE STUDY

Developing a Monitoring System and Thresholds for European Crane Fly in Lawns

European crane fly (*Tipula paludosa* Meigen) is native to Europe and was first reported in eastern North America in 1952. By 1965, it was discovered on the other side of the continent in lower British Columbia. From there, it moved steadily south and currently extends along the Pacific Coast as far south as northern California. Early reports indicated that the larvae of this insect could cause severe damage to lawns, gardens, and pastures.

The first step in developing an IPM monitoring plan for European crane fly requires knowledge of its life cycle. With one generation per year, most adults emerge from late August through early October. Adults mate shortly after hatching (Color Plate 10-2), and females lay eggs in the thatch and soil during September and October (Color Plate 10-3). Eggs generally hatch from September through mid-October. The larvae molt to the third instar by late November (Color Plate 10-4). Larvae overwinter no deeper than 3 inches (7.5 cm) from the soil surface and feed on roots and shoots through the winter and spring periods before molting to the fourth instar by late April or early May (Color Plate 10-5). Pupae form in August, and the cycle is complete.

The third instar causes damage due to its voracious feeding during winter and spring. The fourth instar does not feed much and causes no apparent damage. Adults do not feed during their short life and cause no damage to lawns. Often the only sign of larval damage is turf thinning, which generally shows up from February to early April in most years (Color Plate 10-6). In severe outbreaks, the entire lawn will be destroyed, but in most cases slight to moderate thinning is more common.

When crane fly first moved into the region, damage was often severe, and the general reaction was to spray insecticides as soon as adults were observed. Some sprayed in early fall, late fall, and again in spring. The need for a better control plan was obvious.

Because damage rarely is seen before early spring, monitoring starts around January 1, with sampling occurring at two-week intervals through March, if needed. Sampling involves removing three or more cores 4 to 6 inches (10 to 15 cm) in diameter and 3 inches (7.5 cm) deep. The cores are broken up by hand, and third instar larvae are counted. If no larvae are observed after several consecutive tries, sampling can be discontinued. Empirical observations indicated that lawns that were healthy in fall could handle 25 to 50 larvae per square foot (1000 cm^2) of turf without showing signs of injury. In some cases, larval populations as high as 75 per square foott (1000 cm^2) caused no visible damage. A practical threshold of 25 to 50 larvae per square foot (1000 cm^2) plus visual signs of 10 to 20 percent thinning before deciding to treat with insecticides was established.

Developing a monitoring program and establishing an action threshold revealed several important points:

1. Adult populations are no indication of potential larval activity.
2. Fewer than 1 in 100 lawns are likely to have crane fly populations high enough to cause turf injury.
3. Most damage occurs on lawns where no monitoring was done.
4. Most of the winter and spring lawn damage has nothing to do with crane fly activity.
5. Crane fly damage becomes less frequent and more sporadic within a few years after the first infestations, perhaps due to the buildup of natural predators.

In agriculture, thresholds are based on pest impact on crop production. It is largely economic factors that establish thresholds and defend decisions whether or not to treat a crop. The problem with action thresholds for making treatment decisions in constructed landscapes is that most decisions are based on aesthetic injury. For some, the mere presence of insects or leaf spots demands action. For others, 20 percent foliar damage is no cause for alarm. In other cases where damage is apparent only after the pest is gone, preventive treatment may be the only viable option short of removing the injury-prone plant from the landscape.

Raupp, Koehler, and Davidson (1994) reviewed numerous studies in which researchers attempted to quantify relationships between aesthetic perceptions and insect-related plant injury. In most studies, the action threshold for aesthetic injury was around 10 percent based on visual appearance. In an IPM context, the challenge is to determine what level of insect or disease activity causes 10 percent aesthetic injury.

Selecting Resistant Plants

It is not likely that resistant plants will solve all pest problems, but the advantages of selecting resistant plants should be obvious. Breeders currently pay much more attention to disease resistance, and their efforts are paying off with both disease-resistant and insect-resistant cultivars. Along with these new plants, existing plants that are already resistant to many landscape pests provide designers many choices to deal with common pests. For example, while there are many ways of dealing with dogwood anthracnose (*Discula* spp.) (chemically and culturally), the easiest way involves switching from susceptible flowering dogwood (*Cornus florida*) to more resistant Kousa dogwood (*Cornus kousa*) (Brown, Windham, and Trigiano 1996). In addition, Kousa dogwood is a tougher plant, able to handle more extreme environmental conditions than flowering dogwood.

A review of woody landscape plants susceptible to Japanese beetle (*Popillia japonica* Newman) defoliation yielded a list of resistant and susceptible plant species. Resistance among species of maple (*Acer* spp.) and birch (*Betula* spp.) and among cultivars of crab apple (*Malus* spp.), crape myrtle (*Lagerstroemia* spp.), and linden (*Tilia* spp.) was also observed (Held 2004). Rose (*Rosa* spp.) showed no resistance at all (Potter and Held 2002). The most sustainable method of dealing with damage from Japanese beetle was by selecting resistant plants (Held 2004).

Disease-resistant lawn grasses have been developed through selection and breeding work. Notable examples are resistance to leaf spot diseases (*Drechslera* spp.), rust (*Puccinia* spp.), and, more recently, gray leaf spot (*Pyricularia grisea*). Current resistance ratings for newer cultivars can be gleaned from variety trials conducted at research stations worldwide. In the United States, data is available from the National Turfgrass Evaluation Program at www.ntep.org.

There are limitations to using resistant plants in landscape settings. Because most landscape plants are long-lived perennials, it is possible that plants currently considered pest resistant will eventually succumb to new or imported pest problems. Dutch elm disease (*Ophiostoma ulmi*) on American elm (*Ulmus americana*) and emerald ash borer (*Agrilus planipennis*) on many tree species are examples of pests introduced into the United States from other countries. These pests have caused widespread destruction as they have moved across the continent. In spite of this problem, it makes sense to select resistant plants when the opportunity arises.

INSECT CONTROL STRATEGIES

Monitoring indicates whether pests are present, and action thresholds indicate what, if anything, needs to be done. The next critical step is developing a control strategy. Control tactics take many forms, including doing nothing, removing problem plants, installing resistant plants, applying biological control options, and treating with synthetic pesticides.

Biological Insect Control Options

Biological control of insects involves suppression of pest populations by living organisms or their by-products (Vittum, Villani, and Tashiro 1999). In nature, there is essentially a balance between competing organisms so that pest species may be held in check by the activity of vertebrate and invertebrate predators, various parasitoids, and microbial pathogens (Vittum, Villani, and Tashiro 1999). If pest species are introduced into a situation where none of the normal biological control species are present, an epidemic is likely to occur. Biological control depends on appropriate species of antagonists that attack pest organisms. There are three basic strategies used in biological control: introduction, augmentation, and conservation.

1. *Introduction.* In this case, natural enemies of pests are introduced into the area where the new pest is with the hope that they will become established and effectively check the spread of the introduced pest. This approach may work if the introduced control species thrives in the new surroundings.
2. *Augmentation.* Importing artificially reared predators to bolster those already present is another means of biological control. Releasing lady beetles to combat aphids or introducing entomopathogenic nematodes for controlling root weevils are examples of augmentation. Because there is no guarantee that the predators will establish (or stay where they are released), this strategy may amount to a short-term solution.
3. *Conservation.* In a healthy environment, beneficial organisms thrive and perform their normal control activities, which keep pest populations in check. By developing a healthy environment through cultural practices that keep soils aerated, maintain healthy soil pH, and minimize the input of broad-spectrum toxins that might kill beneficial organisms, strong populations of natural enemies can be maintained. Diverse plantings, which are common in many landscapes, often support an extensive array of beneficial organisms and facilitate natural control.

Currently, a number of biological control measures are available for landscape pest management. These controls can be categorized as predators, parasitoids, microbials, nematodes, endophytes, pheromones, insect growth regulators, and botanical insecticides.

Predators

Predators are generally other insects or spiders that eat pest species. As a rule, predator populations build up as pests build up. The implication is that a certain level of pest activity has to precede predator activity. Therefore, owners need to accept some level of pest development if predators are going to have an opportunity to control outbreaks (Figure 10-1). Green lacewings (*Chrysoperla rufilabris*), lady beetles (Figure 10-2), and assassin bugs (Figure 10-3) are examples of predators that control aphids on a wide range of woody and herbaceous plants. Where a broad range of predators are present on-site, the best strategy is conservation. If long-term application of nonselective insecticides has occurred, then augmentation may be required to re-establish populations. If a new pest is present, introduction may be necessary (Mizell and Hagan 2000).

Parasitoids

Parasitoids are insects that kill pest insects by laying eggs on or in the host. After hatching, these parasitoids eat internally or externally, ultimately killing the pest insect. Parasitoids are often specific in attacking hosts at the genus and species levels and at specific life stages. Parasitoid insects as a group

Figure 10-1 In order for predators to do their job, there have to be enough pests to provide a food source. These roses have a healthy population of aphids that will fuel predator activity.

Figure 10-3 Assassin bug adults are very active aphid predators.

help control a wide range of pest species. Three parasitoids collected in Asia have been introduced in the United States for control of the emerald ash borer (*Agrilus planipennis*). This is an example of the introduction of natural enemies to combat an introduced pest.

Microbials

Microbial insecticides include fungi, bacteria, rickettsias, viruses, and protozoans. Spinosad is a natural by-product of bacterial fermentation that is used as a microbial insecticide. The following discussion will focus on fungi, bacteria, and spinosad.

(a)

(b)

Figure 10-2 (a) Lady beetle adults feed on aphids. (b) Lady beetle larvae are even more aggressive aphid predators.

Fungi useful in insect control have been used for some time. For instance, *Beauveria bassiana* has been used in Asia for insect control and is currently registered for use on turf and ornamentals in the United States. Insects controlled by this fungus include aphids, caterpillars, mealybugs, mites, and weevils. As a naturally occurring soil fungus, it has also been associated with natural control of chinch bugs in lawns in the United States. Another fungus, *Metarhizium anisopliae*, has been used for insect control in South America and has shown promise for control of Japanese beetle (*Popillia japonica* Newman) and black vine weevil (*Otiorhynchus sulcatus*). It is currently registered only for termite control in the United States.

Bacteria are a mainstay of biological insect control. Several strains of *Bacillus thuringiensis* (commonly known as *Bt*) have been developed for specific insect pests. There are many subspecies and varieties of this bacterium, all of which produce toxic protein crystals. The most common commercial *Bt*s are *Bt kurstaki* and *Bt aizawai* for caterpillar control, *Bt israelensis* for mosquitoes, and *Bt tenebrionis* for leaf beetles (Vittum, Villani, and Tashiro 1999). Once ingested by susceptible insects, the protein crystals dissolve in the gut and ultimately cause paralysis. Host insects die within a few days. *Bt* offers no residual control and is widely used as a targeted application for short-term control. It has been effective for gypsy moth (*Lymantria dispar*) control.

Another bacterium, *Bacillus popilliae*, causes milky spore disease in Japanese beetle (*Popillia japonica* Newman) grubs. Once ingested, spores germinate in the gut of larvae and multiply and sporulate. The massive buildup of bacterial spores effectively fills the inner cavity of the grubs and results in a slow death. As good as it seems, *B. popilliae* does not have an impressive track record as a targeted control application for Japanese beetle. It does appear to serve a purpose in general population suppression rather than as a biological insecticide (Klein 1995). There is also evidence of host resistance to this bacterial pathogen, which may account for observed decreases in pathogenesis over time (Redmond and Potter 1995).

Spinosad is a relatively new material composed of two complex organic molecules synthesized by soil bacteria. Once ingested, it causes hyperactivity of the nervous system, which ultimately leads to the death of target insects. It controls a broad range of insects, has minimal impact on beneficial organisms, and has very low toxicity. It has low residual activity and may require repeat applications during the growing season.

Nematodes

Entomopathogenic nematodes are small round worms that attack a wide variety of insect pests. *Steinernema* and *Heterorhabditis* are the only genera currently used for insect control in landscape situations. Between them, seven species are registered for specific insect pests and are available for sale in Europe, Japan, China, and the United States. These nematodes carry pathogenic bacteria that multiply and produce toxins once introduced into target insects.

Successful control of pest insects with nematodes has been somewhat elusive. Applicators need to obtain the correct species, avoid nematode exposure to sunlight, apply to moist soil, avoid application to saturated soils, and apply at the optimum temperature range for the specific nematode. Nematodes cannot tolerate drying, cannot be stored for long periods, and will not survive under high-temperature storage conditions. Low-pressure application equipment is necessary to ensure nematode survival. The best times for applications are early in the morning or late in the evening.

Endophytes

The discovery of endophytic fungi (*Neotyphodium* spp. and *Epichloe festucae*) associated with perennial ryegrass (*Lolium perenne*), fine fescues (*Festuca* spp.), and tall fescue (*Schedonorus arundinaceus* (Schreb.) Dumort.) has had a significant impact on the control of several common turfgrass insect pests, including billbug (*Sphenophorous* spp.), hairy chinch bug (*Blissus leucopterus hirtus*), sod webworm (various species), fall armyworm (*Spodoptera frugiperda*), and greenbugs (*Schizaphis graminum*). Endophytic fungi colonize shoots and crowns but not roots and confer insect resistance to grasses by producing alkaloids. Alkaloids can kill foliar-feeding insects directly or act as feeding deterrents. Root-feeding grubs are not affected by endophytic fungi. Numerous cultivars of turfgrass have been bred to contain endophytes. Unfortunately, some of the most common cool-season grasses like Kentucky bluegrass (*Poa pratensis*) and bentgrass (*Agrostis* spp.) do not develop endophytic associations. Endophytes have not been documented in warm-season grasses.

Endophytes are transmitted by seed so application is as simple as planting a lawn. The main caveat is that endophyte viability decreases the longer seed is stored, particularly if seed is subjected to high temperatures. Only fresh seed of known endophyte content should be used to ensure high levels of infection.

Pheromones

Pheromones are chemicals released by insects that attract nearby insects of the same species. Historically, pheromones have been used for monitoring purposes by drawing adults to traps where they adhere to sticky paper. This is the most successful use of pheromones.

Attempts to use pheromones for mass trapping to control Japanese beetle failed to prevent defoliation of nearby ornamental plants (Gordon and Potter 1985). In fact, in this trial as trap density increased, the rate of defoliation also increased. The traps simply attracted more beetles to the site and increased the number of beetles that found the plants. Using pheromones for mating disruption is most likely to be effective when pest populations are low and the chance for immigration from surrounding areas is low (Vittum, Villani, and Tashiro 1999).

Insect Growth Regulators

Insect growth regulators (IGRs) include natural and synthetic chemicals that interfere with molting of insect larvae from one instar to another. In some cases, IGRs stimulate the molting process, and in others, they retard the process. Activity and insect death are slow compared to other insecticides. In lawns IGRs have shown activity against scarab beetle larvae, cutworms, and sod webworms. They are most effective when applied at times when larvae are actively feeding. Younger larvae are more sensitive than larger, more mature larvae.

Botanical Insecticides

Botanical insecticides encompass numerous chemicals derived from plants. While they are natural products, they range in toxicity to mammals from practically benign to extremely lethal. For example, rotenone is a carcinogen, and nicotine is highly poisonous if inhaled. Currently available botanical insecticides for use on turf and ornamentals include neem oil, citrus and other essential oils, and pyrethrum. Oils kill on contact and have short residuals. Neem acts as an insect growth regulator, deters feeding, and displays several other minor insecticidal properties. Neem also exhibits fungicidal properties on ornamental plants.

Control Options with Synthetic Insecticides

Synthetic insecticides are mostly organic compounds developed specifically for insect control. Early products include chlorinated hydrocarbons (e.g., DDT and related compounds), organophosphates (e.g., diazinon and chlorpyrifos), and carbamates (e.g., carbaryl). More recently, synthetic pyrethroids have become widely used for insect control. Current efforts are moving toward new classes of compounds that have fewer environmental and toxicological consequences for mammals and nontarget organisms. Because pesticide regulations vary from country to country, it is difficult to produce a concise guide to selection and use of these chemicals. This discussion will be limited to chemistries that show promise as lower-risk chemicals for use in sustainable landscape pest management, including horticultural oils, soaps, sugar esters, and neonicotinoids.

Horticultural Oils

Horticultural oil is the name for a variety of widely used petroleum- and plant-derived oils. These include dormant oils, supreme oils, and superior oils, all of which are highly refined to reduce the potential for phytotoxicity (foliage damage). These oils have been developed to the point where there is little difference between them. Horticultural oils kill insects and eggs primarily by smothering them and causing asphyxiation. Applied in the dormant season to deciduous woody plants, they are very effective in killing overwintering eggs of aphids and caterpillars. Applied during the summer, they are effective on many different insects, including aphids, scales, and mites. They have limited impact on the environment when used according to the label.

Soaps

Soaps are salts of fatty acids and can be derived from plants or animals. They have been formulated to be nonphytotoxic when used as directed. Soaps act as contact killers of soft-bodied insects such as aphids and larvae. They are "knock down" products with no residual activity and may have to be applied frequently. They are environmentally benign and have little impact on most beneficial insects.

Sugar Esters

Sugar esters are a relatively new class of insecticide, produced by reacting sugars with fatty acids. They kill insects by suffocation and disrupting the insect cuticle and causing dehydration. There is no indication that they injure beneficial organisms. As a food grade material, they pose no threat to humans. Currently registered products are effective against adelgids, aphids, scale insects, and thrips.

Neonicotinoids

This group of synthetic insecticides has been used worldwide for a variety of insect problems, including aphids, scales, leaf beetles, lace bugs, some borers, and adelgids. Neonicotinoids are systemic in plants and have a long residual period of activity. For example the neonicotinoid imidacloprid reduced defoliation by Japanese beetle for up to two years (Frank, Ahern, and Raupp 2007). These compounds have lower mammalian toxicity than older products.

DISEASE CONTROL STRATEGIES

The conventional approach to disease control in plants involves using registered synthetic fungicides alone or in rotation. These materials are applied for curative control after disease is present or preventively for diseases that are difficult to control after they appear. It is an effective way to control diseases in landscapes.

Fungicides can be contact, locally systemic, or systemic. Contact fungicides tend to have multiple modes of action, have short residual activity, and are most effective when applied frequently. Systemic products typically have only one mode of action, have longer residual activity, and can be applied less often. A detailed listing of fungicides for use in landscape settings can be found at http://plant-disease.ippc.orst.edu/articles.cfm?article_id=13.

In situations where fungicides are used repeatedly, there is always the potential for the development of resistant fungi. Understanding fungicide classes and the potential for resistance buildup is important for achieving consistently good disease control. Rotating fungicide classes and using mixtures of different types of fungicides to avoid the potential development of resistance is the standard recommendation of pest control advisers. To better understand the resistance problem, see a detailed discussion at http://plant-disease.ippc.orst.edu/articles.cfm?article_id=22.

The sustainable approach to disease control starts with the selection of resistant plants, optimal placement of plants, and intelligent maintenance. The final step involves using fungicides of natural origin or those with the least toxic characteristics. Only a few environmentally innocuous products are available, including sulfur, several copper products, kaolin clay, potassium bicarbonate, and neem oil.

Natural-origin fungicides are best used at 7- to 14-day intervals throughout the disease season for preventive control and weekly for curative control. Reports are variable regarding success depending on local environmental conditions and the severity of disease pressure. Thorough spray coverage is needed with these products. Conventional fungicides often allow intervals of 21 to 28 days between applications, which fits more easily into scheduling cycles. Simply substituting natural products for synthetic products does not address the real problem of failing to initially select resistant plants.

WEED CONTROL STRATEGIES

Weed scenarios can be divided into three basic categories: tree, shrub, and flower bed weeds; cool-season lawn weeds; and warm-season lawn weeds. Since the development of modern synthetic herbicides, chemical control of weeds has become standard for commercial landscapes.

The means by which weeds colonize beds and lawns and conventional chemical strategies will be presented first, followed by alternative methods of weed control. Emphasis will focus on methods that minimize herbicide use while maintaining acceptable aesthetic quality.

Weed Encroachment in Landscape Beds

Weed problems in beds arise from weeds imported with soil used in constructing the beds; lack of plant cover due to planting design, pruning, or attrition; and weeds deposited in bed areas by natural means (birds, squirrels, wind, container plants, etc.). Dealing with weeds is ultimately an ongoing process for any given landscape. Weeds can be minimized and managed but never completely eradicated.

Imported soil is often topsoil associated with gravel mining operations, which is usually sandy or loam-type soils. In addition to carrying a full complement of annual weed seeds, these soils may contain perennial weeds such as horsetail (*Equisetum* spp.), quackgrass [*Elymus repens* (L.) Gould], torpedograss (*Panicum repens*), sedges (*Cyperus* spp.), or thistles (*Cirsium* spp.). All of these weeds can be difficult to control after beds are planted (Figure 10-4).

Many landscape beds have sparsely arranged shrubs in a sea of bark or other mulch material. This is an invitation for weeds to move in and colonize the area. As mulch ages and partially decomposes, it provides an ideal environment for weeds to germinate and grow. By design, a never-ending weed management problem has been created. A related problem arises when beds are planted with poorly adapted species that die out and leave large open areas where weed seeds can germinate freely (Figure 10-5). Finally, pruning practices that isolate individual plants or

Figure 10-4 Soil imported during landscape construction often contains horsetail (*Equisetum* spp.) plant fragments that develop into serious weed problems as in this photo.

(a)

(b)

Figure 10-5 (a) The original ground cover in this high-traffic area died, leaving bare ground. (b) The native plants in this bed died because they were not adapted to the exposed site, leaving a large mulch bed.

remove all lower foliage create open surfaces, which are likely to be invaded by weeds (Figure 10-6).

Other unwanted and undesirable plant material arrives from birds, squirrels, and other animals that can deposit seeds from nut and fleshy fruited trees and shrubs (Table 10-1). Windborne seeds add to the colonization of beds with unintended plants. Some weeds arrive with the plant material: wood sorrel (*Oxalis* spp.), mouse-ear chickweed (*Cerastium vulgatum*), and pearlwort (*Sagina procumbens*) are examples of weeds introduced with container planting stock. Self-seeding herbaceous ornamental plants, such as fountain grass (*Pennisetum* spp.) and blue fescue (*Festuca glauca*), also contribute to weeds in beds.

(a)

(b)

Figure 10-6 (a) These rhododendrons (*Rhododendron* spp.) have dense foliage from top to bottom that reduces weed encroachment and the need for herbicides. (b) These rhododendrons (*Rhododendron* spp.) were pruned into small tree forms, which opened up the bed surface to weed invasion, increasing the need for herbicides.

TABLE 10-1 Weeds Introduced by Animals and Wind into a Cool Temperate Marine Climate Garden

Common Name	Scientific Name
Alder	*Alnus* spp.
Barberry	*Berberis* spp.
Blackberry	*Rubus* spp.
Camellia	*Camellia* spp.
Coast redwood	*Sequoia sempervirens*
Cotoneaster	*Cotoneaster* spp.
Cottonwood	*Populus* spp.
Douglas fir	*Pseudotsuga menziesii*
English ivy	*Hedera* spp.
Hawthorn	*Crataegus* spp.
Hazelnut	*Corylus* spp.
Hibiscus; Rose of Sharon	*Hibiscus syriacus*
Holly	*Ilex* spp.
Laurel	*Prunus* spp.
Maple	*Acer* spp.
Oak	*Quercus* spp.
Port Orford cedar	*Chamaecyparis lawsoniana*
Pyracantha	*Pyracantha* spp.
Sweet gum	*Liquidambar styraciflua*
Black walnut	*Juglans nigra*

Conventional Weed Control Strategies in Landscape Beds

With so much weed encroachment from a variety of sources, it is easy to see how herbicides become the tool of choice to solve the problem in commercial landscapes. The most common products include pre-emergent herbicides and nonselective postemergent herbicides. Target weeds may be summer annuals, winter annuals, biennials, or perennials. Some common herbicides intended for use in landscape beds are listed in Table 10-2.

TABLE 10-2 Selected Pre-emergent Herbicides Registered for Professional Use for Shrub Bed Weed Control in the United States*

Common Name†	Target Plants
Benefin	Annual grasses and some dicots
Benefin + oryzalin	Annual grasses and annual and perennial dicots
DCPA	Annual grasses and some dicots
Dichlobenil	Annual grasses and annual and perennial dicots
Dithiopyr	Annual grasses and some dicots
Imazaquin	Annual grasses and some dicots
Isoxaben	Annual and perennial dicots
Isoxaben + trifluralin	Annual grasses and annual and perennial dicots
Metolachlor	Annual grasses and some dicots
Metolachlor + simazine	Annual grasses and some dicots
Napropamide	Annual grasses and annual and perennial dicots
Napropamide + oxadiazon	Annual grasses and some dicots
Oryzalin	Annual and perennial dicots
Oxadiazon	Annual and perennial dicots
Oxadiazon + prodiamine	Annual grasses and some dicots
Pendimethalin	Annual grasses and some dicots
Prodiamine	Annual grasses and some dicots
Simazine	Cool-season grasses and dicots

*Herbicide availability varies significantly in different countries. These examples are for the United States only.

†Read labels carefully as plant tolerance varies significantly by species.

The following five guidelines should be considered when attempting to achieve effective weed control in beds:

1. *Select herbicides appropriate for specific weeds.* Even the most versatile herbicides cannot control all weeds. Start by identifying

weeds and then research chemicals to find the most effective and least toxic products for specific site problems.

2. *Apply at appropriate times.* Pre-emergent herbicides prevent germination. If applied after weeds have emerged, many will have no effect. Difficult-to-kill perennial weeds are often more susceptible to nonselective herbicides at early flower stages. Other perennials are easier to kill in the fall than during the spring and summer. Understanding weed characteristics is important to obtain good control.
3. *Rely on multiple strategies.* Use nonselective directed sprays to kill existing vegetation, followed by pre-emergent herbicides to prevent new weeds. In some cases, removing weeds by hand first is a more efficient method for getting weeds under control before applying herbicides. Follow pre-emergent herbicide treatments with mulch applications to improve control.
4. *Think long term.* When dealing with existing weed problems, realize that it may take more than one growing season to get things under control. Success can only be measured over time in terms of weed population reduction. The first year may yield only 50 to 75 percent control, but with continued efforts in the following years, the control percentage will increase. It takes time to break the seed production cycle and to control rhizomatous perennials. The early control cycle will require more effort than long-term maintenance.
5. *Adjust herbicides to account for species shifts.* Some herbicides are very effective on germinating grasses but weak on germinating dicot weeds. Using the same herbicide over a period of years may essentially select for weeds it does not control, eventually rendering the herbicide ineffective. Evaluating the developing weed populations will allow for timely changes as needed. Resources for planning weed control programs with herbicides are given in the suggested reading at the end of this chapter.

The appearance of most commercially maintained landscape beds indicates that a majority of landscape contractors are successful in their quest to control weeds. The problem with chemical weed control is that it becomes habitual and there is a tendency to rely on herbicides exclusively. Excessive use of herbicides is also a result of the way many commercial landscapes are designed with large open areas covered in mulch serving as an open invitation for weeds to invade.

Sustainable Weed Control in Landscape Beds

There are many instances where managers have simply quit using herbicides for weed control, resulting in massive weed invasion (Color Plate 10-7). Reducing herbicide use requires a coordinated approach, including redesigning beds, changing plantings, using hand labor and other mechanical means, using landscape fabrics when appropriate, using deep mulch at key times of the year, skipping noncritical herbicide applications, experimenting with alternative herbicides, using conventional herbicides to get weeds under control when needed, and altering expectations. A multilevel approach with higher or lower standards based on the priority status of specific areas allows for different strategies on the same property.

Bed Design and Plant Compositions

In landscape plantings, shrub beds and tree wells seem to expand slowly over time. As this occurs, the amount of open area increases, which leads to more weeds. An analysis of beds will determine if they need to be made smaller or redesigned. Tree wells can often be reduced dramatically in size and still protect trees from errant lawn mowers. Creating competition by using dense-growing ground covers can help reduce the need for herbicides

Figure 10-7 Dense-growing ground covers reduce the need for herbicides. This stand of (*Pachysandra terminalis*) is thriving on the north side of this office building.

Figure 10-8 Nonwoven needle-punched fabrics prevent the emergence of dicot weeds, but grasses grow right through the loose fiber mesh as shown on the right side in this trial. The weed-free plot on the left has a nonwoven thermally fused fabric.

(Figure 10-7). Ground covers also offer the option of periodic mowing as a means for mechanical weed control.

Hand Weeding and Mechanical Weed Removal

Sometimes the fastest way to achieve complete cover from newly planted ground covers is to hand-weed the first year (particularly in high-profile areas). Doing so will ensure there are no problems with nontarget root stunting from pre-emergent herbicides or foliar injury from postemergent nonselective herbicides. Avoid using scuffle hoes because they disturb the mulch surface and expose soil. Most soils have extensive seed banks, and anything that disturbs the surface will encourage new weeds from seed.

Landscape Fabrics

Landscape fabrics cover the ground and provide a physical barrier that prevents weeds from emerging. Most research shows fabrics are effective at least in the short term for controlling emerging dicots from seed, in preventing the emergence of bulbs such as wild garlic (*Allium* spp.), and in preventing the emergence of rhizomatous perennial dicots like horsetail (*Equisetum* spp.) or Canada thistle [*Cirsium arvense* (L.) Scop.] (Cook 1987; Derr and Appleton 1989) (Figure 10-8).

Landscape fabrics are less effective at controlling weeds in the long term and are associated with several other problems. For instance, if organic mulch is placed over a fabric in spring, weed control through the first summer will probably be excellent. Between fall and spring, seed that has blown in or otherwise found its way to the mulch will germinate and grow in the mulch (Color Plate 10-8). On most products (except laminated fabrics and heavyweight nonwoven bonded fabrics), weed roots will grow through the fabric and into the soil (Color Plate 10-9). The result is a weed problem that will require the use of herbicides or hand weeding every year. The problems continue as tree and shrub roots begin to accumulate beneath the fabric and grow into and through the material, making it almost impossible to remove the fabric at a later date (Appleton and Derr 1990; Appleton, Derr, and Ross 1990).

Fabrics have limited value for long-term weed control in beds due to complications associated with placing organic mulches over them. The best weed control with fabrics comes from heavyweight laminated products and heavyweight fused spun materials.

Weed Control with Mulch

Achieving weed control with mulch requires thoughtful selection of materials. For example, mulches such as fine-textured bark and composts generally fail to provide weed suppression because they are good media for germination and growth. Composted materials often contain significant nitrogen, phosphorus, and potassium, which further stimulate weed growth. Hemlock bark is a poor choice for weed control because it naturally contains nitrogen (Figure 10-9).

Coarser materials such as pine needles, bark nuggets, and coarse wood (cellulose) chips provide reasonably good weed control. The coarse particle size provides a poor environment for germinating seeds. These same mulches have high carbon-to-nitrogen (C/N) ratios, which creates a nitrogen-poor environment that reduces the vigor of seedlings. Rock is generally effective as mulch in the short run with fewer weed encroachment problems than most organic mulches (Color Plate 10-10).

Mulch depth is also important. Coarse mulches applied at a depth of 4 inches (10 cm) may provide good weed suppression for one or more years, depending on local conditions and the irrigation method (overhead irrigation facilitates weed germination). In addition to providing poor initial weed suppression, fine-textured mulches also tend to hold more water than coarser mulches, resulting in a better environment for weed growth.

Figure 10-9 Hemlock bark contains nitrogen and makes a very good seed bed for wind-borne weed seed so it is a poor choice for weed control purposes.

Softwood mulches (conifers) are relatively slow to decompose and may last longer than hardwood mulches (deciduous trees). Coarser-textured organic mulches will also be slower to decompose. Most organic mulch materials require annual to biannual renewal to maintain depth. The effectiveness in controlling weeds decreases as the depth decreases.

Because herbicides are so often used in mulched beds, it often appears like beds are naturally weed-free, which leads to the mistaken conclusion that mulches provide permanent weed control. Other than short-term control (one season or less), mulches alone are not likely to provide weed control by themselves.

Organic mulch may increase or decrease the effectiveness of pre-emergent herbicides. Volatile herbicides like dichlobenil are more active under mulch than on bare soil. Dichlobenil also works well applied on top of mulch. Oxadiazon provides the best weed control when applied to bare soil and is less effective in association with mulch due to inactivation by organic matter (Color Plate 10-11).

Alternative Herbicides for Bed Weed Control

Alternative postemergent herbicides include soaps, acids, and plant oils. All are contact herbicides and do not translocate through the plant. They kill only the plant parts they contact so thorough coverage via high spray volumes is necessary. Research indicates that they are effective in killing small seedlings of annual and perennial weeds. They can burn down foliage on larger plants but generally do not kill them. They are ineffective on mature perennials even though they may cause initial injury to foliage. They are not as effective as glyphosate, which is the industry standard for postemergent, nonselective weed control.

While alternative herbicide products are considered low-risk pesticides and exempt from most toxicology testing, some do pose significant health risks to applicators. Acetic acid herbicides at concentrations of 20 percent have a DANGER signal word due to potential irreversible eye damage, dermal irritation, and inhalation dangers. The active ingredient in clove oil (methyl eugenol) is a suspected carcinogen, and soap products can cause eye injury.

All alternative herbicides have very short half-lives in the environment and are considered unlikely to cause environmental damage. Relative costs per hectare are as much as 30 times greater than that of glyphosate. The best use for contact herbicides involves spot treatment of small annual weeds and use in situations where glyphosate is not an acceptable choice.

Corn gluten meal is a natural pre-emergent herbicide for crabgrass (*Digitaria* spp.) control. Research results with this herbicide have been variable, and additional research is needed to learn more about its potential as an herbicide for use in landscape settings (Christians 1993; Hilgert 2003) (Figure 10-10).

Weed Control in Lawns

Lawns in cool temperate climates are associated with several summer annual weeds (monocots and dicots) and numerous perennial dicot weeds. Perennial grass weeds are present but generally are less important in lawns than in sports turf. Summer annual grasses pose significant problems in some cool temperate climates such as the entire Midwest and New England and the lower midwestern and southeastern parts of Canada.

Figure 10-10 Corn gluten meal applied to bare soil as a pre-emergent herbicide failed to control annual grasses and annual dicots in this trial. Because it contains nitrogen, it stimulated weed growth.

Transition-zone lawns are among the weediest lawns due to the difficult climate and the challenges of maintaining dense grass cover. Warm-season annual grasses pose consistent challenges during summers, and a wide range of dicot weeds (annual and perennial) make weed-free lawns a rarity.

Warm temperate and tropical zones are host to a significant number of weed problems, including annual and perennial grasses and many annual and perennial dicot plants. Weed control in these climates is an ongoing activity.

Conventional Weed Control Strategies for Lawns

The conventional approach to weed control relies heavily on appropriately timed synthetic herbicide applications. If herbicides are used in conjunction with cultural practices designed to produce dense turf, it is possible to produce relatively weed-free lawns using a modest number of herbicide treatments. If lawn culture does not produce dense competitive turf, weeds will be a constant problem.

Dicot weeds in cool-season grass lawns are generally treated with mixtures of two or more herbicides. This yields better weed control with fewer applications. Warm-season grass lawns have a somewhat different palette of broadleaf weed problems, and additional herbicides are recommended for control. In addition, there are notable differences in tolerance of warm-season grasses to common herbicides. Selection and use of selective postemergent broadleaf herbicides on lawns are best based on local recommendations. A detailed study of product labels is required to determine the weed control spectrum and safety of herbicides for specific lawn grasses. Common postemergent broadleaf herbicides and mixtures for dicot control in cool-season grass lawns are presented in Table 10-3, while those for warm-season grass lawns are presented in Table 10-4. Links to

TABLE 10-3 Postemergent Broadleaf Herbicides Registered for Professional Use on Cool-Season Lawns in the United States*

Common Name	Target Plants
Single Chemicals†	
2,4-D	False dandelion *Hypochaeris,* Plantains *Plantago,* Common dandelion *Taraxacum*, etc.
2,4-DP	Similar to 2,4-D
Carfentrazone-ethyl	Bryophytes; enhanced broadleaf control when used in mixtures
Dicamba	Yarrow *Achillea*, Mousear chickweed *Cerastium*, Clovers *Trifolium*, etc.
Fluroxypyr	Yarrow *Achillea*, Mousear chickweed *Cerastium*, Wood sorrel *Oxalis*, Clovers *Trifolium*, Violets *Viola*, etc.
MCPA	Similar to 2,4-D
MCPP	Mousear chickweed *Cerastium*; enhanced broadleaf control when used in mixtures
Quinclorac	Similar to 2,4-D
Triclopyr	Wood sorrel, *Oxalis*, Clovers *Trifolium*, other hard-to-kill plants
Two-Way Mixtures	
2,4-D + dicamba	Broad spectrum of broadleaf plants, including hard-to-kill plants
2,4-D + fluroxypyr	Broad spectrum of broadleaf plants, including hard-to-kill plants
2,4-D + MCPP	Broad spectrum of broadleaf plants, including hard-to-kill plants
2,4-D + triclopyr	Broad spectrum of broadleaf plants, including hard-to-kill plants
MCPA + dicamba	Broad spectrum of broadleaf plants, including hard-to-kill plants
MCPA + fluroxypyr	Broad spectrum of broadleaf plants, including hard-to-kill plants
Three-Way Mixtures	
2,4-D + 2,4-DP + dicamba	Broad spectrum of broadleaf plants, including hard-to-kill plants
2,4-D + MCPP + dicamba	Broad spectrum of broadleaf plants, including hard-to kill-plants
2,4-D + fluroxypyr + dicamba	Broad spectrum of broadleaf plants, including hard-to-kill plants
2,4-D + quinclorac + dicamba	Broad spectrum of broadleaf plants, including hard-to-kill plants
MCPA + MCPP + dicamba	Broad spectrum of broadleaf plants, including hard-to-kill plants
MCPA + fluroxypyr + dicamba	Broad spectrum of broadleaf plants, including hard-to-kill plants
Four-Way Mixtures	
2,4-D + MCPP + dicamba + carfentrazone-ethyl	Broad spectrum of broadleaf plants, including hard-to-kill plants
MCPA + MCPP + dicamba + carfentrazone-ethyl	Broad spectrum of broadleaf plants, including hard-to-kill plants

*Herbicide availability varies significantly in different countries. These examples are for the United States only.

†Grass species tolerance varies according to chemical. Study labels to determine the tolerance of specific grasses.

TABLE 10-4 Postemergent Broadleaf Herbicides Registered for Professional Use on Warm-Season Lawns in the United States*

Common Name	Target Plants
Single Chemicals†	
2,4-D	False dandelion *Hypochaeris*, Plantains *Plantago*, Common dandelion *Taraxacum*, etc.
2,4-DP	Similar to 2,4-D
Atrazine	Winter annual weeds
Bentazon	Broadleaf weeds and sedges
Bromoxynil	Winter annual weeds
Carfentrazone-ethyl	Bryophytes; enhanced broadleaf control when used in mixtures
Chlorsulfuron	Annual and perennial broadleaf weeds, some grasses
Dicamba	Yarrow *Achillea*, Mousear chickweed *Cerastium*, Clovers *Trifolium*, etc.
Fluroxypyr	Yarrow *Achillea*, Mousear chickweed *Cerastium*, Wood sorrel *Oxalis*, Clovers *Trifolium*, Violets *Viola*, etc.
Halosulfuron	Yellow nutsedge *Cyperus esculentus*
Imazaquin	Summer and winter annual weeds and sedges
MCPA	Similar to 2,4-D
MCPP	Mousear chickweed *Cerastium*; enhanced broadleaf control when used in mixtures
Mesotrione	Annual grasses and annual and perennial broadleaf weeds
Metsulfuron	Annual grasses and annual and perennial broadleaf weeds
Pyraflufen-ethyl	Annual grasses and annual and perennial broadleaf weeds
Quinclorac	Similar to 2,4-D plus postemergence on crabgrass *Digitaria*
Simazine	Annual grasses and annual broadleaf weeds
Triclopyr	Wood sorrel *Oxalis*, Clovers *Trifolium*, other hard-to-kill plants
Two-Way Mixtures	
2,4-D + dichlorprop	Broad spectrum of broadleaf plants, including hard-to-kill plants
2,4-D + MCPP	Broad spectrum of broadleaf plants, including hard-to-kill plants
2,4-D + triclopyr	Broad spectrum of broadleaf plants, including hard-to-kill plants
Three-Way Mixtures	
2,4-D + fluroxypyr + dicamba	Broad spectrum of broadleaf plants, including hard-to-kill plants
2,4-D + MCPP + dicamba	Broad spectrum of broadleaf plants, including hard-to-kill plants
2,4-D + MCPP + dichlorprop	Broad spectrum of broadleaf plants, including hard-to-kill plants
MCPA + MCPP + dichlorprop	Broad spectrum of broadleaf plants, including hard-to-kill plants
Four-Way Mixtures	
2,4-D + dicamba + MCPP + sulfentrazone	Broad spectrum of broadleaf plants, including hard-to-kill plants
2,4-D + dicamba + quinclorac + sulfentrazone	Broad spectrum of broadleaf plants, including hard-to-kill plants
2,4-D + MCPP + dicamba + carfentrazone-ethyl	Broad spectrum of broadleaf plants, including hard-to-kill plants
MCPA + MCPP + dicamba + carfentrazone-ethyl	Broad spectrum of broadleaf plants, including hard-to-kill plants

*Herbicide availability varies significantly in different countries. These examples are for the United States only.

†Grass species tolerance varies according to chemical. Study labels to determine the tolerance of specific grasses.

TABLE 10-5 Pre-emergent Herbicides* Registered for Professional Use on Cool-Season Lawns in the United States†

Common Name	Target Plants
Benefin	Annual grasses
Benefin + trifluralin	Annual grasses
Bensulide	Annual grasses
Dithiopyr	Annual grasses
Ethofumesate	Annual grasses, clovers
Isoxaben	Annual and perennial dicots
Oxadiazon	Annual grasses
Pendamethalin	Annual grasses
Prodiamine	Annual grasses and dicots
Siduron	Annual warm-season grasses

*Read labels carefully as tolerance to herbicides varies by lawn grass species.

†Herbicide availability varies significantly in different countries. These examples are for the United States only.

TABLE 10-6 Pre-emergent Herbicides Registered for Professional Use on Warm-Season Lawns in the United States*

Common Name†	Target Plants
Atrazine	Annual grasses and annual and perennial dicots
Benefin	Annual grasses and some dicots
Benefin + oryzalin	Annual grasses and annual and perennial dicots
Benefin + trifluralin	Annual grasses and some dicots
Bensulide	Annual grasses
Bensulide + oxadiazon	Annual grasses
Dithiopyr	Annual grasses and some dicots
Ethofumesate	Annual grasses and some dicots
Fenarimol	Annual bluegrass
Isoxaben	Annual and perennial dicots
Mesotrione	Pre- and postemergence on many annual grasses and dicots
Metolachlor	Annual grasses
Napropamide	Annual grasses and annual and perennial dicots
Oryzalin	Annual and perennial dicots
Oxadiazon	Annual grasses
Pendimethalin	Annual grasses and some dicots
Prodiamine	Annual grasses and some dicots
Pronamide	Cool-season grasses and dicots
Simazine	Cool-season grasses and dicots

*Herbicide availability varies significantly in different countries. These examples are for the United States only.

†Read labels carefully as lawn grass tolerance varies significantly by species.

regional guidelines for major climates in the United States are listed in the suggested reading at the end of this chapter.

Pre-emergent herbicides are applied before expected germination of target weeds. In cool temperate climates, these herbicides are used primarily to control summer annual grasses such as crabgrass (*Digitaria* spp.), foxtail (*Setaria* spp.), and goosegrass (*Eleusine indica*). In warm temperate and tropical environments, they are used to control both annual grasses and broadleaf weeds from seed. Table 10-5 lists pre-emergent herbicides registered for control of weeds in cool-season grasses. Table 10-6 lists herbicides registered for pre-emergent control in warm-season lawns. Nonselective products, primarily glyphosate, are used for spot treatments and for complete kill of existing lawns prior to reseeding.

Sustainable Weed Control Strategies for Lawns

There are limited options available for controlling weeds by alternative methods. Available natural herbicides are the same as discussed earlier for alternative herbicides in beds. Acids, soaps, and plant oils are all nonselective contact herbicides suited for spot spraying. They are most effective on young weeds and may only cause foliar kill on perennial tap root or rhizomatous species. The most widely touted herbicide is corn gluten meal, and its effectiveness as an herbicide can be unpredictable. In cool temperate marine climates, it has not effectively controlled crabgrass (*Digitaria* spp.) in cool-season lawns (Figure 10-11).

The first step when using alternative weed control strategies is maintaining dense healthy turf via optimum mowing, fertilization, and irrigation practices. Dense turf is an effective means of reducing weed encroachment.

The second step in developing a sustainable approach to weed management in lawns involves reducing expectations. Accepting weeds such as clover (*Trifolium* spp.), speedwell (*Veronica* spp.), wood sorrel (*Oxalis* spp.), common yarrow (*Achillea millefolium*), and other low-growing turf-compatible species is imperative. Objectionable rosette weeds such as false dandelion (*Hypochaeris radicata*) and plantain (*Plantago* spp.) may be controlled by hand or by use of spot sprays.

Figure 10-11 Barricade (left), a synthetic pre-emergent herbicide, gave 100 percent control of crabgrass (*Digitaria* spp.) compared to no control from corn gluten meal (right).

SUMMARY

Experience shows that IPM in landscapes can reduce synthetic insecticide use significantly. Monitoring programs and action thresholds have become powerful tools for avoiding calendar-based cover sprays and moving to targeted sprays often with environmentally benign natural or synthetic products. Similar approaches to disease management are also effective. The current shortcoming is the lack of effective alternative weed control materials. Until natural control technologies catch up with the desire to replace synthetic pest control products with natural ones, efforts to reduce herbicide use will continue to be unsatisfactory.

The ultimate challenge in developing acceptable sustainable pest control strategies is to reshape the public's view of the landscape, how it is designed, and how it is managed. By altering designs, changing planting schemes, selecting resistant plants, developing multiple quality standards for individual sites, and generally learning to accept less than perfect as good enough, the need for and use of pesticides in landscapes will decline. Further, by seriously exploring environmentally benign pest control options, contractors will determine how to get maximum benefit from available products. The end result will be a different style of working with landscape pests. In the end, fewer pesticides will be used, landscapes will be hardier, and negative environmental impacts will be reduced.

STUDY QUESTIONS

1. As far as pesticides are concerned, what are the goals of sustainable pest management?
2. Why does IPM result in fewer pesticide applications than a calendar-based pest management approach?
3. Explain the concept of key plants and key pests. What do they have to do with IPM?

4. What is the relationship between monitoring and action thresholds? Why are action thresholds important?
5. What role do pest-resistant plants play in sustainable landscape management? Are there limitations to using resistant plants?
6. How do the following biological control strategies differ from each other?
   a. Introduction
   b. Augmentation
   c. Conservation
7. What role do predators play in biological control of insect pests? What landscape practices influence their success or failure?
8. What are microbial insecticides? Explain how *Bt* strains work when applied as insecticides. Does it matter which strain is used?
9. Entomopathogenic nematodes sound like a great way to control insect pests. What problems limit their use in commercial landscapes?
10. What are endophytes? What kinds of plants contain endophytes? What kind of insects do they control?
11. Can insect pests be controlled with pheromone traps? Explain.
12. Explain how each of the following materials kills insect pests:
    a. Horticultural oils
    b. Insecticidal soaps
    c. Sugar esters
13. What major advantage do synthetic fungicides have over natural-origin fungicides in a disease control program?
14. Where do weeds in landscapes come from?
15. Synthetic herbicides have long been used for control of weeds in landscape beds. What factors do you need to consider for achieving good weed control with an absolute minimum of herbicide applications?
16. If herbicides are not used for weed control in beds, what options does the landscape manager have for achieving acceptable levels of weed control?
17. Landscape fabrics are popular for weed control. Explain how well they work in the short and long term. What problems are associated with fabrics under landscape conditions? Answer the same questions for mulch.
18. Are natural-based herbicides effective and economical for weed control in commercial situations? What kind of residual control can be expected from natural-based herbicides?
19. What are pre-emergent and selective postemergent synthetic herbicides supposed to control on lawns?
20. If synthetic herbicides were banned tomorrow, could we expect the same level of weed control from available natural-based herbicides? Explain.

SUGGESTED READING

The science of degree-day models is explained at several Web sites, including: http://www.ipm.ucdavis.edu/WEATHER/ddconcepts.html.

Regional degree-day calculators are also available at numerous Web sites, including: http://ippc2.orst.edu/cgi-bin/ddmodel.pl.

For a detailed account of herbicides for weed control in warm-season grass lawns, see: http://www.clemson.edu/extension/horticulture/turf/pest_guidelines/pest_handbook/section1.pdf.

For information on biological control with nematodes, see: http://www.nysaes.cornell.edu/ent/biocontrol/pathogens/nematodes.html.

References

CHAPTER 1

Bailey, R. 2000. Earthday, then and now. *Reason Online* (May), http://www.reason.com/news/show/27702.html (accessed June 8, 2009).

———. 2002. *Silent spring* at 40. *Reason Online* (June), http://reason.com/archives/2002/06/12/silent-spring-at-40/singlepage (accessed February 14, 2010).

Bryson, B. 2006. *The life and times of the thunderbolt kid.* New York: Broadway Books.

Carson, R. 1962. *Silent spring.* New York: Houghton Mifflin.

Jevons, W. S. 1865. *The coal question: An inquiry concerning the progress of the nation, and the probable exhaustion of our coal-mines.* London: Macmillan.

LEED. 2009. http://www.usgbc.org/DisplayPage.aspx?CMSPageID=1988 (accessed February 8, 2010).

Leopold, A. 1949. *A Sand County almanac: And sketches here and there.* Oxford: Oxford Univ. Press.

Makson, L. 2003. Rachel Carson's ecological genocide. *Front Page Magazine.com* (July 31), http://97.74.65.51/readArticle.aspx?ARTID=16987 (accessed February 14, 2010).

Malthus, T. R. 1959. *Population: The first essay.* Ann Arbor: Univ. of Michigan Press, 1959.

Marco, G. G., R. M. Hollingworth, and W. Durham, eds. 1987. *Silent spring revisited.* Washington, DC: American Chemical Society.

McHarg, I. L. 1969. *Design with nature.* Garden City, NY: Doubleday/Natural History Press.

Starke, L. 1990. *Signs of hope: Working towards our common future.* New York: Oxford Univ. Press.

Sustainable Sites Initiative. 2009a. The case for sustainable landscapes. http://www.sustainablesites.org/report/The%20Case%20for%20Sustainable%20Landscapes_2009.pdf (accessed February 20, 2010).

———. 2009b. Guidelines and performance benchmarks. http://www.sustainablesites.org/report/Guidelines%20and%20Performance%20Benchmarks_2009.pdf (accessed February 20, 2010).

TerraChoice Environmental Marketing. 2009. The seven sins of greenwashing. http://sinsofgreenwashing.org/ (accessed June 6, 2009).

Whitten, J. L. 1966. *That we may live.* New York: Van Nostrand.

World Commission on Environment and Development. 1987. *Our common future.* Oxford: Oxford Univ. Press.

World conservation strategy: Living resource conservation for sustainable development. 1980. IUCN-UNEP-WWF. http://data.iucn.org/dbtw-wpd/edocs/WCS-004.pdf (accessed June 8, 2009).

CHAPTER 2

Acquaah, G. 1999. *Horticulture: Principles and practices.* Upper Saddle River, NJ: Prentice Hall.

DeJong, G., L. Sheppard, M. Lieber, and D. Chenoweth. 2003. Executive summary: The economic cost of physical inactivity in Michigan. Governor's Council for Physical Fitness, Health, and Sports and the Michigan Fitness Foundation, Lansing, MI.

Dunnett, N. P., and A. Clayden. 2000. Resources: The raw materials of landscape. In *Landscape and sustainability,* ed. J. F. Benson and M. H. Roe, 179–201. London: Spon Press.

Kaplan, R., S. Kaplan, and R. Ryan. 1998. *With people in mind: Design and management of everyday nature.* Washington, DC: Island Press.

Palmer, D. 2009. Landscape installation and maintenance: Are the rules changing? Univ. of Florida Extension. http://prohort.ifas.ufl.edu/files/pdf/publications/HC-RulesChanging.pdf (accessed January 1, 2010).

Ramstad, K., and C. Orlando. 2009. Tree choices: Native? Non-native? Invasive? The terms can be relative. Urban and Community Forestry Assistance Program, Oregon Department of Forestry, Salem, OR.

Sustainable Sites Initiative. 2009a. Guidelines and performance benchmarks. http://www.sustainablesites.org/report/Guidelines%20and%20Performance%20Benchmarks_2009.pdf (accessed January 1, 2010).

———. 2009b. The case for sustainable landscapes. http://www.sustainablesites.org/report/The%20Case%20for%20Sustainable%20Landscapes_2009.pdf (accessed January 1, 2010).

Wann, D. 1996. *Deep design: Pathways to a livable future.* Washington, DC: Island Press.

Wellness Council of America. 2010. http://www.welcoa.org/ (accessed January 1, 2010).

Wikipedia. 2010. Nonpoint source pollution. http://en.wikipedia.org/wiki/Nonpoint_source_pollution (accessed January 1, 2010).

CHAPTER 3

American Wood Preservers Institute. 2004. Treated wood industry in transition. *Treated Wood News*.

Asphalt Pavement Alliance. 2009. Asphalt: The sustainable pavement. http://www.pavegreen.com/pdfs/Better_Water_Quality.pdf (accessed January 1, 2010).

Bean, E. Z., W. F. Hunt, D. A. Bidelspach, and R. J. Burak. 2004. Study on the surface infiltration rate of permeable pavements. Paper presented at the First Water and Environment Specialty Conference of the Canadian Society for Civil Engineering, June 2–5, Saskatoon, SK.

Burak, R., and D. R. Smith. 2008. Meeting sustainability goals with segmental concrete paving. *Interlocking Concrete Pavement Magazine* 15 (4):28–34.

Day, S., and N. L. Bassuk. 1994. A review of the effects of soil compaction and amelioration treatments on landscape trees. *Journal of Arboriculture* 20:9–17.

Elmendorf, W., H. Gerhold, and L. Kuhns. 2005. A guide to preserving trees in development projects. Pennsylvania State Univ. http://pubs.cas.psu.edu/FreePubs/pdfs/uh122.pdf (accessed January 1, 2010).

Interlocking Concrete Pavement Institute. 2008. *Permeable interlocking concrete pavement: A comparison guide to porous asphalt and pervious concrete*. Washington, DC: Interlocking Concrete Pavement Institute.

National Pollutant Discharge Elimination System. 2009. http://cfpub.epa.gov/npdes/stormwater/swbasicinfo.cfm (accessed January 1, 2010).

National Ready Mixed Concrete Association. 2009. http://www.perviouspavement.org/ (accessed January 1, 2010).

Sustainable Sites Initiative. 2009. Guidelines and performance benchmarks. http://www.sustainablesites.org/report/Guidelines%20and%20Performance%20Benchmarks_2009.pdf (accessed January 1, 2010).

Thompson, J. W., and K. Sorvig. 2008. *Sustainable landscape construction: A guide to green building outdoors*. 2nd ed. Washington, DC: Island Press.

U.S. Environmental Protection Agency. 2009. Clean Water Act of 1972. http://www.epa.gov/watertrain/cwa/ (accessed January 1, 2010).

U.S. Green Building Council. 2009. http://www.usgbc.org/DisplayPage.aspx?CategoryID=19 (accessed January 1, 2010).

Wilson, A. 2002. Treated wood: An update. *Landscape Architecture* 92 (1):46–50.

CHAPTER 4

Sustainable Sites Initiative. 2009. Guidelines and performance benchmarks. http://www.sustainablesites.org/report/Guidelines%20and%20Performance%20Benchmarks_2009.pdf (accessed January 1, 2010).

Thompson, J. W., and K. Sorvig. 2008. *Sustainable landscape construction: A guide to green building outdoors*. 2nd ed. Washington, DC: Island Press.

U.S. Environmental Protection Agency. 2007a. Why water efficiency? http://www.EPA.gov/WaterSense/water/why.htm (accessed January 1, 2010).

———. 2007b. Outdoor water use in the United States. EPA-832-F-06-005.

Wikipedia. 2010a. Greywater. http://en.wikipedia.org/wiki/Greywater (accessed January 1, 2010).

———. 2010b. Water framework directive. http://en.wikipedia.org/wiki/Water_framework_directive (accessed January 1, 2010).

CHAPTER 5

Ahern, J., E. Leduc, and M. L. York. 2006. *Biodiversity planning and design: Sustainable practices*. Washington DC: Island Press.

Bell, N., A. M. VanDerZanden, and L. McMahan. 2001. *Water efficient landscape plants*. EC 1546, Oregon State Univ. Extension Service, Corvallis, OR.

Benson, J. F., and M. H. Roe. 2000. *Landscape and sustainability*. London: Spon Press.

Breshears, D. D., T. E. Huxman, H. D. Adams, C. B. Zou, and J. E. Davison. 2008. Vegetation synchronously leans upslope as climate warms. *Proceedings National Academy of Sciences USA* 105 (33):11591–92.

Brooker, R., and M. Corder. 1986. *Environmental economy*. London: E & FN Spon.

Brooklyn Botanic Garden. 2009. Disturbance and succession. http://www.bbg.org/gar2/topics/ecology/eco_disturbance.html (accessed January 1, 2010).

California State Parks. 2009. Natural resource management. http://www.parks.ca.gov/?page_id=22197 (accessed January 1, 2010).

Dunnett, N. P., and A. Clayden. 2000. Resources: The raw materials of landscape. In *Landscape and sustainability*, ed. J. F. Benson and M. H. Roe, 179–201. London: Spon Press.

Dunnett, N. P., and J. D. Hitchmough. 1996. Excitement and energy: Sustainable landscape planting. *Landscape Design* (June): 43–46.

Gaublomme, E., F. Hendrickx, H. Dhuyvetter, and K. Desender. 2008. The effects of forest patch size and matrix type on changes in carabid beetle assemblages in an urbanized landscape. *Biological Conservation* 141: 2585–96.

Handley, J. F., and P. Bulmer. 1987. The design and management of cost effective landscapes. In *Proceedings of the 27th Askham Bryan Amenity Technical Course*, ed. B. Rigby. York, UK: Askham Bryan College of Agriculture and Horticulture.

Invasive plant atlas of the United States. 2009. http://www.invasiveplantatlas.org/trees.html (accessed January 1, 2010).

Kelly, A. E., and M. L. Goulden. 2008. Rapid shifts in plant distribution with recent climate change. *Proceedings National Academy of Sciences USA* 105 (33):11823–26.

Kendle, T., J. E. Rose, and J. Oikawa. 2000. Sustainable landscape management. In *Landscape and sustainability*, ed. J. F. Benson and M. H. Roe, 264–93. London: Spon Press.

Lee, H. 2009. Aspects of Ecosystem Dynamics. Univ. Kiel, Ecology Centre, Msc Environmental Science, thesis. http://openlandscapes.zalf.de/openLandscapesWIKI_Glossaries/Aspects%20of%20Ecosystem%20Dynamics.aspx (accessed June 7, 2010).

Loram, A., K. Thompson, P. H. Warren, and K. J. Gaston. 2008. Urban domestic gardens (XII): The richness and composition of the flora in five UK cities. *Journal of Vegetation Science* 19:321–30.

Lyle, J. T. 1985. *Design for human ecosystems: Landscape, land use and natural resources*. New York: Van Nostrand.

Makhzoumi, J., and G. Pungetti. 1999. *Ecological landscape design and planning: The Mediterranean context*. London: E & FN Spon.

Millennium Ecosystem Assessment. 2007. *A toolkit for understanding and action: Protecting nature's services, protecting ourselves*. Washington, DC: Island Press.

Ramstad, K., and C. Orlando. 2009. *Tree choices: Native? Non-native? Invasive? The terms can be relative*. Urban and Community Forestry Assistance Program, Oregon Department of Forestry, Salem, OR.

Stilma, E., K. J. Keesman, and W. Van der Werf. 2009. Recruitment and attrition of associated plants under a shading crop canopy: Model selection and calibration. *Ecological Modeling* 220 (8):1113–25.

Sustainable Sites Initiative. 2009a. Guidelines and performance benchmarks. http://www.sustainablesites.org/report/Guidelines%20and%20Performance%20Benchmarks_2009.pdf (accessed January 1, 2010).

———. 2009b. The case for sustainable landscapes. http://www.sustainablesites.org/report/The%20Case%20for%20Sustainable%20Landscapes_2009.pdf (accessed January 1, 2010).

Thoday, P., T. Kendle, and J. Hitchmough. 1995. Plants for landscape site. *The Horticulturist* 4 (3):29–35.

U.S. Forest Service, Northern Research Station Web site. 2010. http://forest.mtu.edu/kidscorner/ecosystems/definition.html (accessed January 1, 2010).

Wann, D. 1996. *Deep design: Pathways to a livable future*. Washington, DC: Island Press.

Wikipedia. 2010a. Population dynamics. http://en.wikipedia.org/wiki/Population_dynamics (accessed January 1, 2010).

———. 2010b. Invasive species. http://en.wikipedia.org/wiki/Invasive_species (accessed January 1, 2010).

Williams, C. E. 1997. Potential valuable ecological functions of non-indigenous plants. In *Assessment and management of plant invasions*, ed. J. O. Luken and J. W. Thieret. New York: Springer.

CHAPTER 6

Baird, J. H., N. T. Basta, R. L. Huhnke, G. V. Johnson, M. E. Payton, D. E. Storm, C. A. Wilson, M. D. Smolen, D. L. Martin, and J. T. Cole. 2000. Best management practices to reduce pesticide and nutrient runoff from turf. In *Fate and management of turfgrass chemicals*, ed. M. J. Clark and M. P. Kenna, 268–93. Washington, DC: American Chemical Society.

Baker, L. A., D. Hope, Y. Xu, J. Edmonds, and L. Lauver. 2001. Nitrogen balance for the central Arizona–Phoenix (CAP) ecosystem. *Ecosystems* 4:582–602.

Baldwin, D. H., J. A. Spromberg, T. K. Collier, and N. L. Scholz. 2009. A fish of many scales: Extrapolating sublethal pesticide exposures to the productivity of wild salmon populations. *Ecological Applications* 19 (8):2004–15.

Balogh, J. C., and W. J. Walker. 1992. *Golf course management and construction: Environmental issues*. Chelsea, MI: Lewis.

Beard, J. B., and R. L. Green. 1994. The role of turfgrasses in environmental protection and their benefits to humans. *Journal of Environmental Quality* 23 (3):452–60.

Bierman, P. M., B. P. Horgan, C. J. Rosen, A. B. Hollman, and P. H. Pagliari. 2009. Phosphorus runoff from turfgrass as affected by phosphorus fertilization and clipping management. *Journal of Environmental Quality* 39:282–92.

Blair, A., and S. H. Zahm. 1995. Agricultural exposures and cancer. *Environmental Health Perspectives* 103:205–8.

Bormann, F. H., D. Balmori, and G. T. Geballe. 2001. *Redesigning the American lawn: A search for environmental harmony*. 2nd ed. New Haven, CT: Yale Univ. Press.

Bourdieu, P. 1984. *Distinction: A social critique of the judgment of taste*. London: Routledge.

Branham, B. E., and D. J. Wehner. 1985. The fate of diazinon applied to thatched turf. *Agronomy Journal* 77:101–4.

Buckley, J. D., A. T. Meadows, M. E. Kadin, M. M. Le Beau, S. Siegel, and L. L. Robison. 2000. Pesticide exposures in children with non-Hodgkin lymphoma. *Cancer* 89 (11):2315–21.

Clark, M. J., and M. P. Kenna. 2000. *Fate and management of turfgrass chemicals*. Washington, DC: American Chemical Society.

Duncan, R. R., R. N. Carrow, and M. T. Huck. 2009. *Turfgrass and landscape irrigation water quality*. Boca Raton, FL: CRC Press.

Erickson, J. E., J. L. Cisar, J. C. Violin, and G. H. Snyder. 2001. Comparing runoff and leaching between newly established St. Augustinegrass turf and alternative residential landscape. *Crop Science* 41:1889–95.

Frank, K. W., K. M. O'Reilly, J. R. Crum, and R. N. Calhoun. 2006. The fate of nitrogen applied to a mature Kentucky bluegrass turf. *Crop Science* 46:209–15.

Gathercole, W. 2009. April 22, 2009: A date that will live in infamy. *Turf and Recreation* (May), http://www.turfandrec.com/index.php?option=com_annexeditor&task=showissue&issueid=58&Itemid=94/ (accessed February 1, 2010).

Groffman, P. M., N. L. Law, K. T. Belt, L. E. Band, and G. T. Fisher. 2004. Nitrogen fluxes and retention in urban watershed ecosystems. *Ecosystems* 7:393–403.

Harris, S. A., K. R. Solomon, C. S. Bowhey, and G. R. Stephenson. 1990. Homeowner, professional applicator and bystander exposure to 2,4-dichlorophenoxyacetic acid (2,4-D). Research report, Guelph Turfgrass Institute, Guelph, ON.

Harrison, S. A., T. L. Watschke, R. O. Mumma, A. T. Jarrett, and G. W. Hamilton Jr. 1993. Nutrient and pesticide concentrations in water from chemically treated turfgrass. In *Pesticides in urban environments: Fate and significance*, ed. K. D. Racke and A. R. Leslie. Washington, DC: American Chemical Society.

Hart, M. R., B. F. Quin, and M. L. Nguyen. 2004. Phosphorus runoff from agricultural land and direct fertilizer effects: A review. *Journal of Environmental Quality* 33:1954–72.

Hirsch, R., and J. Baxter. 2009. The look of the lawn: Pesticide policy preference and health-risk perception in context. *Environment and Planning C: Government and Policy* 27:468–90.

Hoar, S. K., A. Blair, F. F. Holmes, C. D. Boysen, R. J. Robel, R. Hoover, and J. F. Fraumeni Jr. 1986. Agricultural herbicide use and risk of lymphoma and soft-tissue sarcoma. *Journal of the American Medical Association* 256:1141–47.

Hull, R. J. 1995. The fate of pesticides used on turf. *Turfgrass Trends* (September): 2–11.

Jenkins, V. S. 1994. *The lawn: A history of an American obsession*. Washington, DC: Smithsonian Institution Press.

Khan, F. 2010. CAPE wins New Brunswick pesticide ban. *CAPE Newsletter* (Winter): 1.

Konrad, E. 2009. Fueling debate. *Turf Line News* 215:41–43, 52.

Lanthier, M. 2009. Pesticide safety: The continuum of opinions. *Turf Line News* 215:36–39.

Lehman, J. T., D. W. Bell, and K. E. McDonald. 2009. Reduced river phosphorus following implementation of a lawn fertilizer ordinance. *Lake and Reservoir Management* 25:307–12.

Leonard, J. A., and R. A. Yeary. 1990. Exposure of workers using hand-held equipment during urban application of pesticides to trees and ornamental shrubs. *American Industrial Hygiene Association Journal* 51:605–9.

Milesi, C., C. D. Elvidge, J. B. Dietz, B. T. Tuttle, R. R. Nemania, and S. W. Running. 2005. Mapping and modeling the biogeochemical cycling of turf grasses in the United States. *Environmental Management* 36 (3):426–38.

Mumley, T., and R. Katznelson. 1999. Diazinon sources in runoff from the San Francisco Bay region. *Watershed Protection Techniques* 3 (1):613–16.

Niemczyck, H. D., H. R. Krueger, and K. O. Lawrence. 1977. Thatch influences movement of soil insecticides. *Ohio Reports* 62:26–28.

Ottoboni, M. A. 1997. *The dose makes the poison*. 2nd ed. New York: Van Nostrand Reinhold.

Pest Management Regulatory Agency. 2008. Information Note: Health Canada Releases Final Re-evaluation Decision on 2,4-D. http://www.hc-sc.gc.ca/cps-spc/pubs/pest/_fact-fiche/24d/index-eng.php (accessed online May 25, 2010)

Petrovic, A. M., and Z. M. Easton. 2005. The role of turfgrass management in water quality of urban environments. *International Turfgrass Society Research Journal* 10:55–69.

Potter, D. A. 1994. Pesticide and fertilizer effects on beneficial invertebrates and consequences for thatch degradation and pest outbreaks in turfgrass. In *Pesticides in urban environments: Fate and significance*, ed. K. D. Racke and A. R. Leslie. Washington, DC: American Chemical Society.

Potter, D. A., M. C. Buxton, C. T. Redmond, C. G. Patterson, and A. J. Powell. 1990. Toxicity of pesticides to earthworms (Oligochaeta: Lumbricidae) and effect on thatch degradation in Kentucky bluegrass turf. *Journal of Economic Entomology* 83:2362–69.

Priest, M. W., D. J. Williams, and H. A. Bridgman. 2000. Emissions from in-use lawn-mowers in Australia. *Atmospheric Environment* 34:657–64.

Racke, K. D., and A. R. Leslie. 1993. *Pesticides in urban environments: Fate and significance*. Washington, DC: American Chemical Society.

Richardson, A. W. 2008. Municipal water use policies. In *Water quality and quantity issues for turfgrasses in urban landscapes*, ed. J. B. Beard and M. P. Kenna. Ames, IA: Council for Agricultural Science and Technology.

Ritter, L., C. Heath Jr., E. Kaegi, H. Morrison, and S. Sieber. 1997. Report of a panel on the relationship between public exposure to pesticides and cancer. *Cancer* 80 (10):2019–33.

Robbins, P. 2007. *Lawn people: How grasses, weeds, and chemicals make us who we are.* Philadelphia: Temple Univ. Press.

Robbins, P., and J. Sharp. 2003. The lawn-chemical economy and its discontents. *Antipode* 35:955–79.

Rosen, C. J., and B. P. Horgan. 2005. Regulation of phosphorus fertilizer application to turf in Minnesota: Historical perspective and opportunities for research and education. *International Turfgrass Society Research Journal* 10 (1):130–35.

Sandberg, L. A., and J. Foster. 2005. Challenging lawn and order: Environmental discourse and lawn care reform in Canada. *Environmental Politics* 14 (4):478–94.

Sears, M. K., C. Bowhey, H. Braun, and G. R. Stephenson. 1987. Dislodgeable residues and persistence of diazinon, chlopyrifos and isofenphos following their application to turfgrass. *Pesticide Science* 20:223–31.

Soldat, D. J., and A. M. Petrovic. 2008. The fate and transport of phosphorus in turfgrass ecosystems. *Crop Science* 48:2051–65.

Steinberg, T. 2006. *American green: The obsessive quest for the perfect lawn.* New York: Norton.

Stone, W. B., and P. B. Gradoni. 1985. Wildlife mortality related to use of the pesticide diazinon. *Northeastern Environmental Science* 4 (1):30–38.

Thompson, D. G., G. R. Stephenson, and M. Sears. 1984. Persistence, distribution and dislodgeable residues of 2, 4-D following its application to turfgrass. *Pesticide Science* 15:353–60.

U.S. Environmental Protection Agency. 1998. Small engine emission standards. EPA-420-F-98-025.

———. 2008. EPA finalizes emission standards for new nonroad spark-ignition engines, equipment, and vessels. EPA-420-F-08-013.

U.S. General Accounting Office. 1990. Lawn care pesticides: Risks remain uncertain while prohibited safety claims continue. Report to the chairman, subcommittee on toxic substances, environmental oversight, research and development and public works, U.S. Senate. General Accounting Office, Gaithersburg, MD.

White, J. J., J. N. Carroll, C. T. Hare, and J. G. Lourenco. 1991. Emission factors for small utility engines. Technical Paper Series 910560, Society of Automotive Engineers, Warrendale, PA.

Wikipedia. 2010. The precautionary principle. http://en.wikipedia.org/wiki/Precautionary_principle (accessed May 25, 2010).

CHAPTER 7

Aubertin, G. M., and L. T. Kardos. 1965. Root growth through porous media under controlled conditions. *Soil Science of America Proceedings* 29:290–93.

Bardgett, R. D. 2005. *The biology of soil: A community and ecosystem approach.* Oxford: Oxford Univ. Press.

Bullock, P., and P. J. Gregory. 1991. *Soils in the urban environment.* London: Blackwell.

Cheng, Z., D. S. Richmond, S. O. Salminen, and P. S. Grewal. 2008. Ecology of urban lawns under three common management programs. *Urban Ecosystems* 11:177–95.

Coleman, D. C., and D. H. Wall. 2007. Fauna: The engine for microbial activity and transport. In *Soil microbiology, ecology and biochemistry*, ed. E. A. Paul. 3rd ed. Amsterdam: Elsevier.

Craul, P. J. 1999. *Urban soils: Applications and practices.* New York: Wiley.

Day, S., and N. L. Bassuk. 1994. A review of the effects of soil compaction and amelioration treatments on landscape trees. *Journal of Arboriculture* 20:9–17.

Dick, R. P. 1997. Soil enzyme activities as integrative indicators of soil health. In *Biological indicators of soil health*, ed. C. E. Pankhurst, B. M. Doube, and V. V. S. R. Gupta, 121–56. New York: CAB International.

Doran, J. W., and M. Safley. 1997. Defining and assessing soil health and sustainable productivity. In *Biological indicators of soil health*, ed. C. E. Pankhurst, B. M. Doube, and V. V. S. R. Gupta, 1–28. New York: CAB International.

Evans, C. V., D. S. Fanning, and J. R. Short. 2000. Human influenced soils. In *Managing soils in an urban environment*, ed. R. B. Brown, J. H. Huddleston, and J. L. Anderson, 33–68. Madison, WI: American Society of Agronomy.

Fenton, T. E., and M. E. Collins. 2000. The soil resource and its inventory. In *Managing soils in an urban environment*, ed. R. B. Brown, J. H. Huddleston, and J. L. Anderson, 1–32. Madison, WI: American Society of Agronomy.

Ferris, H., and M. M. Matute. 2003. Structural and functional succession in the nematode fauna of a soil food web. *Applied Soil Ecology* 23:93–110.

Grabosky, J., N. Bassuk, and P. Trowbridge. 2002. *Structural soils.* Washington, DC: American Society of Landscape Architects.

Grime, J. P., J. M. Mackey, S. H. Hillier, and D. J. Read. 1987. Floristic diversity in a model system using experimental microcosms. *Nature* 328:420–22.

Hascher, W., and C. E. Wells. 2007. Effects of soil decompaction and amendment on root growth and architecture in red maple (*Acer rubrum*). *Arboriculture and Urban Forestry* 33:428–32.

Lloyd, J. E., D. A. Herms, B. R. Stinner, and H. A. J. Hoitink. 2002. Comparing composted yard trimmings and ground wood as mulches. *BioCycle* 43 (9):52–55, 69.

Maechling, P., H. Cooke, and J. G. Bockheim. 1974. Nature and properties of highly disturbed urban soils. *Agronomy Abstracts*, 161.

Pankhurst, C. E. 1994. Biological indicators of soil health and sustainable productivity. In *Soil resilience and sustainable land use*, ed. D. J. Greenland and I. Szabolcs, 331–51. Wallingford, UK: CAB International.

Pankhurst, C. E., B. M. Doube, and V. V. S. R. Gupta. 1997. Biological indicators of soil health: Synthesis. In *Biological indicators of soil health*, ed. C. E. Pankhurst, B. M. Doube, and V. V. S. R. Gupta, 419–35. New York: CAB International.

Pittenger, D. R., and T. Stamen. 1990. Effectiveness of methods used to reduce harmful effects of compacted soil around landscape trees. *Journal of Arboriculture* 16:55–57.

Potter, D. A., A. J. Powell, and M. S. Smith. 1990. Degradation of turfgrass thatch by earthworms (Oligochaeta: Lumbricidae) and other soil invertebrates. *Journal of Economic Entomology* 83:205–11.

Rivenshield, A., and N. L. Bassuk. 2007. Using organic amendments to decrease bulk density and increase macroporosity in compacted soils. *Arboriculture and Urban Forestry* 33 (2):140–46.

Rolf, K. 1992. Soil physical effects of pneumatic subsoil loosening using a Terralift soil aerator. *Journal of Arboriculture* 18:235–40.

Smiley, E. T. 2001. Terravent: Soil fracture patterns and impact on bulk density. *Journal of Arboriculture* 27: 326–30.

Smiley, E. T., L. Calfee, B. R. Fraedrich, and E. J. Smiley. 2006. Comparison of structural and noncompacted soils for trees surrounded by pavement. *Arboriculture and Urban Forestry* 32 (4):164–69.

Smiley, E. T., G. W. Watson, B. R. Fraedrich, and D. C. Booth. 1990. Evaluation of soil aeration equipment. *Journal of Arboriculture* 16:118–23.

Spomer, L. A. 1983. Physical amendment of landscape soils. *Journal of Environmental Horticulture* 1 (3):77–80.

Tiquia, S. M., J. Lloyd, D. A. Herms, H. A. J. Hoitink, and C. M. Frederick Jr. 2002. Effects of mulching and fertilization on soil nutrients, microbial activity and rhizosphere bacterial community structure determined by analysis of TRFLPs of PCR-amplified 16s rRNA genes. *Applied Soil Ecology* 21:31–48.

Urban, J. 2008. *Up by roots: Healthy soils and trees in the built environment*. Champaign, IL: International Society of Arboriculture.

CHAPTER 8

Anella, L., T. C. Hennessey, and E. M. Lorenzi. 2008. Growth of balled and burlapped versus bare root trees in Oklahoma, U.S. *Arboriculture and Urban Forestry* 34:200–203.

Appleton, B., J. Koci, S. French, M. Lestyan, and R. Harris 2003. Mycorrhizal fungal inoculation of established street trees. *Journal of Arboriculture* 29:107–10.

Brickell, C., and D. Joyce. 1996. *The American Horticultural Society pruning and training*. New York: DK Publishing.

Brown, G. E., and T. Kirkham. 2004. *The pruning of trees, shrubs and conifers*. 2nd ed. Portland: Timber Press.

Costello, L., and J. L. Paul. 1975. Moisture relations in transplanted container plants. *HortScience* 10:371–72.

Costello, L. R., N. P. Matheny, J. R. Clark, and K. S. Jones. 2000. *Estimating irrigation water needs of landscape plantings in California*. Univ. of California Cooperative Extension and California Department of Water Resources.

Craul, P. J. 1999. *Urban soils: Applications and practices*. New York: Wiley.

Day, S. D., and J. R. Harris. 2007. Fertilization of red maple (*Acer rubrum*) and littleleaf linden (*Tilia cordata*) trees at recommended rates does not aid tree establishment. *Arboriculture and Urban Forestry* 33:113–21.

Ferrini, F., A. Fini, P. Frangi, and G. Amoroso. 2008. Mulching of ornamental trees: Effects on growth and physiology. *Arboriculture and Urban Forestry* 34:157–62.

Gilman, E. F. 2001. Effect of nursery production method, irrigation, and inoculation with mycorrhizae forming fungi on establishment of *Quercus virginiana*. *Journal of Arboriculture* 27:30–39.

———. 2004. Effects of amendments, soil additives, and irrigation on tree survival and growth. *Journal of Arboriculture* 30:301–10.

Gilman, H., J. Grabosky, A. Stodola, and M. D. Marshall. 2003. Irrigation and container type impact red maple (*Acer rubrum* L.) 5 years after landscape planting. *Journal of Arboriculture* 29:231–36.

Green, T. L., and G. W. Watson. 1989. Effects of turfgrass and mulch on establishment and growth of bare root sugar maples. *Journal of Arboriculture* 15:268–71.

Harris, R. W., J. R. Clark, and N. P. Matheny. 2003. *Integrated management of trees, shrubs, and vines*. 4th ed. New York: Prentice Hall.

Harris, R. W., A. T. Leiser, and W. B. Davis. 1978. Staking landscape trees. Leaflet 2576, Univ. of California Cooperative Extension.

Iyer, J. G., R. B. Corey, and S. B. Wilde. 1980. Mycorrhizae: Facts and fallacies. *Journal of Arboriculture* 6:213–20.

Lowenfels, J., and W. Lewis. 2006. *Teaming with microbes: A gardener's guide to the soil food web*. Portland: Timber Press.

Messenger, S. A. 1976. Root competition: Grass effects on trees. *Journal of Arboriculture* 2:228–30.

Miller, R. W. 2000. Practical applications: Are we asking the right questions and looking in the right places? In *Tree and shrub fertilization: Proceedings from an international conference on tree and shrub fertilization*, ed. A. Siewart

A. Siewart, B. Rao, and D. Marion, 15–19. Champaign, IL: International Society of Arboriculture.

Montague, T., C. McKenney, M. Maurer, and B. Winn. 2007. Influence of irrigation volume and mulch on establishment of select shrub species. *Arboriculture and Urban Forestry* 33:202–9.

Scharenbroch, B. C., and J. E. Lloyd. 2004. A literature review of nitrogen availability indices for use in urban landscapes. *Journal of Arboriculture* 30:214–30.

Siewart, A., A. Siewart, B. Rao, and D. Marion. 2000. *Tree and shrub fertilization: Proceedings from an international conference on tree and shrub fertilization.* Champaign, IL: International Society of Arboriculture.

Smalley, T. J., and C. B. Wood. 1995. Effect of backfill amendment on growth of red maple. *Journal of Arboriculture* 21:247–50.

Spomer, L. A. 1980. Container soil water relations: Production, maintenance, and transplanting. *Journal of Arboriculture* 6:315–20.

Steinfeld, D., M. P. Amaranthus, and E. Cazares. 2003. Survival of ponderosa pine (*Pinus ponderosa* Dougl. ex Laws.) seedlings outplanted with Rhizopogon mycorrhizae inoculated with spores at the nursery. *Journal of Arboriculture* 29:197–208.

Urban, J. 2008. *Up by roots: Healthy soils and trees in the built environment.* Champaign, IL: International Society of Arboriculture.

van de Werken, H. 1981. Fertilization and other factors enhancing the growth of young shade trees. *Journal of Arboriculture* 7:33–37.

Watson, G. W., and E. B. Himelick. 1997. *Principles and practice of planting trees and shrubs.* Champaign, IL: International Society of Arboriculture.

Whitcomb, C. E. 1975. Effects of soil amendments on growth of silver maple trees in the landscape. *Proceedings of the SNA Research Conference* 20:49–50.

———. 1987. *Establishment and maintenance of landscape trees.* Stillwater, OK: Lacebark.

CHAPTER 9

Ashby, M. 1969. *Introduction to plant ecology.* London: Macmillan.

Baxendale, F. P., and R. E. Gaussoin. 1997. *Turfgrass management for the northern great plains.* EC97-1557, Univ. of Nebraska Cooperative Extension, Lincoln, NE.

Beard, J. B., and H. T. Beard. 2005. *Beard's turfgrass encyclopedia.* East Lansing: Michigan State Univ. Press.

Bormann, F. H., D. Balmori, and G. T. Geballe. 2001. *Redesigning the American lawn: A search for environmental harmony.* 2nd ed. New Haven, CT: Yale Univ. Press.

Brede, D. 2000. *Turfgrass maintenance reduction handbook: Sports, lawns, and golf.* Chelsea, MI: Ann Arbor Press.

Carrow, R. N., D. V. Waddington, and P. E. Rieke. 2001. *Turfgrass soil fertility and chemical problems.* Chelsea, MI: Ann Arbor Press.

Christians, N. 1998. *Fundamentals of turfgrass management.* Chelsea, MI: Ann Arbor Press.

Cook, T. 1993. Low maintenance turf. *Hardy Plant Society of Oregon Bulletin* 9 (1):9–15.

Cook, T. W., and E. Ervin. 2010. Lawn ecology. In *Urban ecosystem ecology*, ed. J. Aitkenhead-Peterson and A. Volder. Madison, WI: American Agronomy Society.

Duble, R. L. 1996. *Turfgrasses: Their management and use in the southern zone.* 2nd ed. College Station: Texas A&M Univ. Press.

Dunn, J., and K. Diesburg. 2004. *Turf management in the transition zone.* Hoboken, NJ: Wiley.

Fry, J., and B. Huang. 2004. *Applied turfgrass science and physiology.* Hoboken, NJ: Wiley.

Horne, B., G. Stewart, C. Meurk, M. Ignatieva, and T. Braddick. 2005. The origin and weed status of plants in Christchurch lawns. dspace.lincoln.ac.nz/dspace/bitstream/10182/1242/.../Horne_The_Origin.pdf (accessed December 15, 2009).

Minner, D. D. 1987. Irrigation scheduling of Kentucky bluegrass. *Proceedings of the 33rd Annual Rocky Mountain Regional Turfgrass Conference.*

Muller, N. 1990. Lawns in German cities: A phytosociological comparison. In *Urban ecology,* ed. H. Sukopp et al., 209–22. The Hague: SPB Academic Publishing.

Patton, A. J. 2009. Selecting zoysiagrass cultivars: Turfgrass quality, growth, pest and environmental stress tolerance. *Applied Turfgrass Science.* doi:10.1094/ATS-2009-1019-01-MG (accessed October 19, 2009).

Ruppert, K. C., and R. J. Black. 1997. *Florida lawn handbook: An environmental approach to care and maintenance of your lawn.* 2nd ed. Gainesville: University Press of Florida.

Sheard, R. W. 2000. *Understanding turf management.* Guelph, ON: Sports Turf Association.

Shearman, R. C., T. P. Riordan, and P. Johnson. 2004. Buffalograss. In *Warm-season (C4) grasses,* ed. L. E. Moser, B. L. Burson, and L. E. Sollenberger. Madison, WI: American Society of Agronomy.

Thompson, K., J. G. Hodgson, R. M. Smith, P. H. Warren, and K. J. Gaston. 2004. Urban domestic gardens (III): Composition and diversity of lawn floras. *Journal of Vegetation Science* 15 (3):373–78.

Turgeon, A. J. 2008. *Turfgrass management.* 8th ed. Upper Saddle River, NJ: Pearson Prentice Hall.

White, R. H., M. C. Engelke, S. J. Morton, and B. A. Ruemmele. 1993. Irrigation water requirement of zoysiagrass. *International Turfgrass Society Research Journal* 7:587–93.

Wiecko, G. 2006. *Fundamentals of tropical turf management.* Cambridge, MA: CAB International.

CHAPTER 10

Appleton, B., and J. Derr. 1990. Tree root surfacing: A potential problem with landscape fabrics? *Nursery Manager* (February): 50.

Appleton, B., J. F. Derr, and B. B. Ross. 1990. The effect of various landscape weed control measures on soil moisture and temperature and tree root growth. *Journal of Arboriculture* 16:264–68.

Brown, D. A., M. T. Windham, and R. N. Trigiano. 1996. Resistance to dogwood anthracnose among *Cornus* species. *Journal of Arboriculture* 22:83–86.

Christians, N. E. 1993. The use of corn gluten meal as a natural preemergence weed control in turf. *International Turfgrass Society Research Journal* 7:284–90.

Cook, T. 1987. Weed control with geotextile fabrics. *Ornamentals Northwest Newsletter* 11:22.

Derr, J., and B. L. Appleton. 1989. Weed control with landscape fabrics. *Journal of Environmental Horticulture* 7 (4):129–33.

Dirr, M. A. 1997. *Dirr's hardy trees and shrubs: An illustrated encyclopedia.* Portland: Timber Press.

Frank, S., R. Ahern, and M. J. Raupp. 2007. Does imidacloprid reduce defoliation by Japanese beetles for more than one growing season? *Arboriculture and Urban Forestry* 33:392–96.

Funk, R. 1988. Davey's plant health care. *Journal of Arboriculture* 14:285–87.

Gordon, F. C., and D. A. Potter. 1985. Efficiency of Japanese beetle (Coleoptera: Scarabaeidae) traps in reducing defoliation of plants in the urban landscape and effect on larval density in turf. *Journal of Economic Entomology* 78:774–78.

Grant, J. A., and C. L. Grant. 1990. *Trees and shrubs for Pacific Northwest gardens.* 2nd ed. Portland: Timber Press.

Held, D. W. 2004. Relative susceptibility of woody landscape plants to Japanese beetle (Coleoptera: Scarabaeidae). *Journal of Arboriculture* 30:328–35.

Hilgert, C. 2003. *Evaluation of natural and synthetic preemergence herbicides used in ornamental landscapes.* Master's thesis, Oregon State Univ.

Holmes, J. J., and J. A. Davidson. 1984. Integrated pest management for arborists: Implementation of a pilot program. *Journal of Arboriculture* 10:65–70.

Klein, M. G. 1995. Microbial control of insect species. In *Handbook of turfgrass insect pests*, ed. R. L. Brandenburg and M. G. Villani. Lanham, MD: Entomological Society of America.

Mizell, R. F., and A. Hagan. 2000. Biological problems and their management in urban soils: Integrated pest management of arthropods and diseases. In *Managing soils in an urban environment*, ed. R. B. Brown, J. H. Huddleston, and J. L. Anderson. Madison, WI: American Society of Agronomy.

Potter, D. A., and D. W. Held. 2002. Biology and management of the Japanese beetle. *Annual Review of Entomology* 47:175–205.

Raupp, M. J. 1985. Monitoring: An essential factor to managing pests of landscape trees and shrubs. *Journal of Arboriculture* 11:349–55.

Raupp, M. J., J. A. Davidson, J. J. Holmes, and J. L. Hellman. 1985. The concept of key plants in integrated pest management for landscapes. *Journal of Arboriculture* 11:317–22.

Raupp, M. J., C. S. Koehler, and J. A. Davidson. 1994. Advances in implementing integrated pest management for woody landscape plants. In *Handbook of integrated pest management for turf and ornamentals*, ed. A. R. Leslie. Boca Raton, FL: Lewis.

Raupp, M. J., and R. M. Noland. 1984. Implementing plant management programs in residential and institutional settings. *Journal of Arboriculture* 10:161–69.

Redmond, C. T., and D. A. Potter. 1995. Lack of efficacy of in-vivo and putatively in-vitro produced *Bacillus popilliae* against field populations of Japanese beetle (Coleoptera: Scarabaeidae) grubs in Kentucky. *Journal of Economic Entomology* 88:846–54.

Schultz, P. B., and D. B. Sivyer. 2006. An integrated pest management success story: Orangestriped oakworm control in Norfolk, Virginia, U.S. *Arboriculture and Urban Forestry* 32:286–88.

Vittum, P. J., M. G. Villani, and H. Tashiro. 1999. *Turfgrass insects of the United States and Canada.* 2nd ed. Ithaca, NY: Cornell Univ. Press.

INDEX

H

I

M

N

O

P

R

For these and other Wiley books on sustainable design, visit www.wiley.com/go/sustainabledesign

Alternative Construction: Contemporary Natural Building Methods, by Lynne Elizabeth and Cassandra Adams

Biophilic Design: The Theory, Science, and Practice of Bringing Buildings to Life, by Stephen R. Kellert, Judith Heerwagen, and Martin Mador

Cities People Planet: Liveable Cities for a Sustainable World, by Herbert Girardet

Contractors Guide to Green Building Construction: Management, Project Delivery, Documentation, and Risk Reduction, by Thomas E. Glavinich, Associated General Contractors

Design with Nature, by Ian L. McHarg

Ecodesign: A Manual for Ecological Design, by Ken Yeang

Green BIM: Successful Sustainable Design with Building Information Modeling, by Eddy Krygiel and Bradley Nies

Green Building Materials: A Guide to Product Selection and Specification, Second Edition, by Ross Spiegel and Dru Meadows

Green Development: Integrating Ecology and Real Estate, by Rocky Mountain Institute

Green Roof Systems: A Guide to the Planning, Design, and Construction of Landscapes over Structure, by Susan Weiler and Katrin Scholz-Barth

The HOK Guidebook to Sustainable Design, Second Edition, by Sandra Mendler, William O'Dell, and Mary Ann Lazarus

Land and Natural Development (LAND) Code, by Diana Balmor and Gaboury Benoit

A Legal Guide to Urban and Sustainable Development for Planners, Developers, and Architects, by Daniel K. Slone and Doris S. Goldstein with W. Andrew Gowder

Site Analysis: A Contextual Approach to Sustainable Land Planning and Site Design, Second Edition, by James A. LaGro

Sustainable Commercial Interiors, by Penny Bonda and Katie Sosnowchik

Sustainable Construction: Green Building Design and Delivery, by Charles J. Kibert

Sustainable Design: Ecology, Architecture, and Planning, by Daniel Williams

Sustainable Design: The Science of Sustainability and Green Engineering, by Daniel A. Vallero and Chris Brasier

Sustainable Healthcare Architecture, by Robin Guenther and Gail Vittori

Sustainable Residential Interiors, by Associates III

Sustainable Urbanism: Urban Design with Nature, by Douglas Farr

Environmental Benefits Statement

This book is printed with soy-based inks on presses with VOC levels that are lower than the standard for the printing industry. The paper, Rolland Enviro 100, is manufactured by Cascades Fine Papers Group and is made from 100 percent post-consumer, de-inked fiber, without chlorine. According to the manufacturer, the use of every ton of Rolland Enviro100 Book paper, switched from virgin paper, helps the environment in the following ways:

Mature trees saved	Waterborne waste not created	Waterflow saved	Atmospheric emissions eliminated	Solid wastes reduced	Natural gas saved by using biogas
17	6.9 lbs.	10,196 gals.	2,098 lbs.	1,081 lbs.	2,478 cubic feet